A SEA OF CONTROVERSY

"Erxleben consumes the criticism."

—front-page headline, *Seattle Times*

"William Erxleben, probably Seattle's most controversial and colorful federal bureaucrat."

—Bruce Ramsey, *Bellevue Journal-American*

Erxleben's supporters said:

"With his regional office transformed into one with national clout, Erxleben's record is a triumph of the idealist."

—*Seattle Business* magazine

"[Erxleben's] efforts in turning around the regional office in Seattle provide one of the best success stories that I know about in the 18 years I have been with Uncle [Sam]. It proves that one man can make a difference."

—Sid Lezak, US attorney for Oregon

"Your commitment to the public will serve as an example to others."

—FTC Award for Distinguished Service

Erxleben's critics said:

"[Erxleben's] entire conduct in this instance was in the finest tradition of the chilling smear and innuendo of the Nixon years."
> —former Seattle mayor Wes Uhlman, in letters to Senators Henry Jackson and Warren Magnuson

"The Portland Retail Druggists Association . . . that the Federal Trade Commission discharge William C. Erxleben, FTC Regional Director, Seattle, Wash., on grounds of actions in excess of authority and gross abuse of authority."
> —Portland Retail Druggists Association, in a letter to the chairman of the FTC, copied to the Oregon congressional delegation and General Haig, President Nixon's chief of staff

"I'm off the Board in a month but fully intend to scrap with you and yours who would turn the practice of law into a flea market."
> —Neil Hoff, member of the Board of Governors of the Washington State Bar Association, in a letter to Erxleben as FTC regional director

Who was right?

A LION
WHERE THERE WERE
LAMBS

A LION
WHERE THERE WERE
LAMBS

THE QUEST FOR TRUTH, JUSTICE, AND THE
RULE OF LAW IN THE PACIFIC NORTHWEST

BILL ERXLEBEN

Forseti
BOOKS

Forseti
BOOKS

Published by Forseti Books LLC
Newcastle, WA 98056

Library of Congress Control Number: 2019901419

Billerxleben.com

Edited and designed by Girl Friday Productions
www.girlfridayproductions.com
Design: Paul Barrett
Project management: Dave Valencia

Image credits:
Cover, "Little One" letter, and pages 28, 34, 48, 65,
76, 195, 231, 274: Courtesy Bill Erxleben
Pages 111, 114, 153, 154, 156, 254, 272: SeattlePI.com/Polaris
Page 220: Steve McKinstry / The Seattle Times, 1974
Page 268: Courtesy of Teamsters Local Union No. 174

ISBN 978-1-7328912-0-3 (paperback)
ISBN 978-1-7328912-1-0 (ebook)
ISBN 978-1-7328912-2-7 (audiobook)

*In memory of my mother, and to
Gayle, David, and Jennifer*

April 23.

Dear Mr. Ersleben:

I am one of the "little people". Not important at all; not very well informed — I know.

What I do know, however, is that we "little people" are very often taken advantage of.

In reading the Seattle Times of April 23 — article by Debby Lowman — I felt compelled to write this short note.

Thank you so very much for what you are trying to do in your work — helping we "little people" get a fair deal — not a hand-out or charity — just _honesty_ in all our dealings.

Please keep up the good work even if you _do_ make a few people "squirm". (Goody-goody!)

Thank you for reading this.

"A Little One."

CONTENTS

Prologue 1

Part I. Coming of Age

CHAPTER ONE: The Making of an Iconoclast 7

CHAPTER TWO: Adventure Bound 25

CHAPTER THREE: The Making of a Lawyer 37

CHAPTER FOUR: A Unique and Unusual Airman 51

Part II. In Pursuit of the Common Good

CHAPTER FIVE: Making My Bones as a Lawyer 75

CHAPTER SIX: Crooked Cops 89

CHAPTER SEVEN: Cleaning House 99

CHAPTER EIGHT: Revolution! 119

CHAPTER NINE: The Tacoma Circus 137

CHAPTER TEN: Saving the Salish Sea 163

CHAPTER ELEVEN: The Fixer 183

CHAPTER TWELVE: Granny on Steroids 193

CHAPTER THIRTEEN: Creative Justice 207

CHAPTER FOURTEEN: The Mountain, the Woodshed, the Farm 227

CHAPTER FIFTEEN: Speaking Truth to Power. 243

CHAPTER SIXTEEN: Biting the Hand That Fed Me 261

CHAPTER SEVENTEEN: Granny the Nanny 269

CHAPTER EIGHTEEN: Dreams of the Future 285

Epilogue: Aftermaths 291

Selected Bibliography 301

Notes 305

Acknowledgments 317

Index 319

About the Author 343

PROLOGUE

A Lion Where There Were Lambs combines memoir, historical non-fiction, and essay. The tale recounts my search for justice and a purposeful life as a lawyer. It is also a paean to the beauty of the entire Pacific Northwest, including British Columbia and Alaska, places I have come to love. I have highlighted many controversial and famous legal events involving the Pacific Northwest that occurred from 1966 to 1979—an extraordinarily turbulent and transformative time in our nation's history. It was a time of anti-war protests against the Vietnam War, the onset of the sexual revolution, the rise and fall of national populist-driven environmental and consumer protection movements, and the rise of political conservatism.

As a personal narrative, this book contains memories of my conversations—perhaps not always precisely accurate to the language expressed, but accurate to the thoughts expressed. The book is based upon available court and congressional hearing transcripts where accessible, newspaper accounts, federal agency internal memoranda, and my own personal correspondence. It is intended not to be a scholarly work, but to reflect my personal memories and beliefs over time and to add to the historical record of some important events. I hope to entertain and sometimes instruct with life lessons learned on my journey. Some of the facts may be inadvertently fictional, and for that I apologize. I must tell you that I have shortened or omitted a few people's names or used pseudonyms, either because I have forgotten the name or to protect the guilty; otherwise my story is true, to the best of my recollection.

The first few chapters of the book are devoted to the early years that forever shaped my life: What motivated me to follow the road less traveled? Why did I start to question authority and step on toes? How did I come to adopt the persona of an outspoken and fearless would-be knight-errant on a crusade in the battle between good and evil, a paladin in search of justice and dedicated to the common good? Was I born a maverick who distrusted and defied authority? Or did my formative years change me?

For me, the choice of the road less traveled was heavily influenced by my experiences witnessing poverty, war, discrimination, and public corruption. Dissembling by governments and the irrationality of religion caused me to question authority and the status quo. It propelled me into a search for truth in a world too often manipulated by mendacity.

While some of the stories are cast in a lighthearted and humorous vein, there is an underlying serious theme throughout the book that is apropos for our times: in the era of fake news, untruthfulness, lack of civility, and government gridlock, American citizens must learn from history and exercise moral responsibility by speaking out to preserve the common good and our democratic institutions.

The closest descriptor of my character—or the person I would like to be remembered as—is found in the ninth sign of the zodiac, the sign of my birth: Sagittarius.

The symbol of a Sagittarian is an ancient Greek centaur, Chiron, half horse and half man—a warrior archer such as he who tutored Achilles, the Greek hero of the Trojan War. Independence is the overriding Sagittarian principle—we crave adventure and excitement; we are idealistic, with a great sense of humor. We will say anything, no matter how undiplomatic. A Sagittarian likes freedom, travel, and being outdoors. A Sagittarian dislikes being constrained, dislikes details. Sagittarians want to make the world a better place, and they choose careers that are well suited to accomplish that objective. This is who I would like to think I am.

***

Socrates once said, "The unexamined life is not worth living." While that sounds a bit harsh, I did try to fathom my rationale for taking on, in recent years, the semimonastic life of a writer, tethered to a desk like a cloistered monk transcribing a medieval manuscript, sorting out my memories as a young man and as a lawyer, when I could be enjoying, at leisure, my retirement. Eight reasons eventually came to mind.

1. To embark on a journey of self-discovery and understanding: Who am I? (Yes, writing has indeed forced me to reflect on the purpose and arc of my life.)
2. To tell some amazing stories. (Yes, that rings true.)
3. To offer life lessons from my accumulated experiences to instruct future generations. (Yes, this sounds quite admirable.)
4. To create a ready reference work for my eulogy. (Yes, although it sounds rather macabre.)
5. To shape the narrative of my professional life before someone else does. (Yes indeed—if it works in politics, why not here?)
6. To settle scores with old enemies. (Yes, although only a few of the most deserving will be so honored.)
7. To write a vanity piece, a hagiography. (No, although at first blush the title is suspect. This indulgence is primarily the province of well-known celebrities, famous and infamous and sometimes both. Like Bill Clinton, who said of presidential memoirs: "A lot are dull and self-serving. I hope mine is interesting and self-serving.")
8. To say, *"Scribo, ergo sum"*: I write, therefore I am. (Yes—with a tip of my pen to Descartes, I'll go with that. It sounds almost erudite, doesn't it?)

PART I

COMING OF AGE

1942–1968

Who in the world am I? Ah, that's the great puzzle.
    —Lewis Carroll, *Alice in Wonderland*

CHAPTER ONE

THE MAKING OF AN ICONOCLAST

What do children really remember from their childhood? I remember everything.

Chicago, 4:40 p.m., December 18, 1942, Swedish Covenant Hospital: I was born. Not an easy birth, mind you. I entered the world reluctantly, in a breech position, struggling to stay safe in the womb. Apparently, I tried to one-up Freud's concept of the human desire to return to the womb: I never wanted to leave.

One month later, I was christened—William Charles Erxleben, after the first names of my grandfathers—and soon was baptized at Saint John's Lutheran Church. My mother, who had a flair for the dramatic, would remind me in my teenage years that mine was a difficult and painful birth. She attributed the problem to the fact that I was stubborn and I simply didn't want to come out. Ever quick with an answer, I would say, "Who would want to be born in the middle of World War II? It wasn't safe."

"You've got an answer for everything, don't you?" she said. "You'll probably be a lawyer." She was prescient.

***

I lived in Chicago until I was ten years old. Chicago was and still is today predominantly a Catholic city—like Boston, Saint Louis, and Spokane; it is an ethnic city where waves of German, Jewish, Polish, Italian, Greek, and Irish immigrants had their own distinct neighborhoods. In the 1950s, black people were relegated to the less desirable south side of the city. Norwood Park on the northwest side of the city, my neighborhood, was more diverse ethnically than most of the city, but virtually all white.

My father, Walter Sr., was as conservative religiously as he was politically. The son of a German immigrant bricklayer, he was the first in his family to attend college. A self-made man and a staunch conservative Republican, he despised Democrats and thought that Roosevelt's New Deal was just a government giveaway.

Father managed to put himself through college and medical school during the Great Depression. After starting a solo medical practice in Chicago, he married my mother and started a family. World War II changed everything. In 1942, at thirty-four years of age, he was drafted into the army as a medical doctor, given the rank of captain, and assigned to the tank corps, where his hearing was damaged during a training exercise, causing tinnitus, a persistent ringing in the ear. He was medically discharged from the army and awarded fifteen dollars a month partial-disability payment, so he returned to Chicago to restart his medical practice.

Like many Germans, my father was a big man: six feet two inches. He had a full head of coal-black hair and weighed 230 pounds. At Wayne State University, in Midtown Detroit, he played football, as a tackle. Later, he would complete medical school at the University of Michigan and do postgraduate work in Poland. As a physician and surgeon, he did it all: family practice, general surgery, and obstetrics. The pace of his practice was grueling—house calls were made many nights of the week, hospital rounds to see patients every weekend, and sleep deprivation from frequently delivering babies in the middle of the night.

Of all my father's German traits, the most difficult one for me to accept was his version of the German notion of discipline. I respected my father and admired his intelligence and his skill as a doctor, but

I greatly feared his wrath. My father didn't countenance nonconformity with either his rules or his beliefs. He was quick to anger and demanded unstinting obedience from his children to his authority. He ruled the roost with an iron hand that was very often applied to my backside.[1]

My mother, Sara Louise Erxleben (*née* Githens), or Sally, as she liked to be called, was the fifth of eight children, a product of German and Scandinavian heritage. Like my father, my mother was an imposing figure, at five feet ten, 180 pounds. A generous woman with a ready smile, auburn hair, and an outgoing personality, she stood out. Given her height, it is not surprising that my adult height is the same as my father's, but to my chagrin, I remain the shortest of the family's offspring.

After attending the University of Toledo and Michigan State University, Mother worked as a dietician for Stouffer's Restaurants in Chicago, where she met my father. She would eventually give birth to four sons: Walter Jr., the oldest; myself, now nicknamed Bill, the second oldest; Richard, five years younger, the son most resembling my father; and Terry, eight years younger, and like me, a redhead.

Religion, politics, and world affairs were of little concern to my mother. She was quite content to put all her time and energy into being a homemaker. One flaw in her character—which I usually found amusing—was that she pretty much said everything that came to mind; there was little self-censoring. One day she said to me, "I really like the fact that your father has little body hair."

"Why?" I said.

"It's a sign a person is further evolved from the apes." Her logic was always interesting, if questionable.

Later, to my astonishment, on a visit to Chicago's Lincoln Park Zoo primate house, I came upon a beautifully marked and vividly colored small primate with the name "Erxleben monkey" splashed across the top of its cage. My mother, it seems, may have had an uncanny insight into the ancient roots of our family tree. This rare species of monkey was named after a famous German naturalist, Johann Polycarp Erxleben (1744–1777), who discovered it. Johann's equally famous mother, Dorothea Erxleben (1715–1762), overcame great odds to

PLATE XXX.

ERXLEBEN'S GUENON.

become the first female physician in Germany. During the 1980's, a commemorative stamp was issued in Germany honoring her.

Mother was strong-willed and independent, stubborn and difficult at times, and politically incorrect most of the time—definitely a one-of-a-kind character, prone to melodrama, a drama queen for sure. But no matter, she was a hoot, and I adored her.

Father's religion, Missouri Synod Lutheran, became the family's religion. It is a conservative religion that espouses a fundamentalist Christian doctrine with German roots. The faith is based upon the teachings of Martin Luther, a law school dropout who became a Roman Catholic Augustinian monk and priest. Luther became a seminal figure in the Protestant Reformation five hundred years ago when he disseminated his Ninety-Five Theses, challenging the practices of the Roman Catholic Church; he is now one of the most historically dramatic examples of telling truth to power. He brazenly charged the church with corruption, particularly for the vile practice of paying indulgences, which were used primarily for the renovation of church properties in Rome, in exchange for forgiveness of sins.

Martin Luther did not mince words in his condemnation of the Catholic Church. The pope, in Luther's view, was not only the Antichrist but, in the hyperbolic vernacular of the day, also a sodomite and a transvestite. Pope Leo X, unsurprisingly, excommunicated him. But the Reformation, a period of violent religious conflict in Europe lasting more than a century, split the Roman Catholic Church and opened the door for the establishment of thousands of churches under a score of denominations, including Lutheranism.

Like many Europeans at the time, Martin Luther was also antagonistic toward Jews. In his later writings, Luther said that Jewish synagogues and homes should be destroyed, Jewish people's money confiscated, and their liberty curtailed. During World War II, the Nazis used Luther's writings, together with eugenics, to justify the Holocaust.

The Lutheran Church—Missouri Synod was organized in Missouri in the mid-1800s and later founded in Chicago. Until World War I, services were conducted in German. Among the church's beliefs are biblical inerrancy and that it is the only true church. The church also supports literal creationism and rejects evolution.

As soon as we were old enough, my older brother and I were duly enrolled at Our Savior Lutheran School, an affiliate of the church, only a short walk from our house in Norwood Park. My most memorable Lutheran religious dogma involved dooming most people while favoring a chosen few. Here's what I remember: Eternal hellfire and damnation await all those whose sins are not forgiven. You are doomed if you are not baptized and confirmed. You are doomed if you do not pray, confess, and repent your sins regularly. Catholics are especially doomed because they venerate Mary and hate Martin Luther.

Then comes the good part, the saving grace: Jesus loves you because you are Missouri Synod Lutheran. You are not doomed: follow the church's rules and you will ascend to heaven on Judgment Day.

That's pretty much all I remember from one hour of catechism each day for five years.

Mr. Christian (how aptly named) was my fourth-grade teacher. I had no third-grade teacher because I skipped third grade. I started in third grade, but after a few weeks was promoted to fourth grade. It seems I finished my classwork quickly and then walked around the room holding my breath to see how many revolutions I could make before I turned beet red and ran out of breath. Both the teacher and my parents thought I needed more to do. Today, they would probably say I had attention deficit disorder and give me a prescription for Ritalin, along with some counseling.

Mr. Christian had been a Lutheran missionary in China; following church doctrine, he had great zeal to convert the unbaptized masses to Lutheranism. "People must be converted to Christianity, to the Lutheran Church," he would say. "Children will go to hell unless they are baptized and saved by the Lord Jesus Christ." I really took his message to heart, and I started to plan my first conversion. Soon thereafter, as I was walking home from school, carrying my Bible encased in white leather with my name emblazoned in gold lettering, I spotted my opportunity: a boy a bit younger than me, probably about six years old, riding a tricycle.

"Have you been baptized?" I said with a feeling of elation, eagerly anticipating the religious conversion that I was sure was about to happen if he said no.

With a dumbfounded expression on his face, the boy said nothing.

"Have you accepted the Lord Jesus Christ as your Savior?" I continued, perplexed by the boy's refusal to answer.

Still, no answer.

"You do want to go to heaven, don't you?"

Silence.

Saving the best for last, I used a surefire Christian missionary conversion technique: I raised my right arm high into the air, Bible in hand, and, overcome with religious fervor, I told him he was on the road to perdition.

"You don't want to burn in hell and meet the devil, do you?" I shouted.

Terrified and screaming, "Mama, help!" the boy, starting to cry at the prospect of a fiery encounter with the devil, turned his trike rapidly around and pedaled quickly away.

It was my first and last attempt at a religious conversion. I guess I shouldn't feel too bad. Mormon missionaries convert only four people a year on average, and they know what they are doing. Soon thereafter, the Christian religion became like Santa Claus: I believed the story for a while, and then I didn't.

BATESVILLE

By the beginning of the 1950s, Father was dissatisfied with Chicago and the ever-increasing congestion of a bustling big city. He yearned for a simpler life in a small town. But he was determined first to obtain his board certification in surgery. He accepted a position as chief surgical resident at Saint Vincent Hospital in Indianapolis, Indiana, and the rest of the family remained at our house in Chicago while he stayed in an apartment in Indianapolis. He was absent for a full year, with only occasional visits by him to Chicago, or to him in Indianapolis by my mother, with her four young sons in tow.

During my father's residency, the city fathers of Batesville—a small manufacturing and farming community in Indiana that needed another doctor, especially one with strong surgical skills—recruited my father to open a medical practice. In small towns, medical doctors were scarce and revered. Father accepted the offer.

Batesville, with a population of only 3,200 at the time, is located in southeastern Indiana, just thirty-five miles from Cincinnati, in the heartland of early German immigration settlements. It had a well-equipped Roman Catholic regional hospital, containing a fully staffed surgical center with only one other doctor in town. Founded in 1852, the city had a solid economic base consisting of the manufacture of caskets, furniture, and hospital supplies.

Batesville Casket Company, the largest company in town, was then and still is the preeminent manufacturer of high-end caskets in the United States. Batesville was known as "Casket City." The company in the 1940s pioneered the metal casket, replacing wooden caskets, and over the years, Batesville Casket Company has continued to innovate. To accommodate the ever-increasing corpulence of the American public, today the company offers expanded-width caskets, formerly twenty-four inches wide, but now twenty-eight inches wide. Batesville Casket calls it "a little extra room for life's final journey."

Batesville had only one movie theater, but there were ten churches and fourteen taverns. It was a meat-and-potatoes German town. Asian cuisine was limited to canned chop suey, and canned salmon was a special treat. The wine of choice was Mogen David, which must have been the best wine, because it tasted just like the wine offered during communion.

The houses were mostly working-class, tidy with small lawns and very well kept. But there was also the town's small elite, the Catholic families who owned the factories, some of whom lived in large mansions at the ends of long driveways, fronted by wide expanses of green lawn. It was a friendly town, where people left their homes unlocked and their car keys in the ignition. Almost everyone knew everyone else—either directly or by reputation. The crime rate was extremely low, and if you needed it, any resident would give you the shirt off their back. When you passed someone on the sidewalk, you always said hello; it was a major affront not to.

But Batesville also had a dark side, or more accurately, a white side. It was a tale of two cities. Only white people lived in the town.[2]

Although the town was north of the Mason-Dixon Line, Batesville had a full set of prejudices and then some. As if little had changed, Batesville mirrored the split following the Protestant Reformation between Protestant northern Germany and the large conservative Roman Catholic southern Free State of Bavaria. Batesville was about equally divided between Catholics and Protestants. They didn't mix much socially, and each side was convinced that they had the keys to heaven. The Catholics often attended their own private religious schools, mostly same-sex schools. Intermarriage was frowned upon, but that didn't stop Protestant high school boys from lusting after Catholic high school girls. They were convinced that these girls—sexually repressed by their isolation in convent-run schools—would enjoy a romp in the hay if only they could be enticed beyond their cloistered walls. But the Protestant boys were ecumenical in their desire: they thought the town's Protestant ministers' daughters equally repressed and just as vulnerable.

In my public high school graduating class, there were sixty students. Only six of us went on to college and graduated. Most of my male classmates joined the military, went to work on the farm, or worked in the local casket or furniture factories. With some notable exceptions, the women got married and raised children.

Batesville was a "whites-only after dark" sundown town. Black people were not allowed to stay overnight in the city, although they were welcome during the day for domestic or other menial work. There were still memories of a black lynching in Versailles, the Ripley County seat, twenty years earlier.

Jews fared better in Batesville: there weren't any, although one of the town's grocers was suspect. No open homosexuals lived in Batesville either. In fact, we didn't believe that homosexual men, let alone lesbians, even existed. But there were rampant rumors of farm boys having sex with an assortment of farm animals. We were sure that rumor was true. And if you owned a foreign car—even a German Volkswagen—there was always a chance you were a pinko communist.

Apart from this wide range of prejudices, Batesville was a really friendly and nice town.[3]

**

My father had bad karma. Only five short years after we moved to Batesville, he was dead. At home early one morning, he had a massive heart attack and died at age forty-nine. My brothers and I were called home from school and told the news. I was fourteen, a sophomore in high school.

I was despondent at his death, but, now emancipated from the authoritarianism of his rule and unburdened from his ultraconservative political and religious beliefs, I was free to forge my own path. My mother had four young sons to raise and educate. The house was paid for, but there was only a small military life insurance policy. (My father didn't believe in life insurance.) His death upended my world and seared into my memory the temporariness of everything, the fragility of life, the uncertainty of expectations.

MIAMI UNIVERSITY

In September of 1959 my mother drove me to the college of my choice—Miami University, in Oxford, Ohio. Forty miles from Batesville, as the crow flies, but almost two hours by car. The trip was over curvy backcountry roads, across two covered bridges, through countless acres of corn and soybeans, and past the acrid smell of small dairy and pig farms; the last ten miles were unpaved. It was Miami University through the back door. I was sixteen.

Miami University was founded in 1809. The redbrick, neo-Georgian architecture of the campus gives it a decided colonial feeling. The university is considered the "public ivy" of Ohio and the "Mother of Fraternities." This refers to the Miami triad: Miami is the founding home of three major national fraternities: Beta Theta Pi, Phi Delta Theta, and Sigma Chi. Most of campus social life was organized around fraternities and sororities.

I went through the fall first-year fraternity rush in hopes of pledging one of the well-known national fraternities. I wasn't too enthusiastic about joining a fraternity—because you had to endure silly rituals and harassment as a pledge—but it was an established part of the Miami tradition. Ignored by the triad, who apparently weren't impressed by my yellow-leather-sleeved, blue-cloth Batesville High School football letter jacket (with the letter *B* removed, but you could still see its outline). I ended up pledging Delta Chi.

The best steak sandwich in Oxford turned out to be the undoing of the only other student from Batesville attending Miami. Nick, I'll call him, the scion of a wealthy and prominent Batesville family, went to high school at an elite private Catholic boarding school and was a junior at Miami when I was a freshman. Early one Sunday morning, after a Saturday night of drinking, drunk as a good German on a bender can be, Nick developed an overwhelming desire for the famous

Mac and Joe's steak sandwich, available only in an alleyway tavern in downtown Oxford. There was a problem, however: it was 1:00 a.m. and the tavern had closed at midnight, which was the female students' weekend curfew hour.

Undeterred by the time, and totally fixated on the sandwich, Nick broke into the tavern, went into the kitchen and turned on the stove, grabbed a big juicy steak from the refrigerator, and began frying it. Regrettably for Nick's college career, before the steak finished cooking and he could savor Oxford's most famous sandwich, the Oxford police noticed smoke coming out of the stove vent on the tavern roof. Nick was arrested, expelled from school, and escaped jail time only by agreeing to join the army. Many people thought his punishment was too harsh. *Nick couldn't help himself,* they thought. *They really are, after all, great sandwiches.*

In my sophomore year, it was time to declare a major. After a disastrous year taking Latin in a public high school class taught by a Catholic priest, Father Aloysius—whom I suspected of not liking Protestants—I felt a liberal arts major was not an option: it had a foreign language requirement. There had been five boys in Father Aloysius's class, including my older brother, Walter. At the end of the course, the priest awarded four Ds and one C. Walter received the C, the only C to besmirch his record as class valedictorian.

I am genetically incapable of learning another language, I convinced myself. I abandoned my dream of becoming a history and government professor, where foreign language proficiency is required for a PhD. But there was no foreign language requirement for a business degree, so I took the easier path and chose to major in general business (the business major that allowed the most courses in the liberal arts) with a minor in economics.

I soon had several qualms about a business career, especially one with a large corporation. In 1959 I had read the best-selling book *The Organization Man,* by William Whyte—now considered one of the most influential books on management. His central thesis was that most Americans believe in a group ethic for decision-making in large organizations, and as a consequence, individual creativity is destroyed by the conformity and risk-averse behavior demanded as the price for success.

The thought of working in the bowels of the bureaucracy of a large corporation subject to groupthink was anathema to me. I knew my personality and temperament would not permit me to become an organization man. I did not like to be told what to do, and I got bored easily—a condition probably caused by my self-diagnosed attention deficit disorder. On the other hand, I thought I might have the predisposition for more-entrepreneurial business ventures. I saw myself as strategic, not detail oriented, as well as self-driven, creative, resilient, and unafraid to take risks.

But there were other significant problems that I had with the idea of a business career: How would working in business and the sole pursuit of economic gain contribute to a sense of purpose, a value-infused and impactful life? And could my creative bent—an itch I wanted to scratch—be satisfied working in an ad agency on Madison Avenue in New York City? But then, who wants to dedicate their life to making up jingles for a cartoon character like Joe Camel or Tony the Tiger?

SEE THE GIRL WITH THE RED DRESS ON

There is a saying: "The odds are good, but the goods are odd." This saying is often attributed to women who go to Alaska to find a mate because of a favorable male-to-female ratio. However, while the goods may be odd in Alaska, the odds are actually not that good: the ratio of men to women there is now only 52 percent to 48 percent. At Miami, however, the odds at the time were good for men—with 46 percent male to 54 percent female students—and the goods were good too. The campus was overflowing with attractive, intelligent women from fine families. *This college may be a wonderful place to look for a mate,* I concluded, and so commenced my search.

Though I was slow getting started, by my junior year in college, things were looking up for me socially. I was finally as old as most of the entering first-year women students. Also, the legal drinking age in Ohio was eighteen, and by midyear I would be old enough to drink 3.2

percent beer at Mac and Joe's and the other weekend social gathering spots.

I was selected as a resident assistant in a new first-year men's dorm, Anderson Hall (a position not available to junior women in women's dorms). For additional income, I quickly secured the only laundry and dry-cleaning franchise permitted in the building. As a resident assistant, I received free room and board and a small stipend; as an additional perk, I also had a room to myself. At the neighboring women's residence, Porter Hall, the sophomore women counselors shared a room and received no compensation; it was considered an honor for them. Anderson and Porter resident halls shared a common dining hall; the prospects for social interaction looked promising.

One night in the fall of 1961, the women counselors from Porter Hall organized a meet and greet with the male resident assistants from Anderson Hall. In the large living room of Porter Hall, I filled out my name tag with a black marking pen and started to circulate among the assemblage of twenty or so female counselors. One tall (five foot seven), strikingly pretty, slender brunette caught my eye. She was wearing the brightest red velvet dress that I had ever seen and stood out among all the other women. I maneuvered my way toward her, glancing at her name tag in the process. I saw that her last name was Reichmuth, German sounding. After a quick count, I calculated it was one letter longer than Erxleben. *A woman with a name like that might be induced to change it,* I deduced, before I had even met her. While it may not have been a *coup de foudre*—love at first sight—it certainly was name at first sight.

She said her first name was Gayle, and she explained that her last name was Swiss, Swiss German to be exact. (An omen for a potential romance, perhaps.) Gayle was a border-state belle from Louisville, Kentucky, who had lived on Sweetbriar Lane and still said, "Hi, y'all." Her father was an executive with Hillerich and Bradsby, the famous Louisville Slugger baseball bat company.

This was going to be a challenging matchup. We started to date, but only sporadically at first. I would call her on a Thursday night for a weekend date, and she would say she already had a date. I knew I would have to compete harder, and I needed a plan. I would make her laugh.

And laugh she did. But here's the best part: We went on a hayride one evening, in a wagon pulled by a tractor, into the farmlands surrounding Oxford, and for some inexplicable reason, I decided to risk it all and sing my favorite love song—"Unchained Melody"—softly in her ear. I was even so brave as to sing the high notes in a falsetto voice. She told me I had a very good voice. I teared up. No one had ever—and I do mean *ever*—said that to me before. (Kenny Krinhop and I were barred from the Batesville Grade School mandatory mixed chorus in the seventh grade because we couldn't carry a tune.)

Of course, Gayle was wrong about the quality of my singing, but it was hard for her to think negatively about anyone.

We had a lot in common; we liked to walk, we liked to talk, and we liked Ingmar Bergman films. We were convinced that the films had deep meanings; we just didn't understand them. We liked music (she played the piano and sang); we liked plays; and of course, we liked to laugh. She was dean's list smart.

ENLIGHTENMENT

I tried atheism, and I can't stick at it: I keep having doubts.

—Ian Hislop, British satirist

By the time I graduated high school, I considered myself a religious agnostic. I really didn't know what to believe. I thought that if we could all agree that life is a great mystery, it would be an admission of what we really know. We shouldn't make up the answers, or be prisoners of the accidents of our births, or accept blindly the cultural inheritance of our parents. Since there are thousands of religions in the world, how can they all be true? Humans, it seems, are highly programmable and subject to the siren call of groupthink and tribal loyalties.

To find one's path in life, everyone has to struggle with the metaphysics of one's own existence. Some will be guided by a religion; others will find their moral direction through philosophy or conscience. Although achieving any adequate answer is impossible because it is unknowable, the search itself is important, I believe. In the end we must all find our own path to lead a purposeful life in a sea of uncertainty.

Every day of college, as I passed under the archway of Upham Hall, I read the inscription carved into the stone: "You shall know the truth, and the truth shall make you free." I was reminded that my goal in college was to become an educated person and as nearly as possible try to discern truth from untruths. Many educational institutions pay homage to the search for truth as the essence of their educational mission. The Latin word *veritas* appears in the mottoes of most colleges. In Roman mythology, Veritas was the goddess of truth. In academic circles, "The truth shall set you free" refers to academic freedom and the power of learning. The original text, however, is from the Bible and speaks to religious, not temporal, truth. I decided that for me, truth would be based upon its accepted secular definition—reality, facts, and science—not an imaginary deity or myth of creation.

In searching for life's meaning, I sought enlightenment from the fashionable college intellectual oasis of the day: existentialism and its philosophers Kierkegaard, Buber, and Nietzsche; as well as novelists who pursued existentialist themes, such as Dostoyevsky, Sartre, and Camus. Existentialists believe that we are born into an indifferent universe, not of our choosing, where humans possess radical freedoms, making us completely responsible for the actions that determine our lives; and, in Sartre's words, we are "condemned to be free."

Søren Kierkegaard, widely considered to be the first existentialist, said that the individual—not society or religion—is solely responsible for giving meaning to life and for living it passionately. Life is random and unfair, beyond the control of the individual. Humans are forced to make sense of the world themselves and to forge their own identities. Joseph Campbell, a twentieth-century writer and philosopher, perhaps put it best when he said, "Life has no meaning. Each of us has meaning and we bring it to life. It is a waste to be asking the question when you are the answer."

As humans, we may be genetically hardwired for religion by an evolutionary need for tribal identity to furnish a sense of community, belongingness, and protection; to counter a natural fear of death by providing confirmation of an afterlife; and to provide a sense of

assurance that we are more than mere specks in a giant unfathom-
able universe. We are also, I believe, hardwired to exhibit empathy for
each other, a principle expressed by the golden rule. This rule may have
begun as an evolutionary survival strategy for human beings, a biolog-
ical imperative. This generosity may have been essential to the survival
of our early ancestors, who lived in small groups of hunter-gatherers.
Scientists view our generosity toward one another as a remarkable
feature of our species. The golden rule, which has both secular and
religious roots, is simply an expression of human empathy. The rule—
predating the ancient Greeks—is the principle that one should behave
toward others as one would have others behave toward oneself. The
golden rule is ordained in the American Constitution itself, which says
that the government should promote the general welfare, the common
good.

I decided that the golden rule would be my guidepost, giving my
life purpose and meaning. It would become my white horse, my moral
compass, and my conscience. My spirituality would be temporal, not
religious: the glory of music, art, live theater, and the quietude of meditation would be the cathedrals where I would celebrate the wonderment of human existence. Nature would be my guardian angel: a hike
in the woods accompanied by my black Labrador retriever, his tail in a
helicopter wag no matter the weather; the sounds of a rushing stream
and the call-and-response of melodies from songbirds; the shimmer-
ing stars in dark night skies. Experiences like these would become my
sources of solace, renewal, and reverie. When you are out in nature, it
clears your mind, your attitude, and makes you think of the real value
of living.

***

As I approached my junior year in college, I began to question the
entire Greek system. There was obvious discrimination against Jews,
foreign students, blacks, and other people of color, all of whom were
usually relegated to their own fraternities or lived independently in
the dormitories. In most cases there was little identifiable social conscience present in the frat house culture. My growing interest in social

justice led me to join the campus YMCA, a secular group interested in the lofty goal of making the world a better place. Dean Stripple, an assistant dean of students and associate professor of religion, was also the faculty advisor to the YMCA and became my mentor. His credo was: "Follow your passion, lead a value-based life; good deeds are self-rewarding."

And so I started down a different path, a path less traveled—at least at Miami. I deactivated from the fraternity and abandoned a Greek scene that I had not actually ever participated in. In my senior year I was elected president of the YMCA.

Now it was time to figure out what I wanted to do next. My father instilled in his sons the importance of a higher education. A graduate education as a goal was strongly encouraged. I could continue my business education and get an MBA, but I already had an undergraduate degree in business and a master's degree seemed redundant. I didn't want to become a doctor, because I couldn't stand the sight of blood and the hours were terrible. That left the law. It would give me maximum flexibility to practice public or private law, enter politics, engage in business, or work in government. I'd figure out what I really wanted to do after I obtained a law degree.

CHAPTER TWO

ADVENTURE BOUND

My guiding philosophy was to work hard and play hard—part of the work ethic of my German heritage, I guess. (I delivered morning papers on my bike—rain, shine, or snow—seven days a week for five years in Batesville.) In college I would be a diligent student throughout the school year, pay for my tuition with a variety of part-time jobs, including as a dishwasher and referee of intermural fraternity football games (my most dangerous job), and pay for my room and board by being a dorm counselor and resident assistant in freshmen dormitories. But during the summer breaks, I would seek adventure, if at the same time I could save money to help pay for my education.

NEW ORLEANS

My sophomore year, Nate Rodgers and I were roommates and counselors in a freshmen men's dorm. For April spring break, we decided to hone our hitchhiking skills by traveling from Oxford, Ohio, to New Orleans, Louisiana—an 850-mile trip—to join spring celebrations in the French Quarter centered on Bourbon Street. On one leg of the journey, we were let out on the north side of Jackson, Mississippi.

While waiting for our next ride, a Mississippi state police car pulled up alongside us with its red emergency lights flashing. The uniformed officer stepped out of the car and approached us. "Need a lift through town, do you, boys?" the officer said with a heavy southern accent, not too happy about our presence.

"We sure do," we answered in tandem, wary of his real interest in us and noting the sawed-off shotgun cradled in a slot by the front seat of his vehicle.

The policeman opened the back door of his prominently marked squad car. "Get in the back seat and I'll give you a ride to the south end of town." Halfway through Jackson we discovered his real interest: "You boys aren't civil rights agitators, are you?"

"No, sir, we're not," Nate said as convincingly as possible. Both of us were aware of recent, simmering civil rights tensions and unjustified arrests of civil rights workers in the South; we didn't want to end up in a Mississippi jail. (Later, we learned that Jackson was on the route for a contingent of three hundred civil rights Freedom Riders headed for New Orleans the next month, in May.)

As the officer sped across town with the red light revolving atop his squad car, in words seared indelibly into my memory like a branding iron, he explained the nuances of Mississippi law enforcement: "Hereabouts, when a white man murders another white man, we arrest him and throw the key away. But when a nigger kills another nigger, we don't even investigate, because, if we're lucky, he'll kill another nigger." The police officer then turned to look at us and smiled to make sure his words had their desired effect. They did. We were appalled, increasingly apprehensive, and dismayed, but said nothing in response. Then to double down on the imagery, the officer said, "Yeah, and last week I took a pregnant nigger mama that was about to hatch to the hospital. I put her in the back seat of my car and told her if her pickaninny started to come out, to push it back in. 'Cause I don't want no mess in my car." Then he laughed uproariously and pulled the squad car over onto the shoulder of the highway to let us out.

This encounter was an eye-opener for me. *How could an officer sworn to uphold the law be so prejudiced?* As we stood by the highway waiting for our next ride, Nate said, "No wonder so many young blacks are joining the Black Panther Party."

EUROPE OR BUST

Skipping commencement exercises after our 1963 graduation from Miami, Nate and I—with our hitchhiking skills still intact and a sign that said, "Europe or Bust!"—hitchhiked from Oxford, Ohio, to Montreal, Canada, a seaport city located on the Saint Lawrence Seaway, another 850-mile journey. The sign was an inspirational piece of marketing. We seldom had to wait long for a ride because people were curious to hear about our adventure. Our plan was to hitchhike to Canada and obtain free passage working as deckhands on a Europe-bound ocean freighter.

One of our rides on our four-day journey to Montreal was with a Catholic priest, who, after hearing our plans in a taxicab-style confession, said with envy, "If I were forty years younger, I'd be there with you." In Clinton, Michigan, he stopped and bought us a couple of beers in a local tavern and, clearly still enamored with our story, took us to the office of the local paper for an interview and picture. After the interview, the newspaper reporter promised to send us a copy of the story to our home address. (When we returned home, a copy of the *Clinton Local* was waiting for us.)

Within a week after arriving in Montreal, by walking the docks and asking to see the captain of the vessel, we secured passage to Europe working as deckhands on a Norwegian tramp freighter sailing to Le Havre, France. The work was far from glamorous: we spent ten days chipping paint with a ball-peen hammer for twelve hours a day, but it was worth it. For two glorious months, on a whirlwind tour, mostly camping out, we traveled from Oslo to Rome and saw much of Western Europe. On the return voyage in late August, as passengers from Europe's largest port, Rotterdam, to New York, we sailed on a low-budget passenger ship full of Dutch students. It was a decrepit 440-foot converted World War II Liberty ship, without stabilizers to reduce the roll of the ship in wind and waves. When we left Rotterdam, the

The Clinton Local   **Thursday June 20, 1963**

ADVENTURE BOUND

The spirit of adventure is not dead. On Monday, George Rogers of Michigan City, Ind., and Bill Erxelben, of Batesville, Ind., stopped in following their graduation from Miami University. They're hitchhiking to Montreal where they will hire out on a Europe-bound freighter and hope to spend the summer touring in England and on the European continent.

weather was balmy, with light winds and mostly sunny skies, but that soon changed. Within three days we were steaming through the eye of the first hurricane of the season on the Atlantic Ocean, a Category 2 with wind speeds of over ninety miles an hour and mountainous waves; I lost twelve pounds from seasickness. Too bad I wasn't dieting. At the end of the trip, we totaled our expenses: about $500 each for the entire summer. Ben Franklin would have approved.

SEATTLE WORLD'S FAIR

Of all my summer adventures, it was during the summer after my junior year of college, when I worked in Seattle, that the trajectory of my life was forever changed.

"Go West, young man" was Horace Greeley's clarion call to young men of the nineteenth century seeking adventure and a new beginning. When Frank Walker, a farm boy from Batesville who was my high school classmate, football teammate, and best high school friend, called me and said that he and a fraternity brother, Bob Heasty, from Hanover College in Indiana, were planning to head west to fight forest fires and possibly make it to the 1962 Seattle World's Fair, I was all ears.

"Are you interested?" he said. "We will work our way across the country to the fair."

I jumped at the chance. "Sign me up," I quickly replied with only a vague understanding of what the trip would entail.

I had never been west of the Mississippi River, but I saw that tracing part of the Lewis and Clark National Historic Trail would be a great opportunity to follow in the footsteps of the best river camping trip ever and see the World's Fair too. It would also be an opportunity to head up into the high country and escape the oppressive humidity of another hot southern Indiana summer.

The trip seemed like a particularly good idea since Bob and Frank had fought forest fires in Idaho the previous summer and saved a ton of money for school. You were paid for twenty-four hours a day while fighting a fire, with tent and board provided. The only catch was, the fire season usually didn't start until mid to late summer. We would have to find other employment and work our way out to Seattle, job to job.

We decided that as soon as college ended in June, Frank and I would drive in Frank's 1939 black Ford sedan from Batesville to Manhattan, Kansas (Bob's hometown). From there we would head west in Bob's car, a mid-1950s Chevy sedan, sharing all expenses.

Our first job was a monthlong stint on a natural gas pipeline crew in Burlington, Colorado, where I worked digging ditches and as a welder's assistant. We managed to save a good chunk of our wages and mail the money home. Then we decided to take a fast track to riches by panning for gold in Estes Park, Colorado, in Rocky Mountain National Park—highly illegal, we later learned. To escape the mosquitoes, we bushwhacked into a remote area of the park and climbed above the tree line until we reached the top of Mount Craig, at twelve thousand feet, and since we had not brought a tent, we camped in a shallow crevice at the base of a giant boulder. Our choice of shelter proved to be misguided when a thunderstorm that evening left us soaking wet in our sleeping bags. After a few days of panning for gold—and no gold—with our rations of beans, bacon, and a canteen full of gin exhausted, we glissaded down the snow-covered north slopes of the mountain in half the time it took us to climb it and headed to Wyoming, applying unsuccessfully for quintessential macho jobs as oil roughnecks and, later, in Missoula, Montana, as smoke jumpers.

Fortunately for us, we were unqualified for these highly dangerous jobs. With our money running low, we took the highway near the difficult Nez Perce Trail, made famous by Lewis and Clark, over the Bitterroot Mountains of Idaho, along the north fork of the Salmon River. We stopped in the Batesville-size city of Salmon, Idaho, where we car camped on an island city park on the Salmon River, waiting for the fire season to start.

To while away the time, Frank one day had the bright idea to float down the Salmon River from our camping area to the Carmen Bridge, which crossed the river about five miles away. Eager to join the fun, I asked Frank if I could come along as a passenger. Bob, eager to facilitate this crazy idea, agreed to pick us up with the car at the bridge. The river flowed out of sight from the highway until the takeout point, leaving us to guess at the river conditions. But no mind, we were young and adventurous; after all, Lewis and Clark didn't know what was beyond the next bend in the river either.

Frank blew up his single-person air mattress, put it in the river, and climbed on top of it, lying facedown on his stomach. I jumped on his back and lay on top of him, and off we went. The river was relatively shallow in places, but the current was so strong that you could not stand up. For a while, things were uneventful, until the mattress sprung a leak; every five minutes or so, Frank had to blow furiously on the inflation tube to keep us afloat. Since we had no way to steer the air mattress, we were at the mercy of the current as we floated down the river past farms and forestlands.

After about an hour afloat, we were relieved to see Bob's car in the distance, where he was waiting at the takeout by the Carmen Bridge.

On the right side of the river, to our horror, we saw a large sign that said, "Diversion Dam (Caution boaters! Go left! Dam on river right!)" There was a spillway over the dam ahead, but without any ability to maneuver the air mattress to the left side of the river, our fate was sealed. In unison we screamed, "Oh shit! Oh shit!"—words immortalized in the movie *Deliverance* as most appropriate when you are on a river in a canoe or, God forbid, on an air mattress and uncontrollably about to go over a waterfall.

Hanging on for dear life to the air mattress, we were soon airborne as we shot over the dam. Fortunately for us, the fall was only about five feet, and the water was deep enough at the bottom to avoid injury. Temporarily separated from the air mattress, we scrambled to catch up to it. We then climbed back aboard and floated downstream a short distance to the takeout, where we met Bob, who had a dumbfounded look on his face that said, "I'm glad it wasn't me."

The Salmon River, famously known in its early days as the "River of No Return," almost became the river of no return for Frank and me.

***

To the dismay of the locals and the Indians in the area, many of whom depended upon summer firefighting jobs each year, it was raining, and the fire season didn't start as usual. One day, Bob got lucky and was arrested for speeding and fined eighty dollars by the local county judge. We didn't have enough money to pay the fine, so the county judge said Bob would have to go to jail until the fine was paid. Frank and I were jealous. Bob received three meals a day and a roof over his head while Frank and I were left to sleep on the ground, warding off mosquitoes and foraging for food. During the day—to make enough money to free Bob from jail—we bucked hay bales on ranches and picked cherries from orchards (eating a few in the process), alongside migrant farmworkers.

Working with migrant laborers was revelatory for us. It was hard not to be sympathetic to the plight of the undocumented workers picking fruit, a job few Americans would do. Since you were paid based upon your production, often the only way for the hardworking Mexican adults to earn enough money to support a family was to have the whole family join in the harvest. We saw children as young as six years old picking cherries on the lower branches while their parents worked the top of the trees on ladders. The living conditions of the workers were abysmal; housing was seldom provided. Many families lived in tents or slept in their cars or trucks without access to bathing or toilet facilities.

In a little less than a week, Frank and I made enough money to post bail for Bob and buy enough gas to get us to Seattle and the World's Fair. The county judge held a court hearing, and Bob was released from jail, looking relaxed and well fed. In a sternly worded warning, the judge told us that we were "indigent itinerants" and had twenty-four hours to get out of Idaho. *So much for Idaho hospitality,* we reckoned.

The next day, we traveled through Spokane, Washington, sleeping in a city park that night, and then headed west through the lake district of open pine forest outside of Spokane until we hit a long stretch of mostly treeless grasslands and wheat fields occasionally punctuated with a pothole lake or the verdant green of an irrigated field. We navigated over the Cascade Mountains by way of Snoqualmie Pass into Seattle. At the crest of the Cascade Mountains, we crossed a political and climatic divide. To the forested west, the climate was wet and temperate and the politics mostly blue. To the wide-open spaces of the east, the climate was dry, the summers hot, the winters cold, and the politics deeply red.[1]

It was a glorious Seattle day—the sun was shining, the humidity was low, and the year-round temperate coastal climate was delightful. We saw no mosquitoes or other biting insects anywhere in the urban area, a big plus for anyone from the Midwest.

Visitors always described Seattle's snow- and ice-capped mountain skyline—anchored by Mount Rainier to the south, Mount Baker to the north, the Cascade Mountains to the east, and the Olympic Mountains to the west—as spectacular. Now I knew why. It was the first word that came to mind when you saw it. Before me lay a New World Eden. I was absolutely smitten by the beauty of it all. It was a feast for the eyes, though not for the stomach. We were nearly broke and very hungry.

The first week, we ate at the Millionair Club, a Seattle charity for homeless people located downtown near the waterfront. Our first "hotel" was camping in Volunteer Park on Capitol Hill; a later one was an asphalt parking lot by the south Seattle Sears store. Our first opportunity for work was picking beans in the Puyallup valley; together with other down-and-outers, we were transported on a school bus from the Pioneer Square district, Seattle's skid row, to the bean fields outside the city of Puyallup thirty miles away. After four hours of picking beans and not much to show for it—"A bad year for beans, too much rain," one transient said—we took the school bus back to Seattle and consoled ourselves with a tour of the Rainier Brewing Company, where a sympathetic bartender in the Mountain Room plied us with all the free beer we could drink.

That night we returned to our favorite camping place under some bushes in Volunteer Park. We settled down for the night in our sleeping bags. Although August was supposed to be a dry month in Seattle, at three in the morning it started to rain, and my two companions raced to the car to spend the night. Not me. I had a waterproof plastic backing on the underside of my sleeping bag, and I turned the bag over and went back to sleep. At six o'clock the sun shone brightly, but for some reason it was still raining. Only then did I realize that I was sleeping under the park's automatic sprinkler system. Frank and Bob thought it was hilarious.

Most people associate homelessness with laziness, addiction problems, and mental illness, but I was surprised by the number of hard-working people of sound mind, addiction-free, who were just down on their luck. Perhaps they had lost a job, were injured or ill, or had faced some other calamity that pulled the financial rug out from under them and spit them onto the streets, into the parks, or under the freeways. Our condition was only temporary, yet I couldn't help but sympathize with the plight of many of the people we met who had no clear path to escape their Dickensian circumstances.

Our luck soon improved when Home Frozen Foods—a meat home-delivery plan—hired us. For a week we traversed the hills around the Queen Anne neighborhood of Seattle as door-to-door lead solicitors. Our sales team was composed of the three of us—and Amelia, an adventuresome eighteen-year-old Englishwoman who had come to Seattle by herself to see the World's Fair, but like us, had run out of money. Our sales manager was named Mr. Lucky, but he wanted to make his own luck. He took us for long coffee breaks that reduced the number of leads we could generate. He said that this would reduce sales, his boss would be fired, and he would be promoted. We suspected that the whole operation was a scam, because the meat plan included an egregiously overpriced freezer, which Mr. Lucky told us not to mention in our sales pitch.

Then the best thing happened. Three jobs as attendants at the United States Science Pavilion (now the Pacific Science Center) suddenly became available. This was the holy grail for job seekers at the World's Fair—and we were immediately hired. The job included dapper uniforms consisting of gray slacks, a blue blazer emblazoned with a Science Pavilion logo, a white shirt, and a striped tie. "There's only one catch," we were told. "You have to join the Teamsters Union." I learned that Washington State was the most unionized state in the country. The Boeing Company and the big unions pretty much called the shots in the state.

Left to right: Bill, Frank, and Bob at the US Science Pavilion.

Our luck continued. Bob ran into one of his college friends, who was working as a barker for Little Egypt, Seattle's reincarnation of the burlesque queen who danced at the 1893 Chicago World's Fair. Bob's friend generously offered us the floor of his apartment living room as a no-cost place to sleep.

In early September it was time to travel home for the start of our senior year in college. Although I didn't fully appreciate it at the time, adventure travel is a great way to learn important life skills: self-reliance, creative problem-solving, and living by your wits when all else fails. My exposure to migrant workers, homelessness, and racial discrimination would also have a profound effect on my future professional choices. It fostered in me an ever-growing commitment to champion the powerless—those exploited and discriminated against, the "little ones."

CHAPTER THREE

THE MAKING OF A LAWYER

Leland Stanford Junior University, adjacent to Palo Alto, California, is known as "the Farm." It was founded in 1885 by one of the robber baron railway magnates of the nineteenth century, Leland Stanford, a former governor of California. The university's formal name is in memory of Stanford's only son, Leland, who died of typhoid fever at the age of fifteen. The school acquired its nickname because the 8,180-acre campus—one of the biggest in the United States, in the heart of Silicon Valley—was formerly Governor Stanford's stock horse farm, a grandiose experiment in breeding racehorses. Acres of open rolling hills, dotted by California oak trees and an occasional lake, place Stanford among the most beautiful campuses in the world.

My arrival at Stanford, a private school known as a training ground for the wealthy and privileged, was not exactly auspicious. It was my first trip to California when I arrived at the campus as a first-year law student in the fall of 1963, making a grand entrance in "Old Blue," my beat-up, faded-blue 1951 Plymouth station wagon. Three months earlier in Batesville, I had purchased our elderly next-door neighbors' old car, left to languish the last few years behind their backyard barn. The price: one dollar. Although the engine ran well and the car had only fifteen thousand miles on it, it had its idiosyncrasies. The body was rusted, the car leaked brake fluid, and every two hundred miles or so, I had to stop and refill the brake fluid or I'd lose the brakes. Since portions of the front-seat floor were rusted through, on a rainy day, even a piece of plywood on top of the frame would not prevent the water from splashing inside.

As I drove down Palm Drive between the stately royal palm trees framing both sides of the road toward the main campus, with Old Blue occasionally backfiring, announcing my arrival, I passed a parade of newly minted Porsches and Corvettes owned by students from wealthy families, many of whom had attended Ivy League schools as undergraduates. I was starting to get intimidated, if not envious. I felt like a hick from the sticks journeying from a tiny Podunk town in Hoosierland to the sophisticated West Coast. I guess I shouldn't complain. Diversity—a goal of the law school's admissions policy—in those days meant geographic diversity. I qualified in spades.

LIFE ON THE FARM

I didn't exactly take Stanford Law School by storm. It would be an understatement to say that law school did not start off well for me. Who would have guessed that within three months of entering law school, I would set a record for the most television watched in Crothers Hall—the law school's single men's residence; be loudly booed in class by a law professor; receive the lowest grade on a practice exam in the school's history; and get caught by the dean's wife stealing from her kitchen. And to add to my stress, after the assassination of President Kennedy on November 22, 1963, and the expansion of the Vietnam War, I was badly depressed. Nevertheless, I was determined to make it through law school, because the alternative was worse. The sword of Damocles—namely, the Vietnam War draft—was hanging over my head. Safety was a student deferment.

Shortly after my arrival on campus, I attended my first Stanford football home game. What a difference from my alma mater, Miami University. There was a demonstrable irreverence toward authority and conventionality at Stanford that was absent at Miami. One example:

Stanford students warmly embraced their sloppily attired, self-governing marching band that during football games performed riotous parodies of the midwestern Big Ten precision marching bands. During one performance, I saw the band kidnap an opponent's drum majorette as she marched down the field. Then the Stanford band dropped their pants and mooned the other team's fans. The university administration, never too pleased with the band, would periodically suspend them from performing, sometimes for years.

Not to be outdone by the shameless band, Stanford cheerleaders led bawdy cheers. At a Miami University football game, a typical cheer would be "Hold that line!" At Stanford, when playing the University of Southern California Trojans, students would yell, "Burst the Trojans!" Or, if the opponent was the University of Washington Huskies, they would yell, "Huck the Fuskies!"

All unmarried male law students were required to live in Crothers Hall their first year. The pressure was on. There were about 150 students in the first-year class. How many would flunk out? Students played mind games to psychologically destroy their perceived competition. Some students would leave the lights on in their room all night to psych out other students, who thought the light meant someone was still up studying. To break the tension, another, larger group of students hit the local bars at night. The favorite hangouts were Rossities and the Oasis on El Camino Real.

I, too, wanted to drown my sorrows with this group, but I could not. I was only twenty when I started law school and still had three more months before it would be legal for me to drink. So I decided to burn the midnight oil. But it wasn't to study; it was to watch TV as a respite from the stress. Since I was taught by my father to be the best that you can be at whatever you do, I gave it my all. Soon I had the unchallenged record in the dorm for the most hours logged in front of the dorm's basement TV.

I wasn't long at Stanford before I wanted out. The law school was located in the Old Quadrangle on the central campus; it was dark, dank, and depressing, with the musty smell of an older building. Once a handsome building with stained glass windows and marble trim, it had been refurbished in 1950 with fluorescent lighting and linoleum.

Heightening my morose mood was the old-style Socratic method and boot camp atmosphere of the school's administration and many of the professors: "Look to your left, look to your right; one of you will not make it." Not making it probably meant being impaled on a punji stick in Vietnam, so the stakes, so to speak, were high. But for fear of the draft, there is no question that I would have quit law school.

Law schools use the Socratic method of inquiry as an intellectual sword to force you to think on your feet. After ample humiliation, you are reborn as a lawyer. It's much like the psychology of a marine corps boot camp, which instills obedience and esprit de corps in new recruits. The brilliant law professors know all the answers to their questions and, with glee, lead you down the path of Socratic inquiry until, at the end of the interrogation, they cut your legs off with one last question that destroys your argument and makes you feel very small. Each encounter left me feeling like a blithering idiot unworthy of admission to the hallowed profession of the law.

Some of my fellow students and I went to great lengths to avoid encounters with these reincarnations of Socrates. Inside the large lecture hall in the law school, behind a partition to the back entryway, a refuge existed—a place to hide for the unprepared, or fearful, student who wanted to hear the lecture but did not want to be seen and risk being called upon and mortified. I was often a member of this esteemed group.

JACK

For me, one of the hardest things about becoming a lawyer was learning how to think like a lawyer. Who knew lawyers had to rewire their brains to join the legal fraternity? When I was a college undergraduate, the answers were important. When I was a law student, the questions—spotting the issues—were the most important. To recast former president Bill Clinton's 1992 campaign mantra, coined by his advisor James Carville, "It's the question, stupid!"

Professor Jack Friedenthal was in his first academic position as a young, freshly minted assistant professor assigned to teach first-year law students civil procedure. He had a few years of trial experience as a California county deputy prosecutor, which was a rarity among law professors, most of whom had never seen the inside of a courtroom. As a graduate of Harvard Law School and a member of the *Harvard Law Review*, Jack otherwise had standard law professor credentials. Note that out of all the professions, the law is the only one in which where you went to school, your class standing, whether you were on law review, and where you clerked matter a lot later in life. In other professions, it is what you accomplished after graduate school, not what you did *in* graduate school and shortly thereafter, that matters most.

Jack was the funniest teacher I ever had. He was stand-up-comic funny. He was a big, beardless, half-bald, funny Jewish Socrates. He had my number early on. Since I was fortunate enough to have a difficult name to pronounce (Erks-lay-ben), in most classes I didn't get called upon for the Socratic humiliation drill as frequently as my classmates did. But Jack soon learned how to pronounce my name, and call upon me he did. It is bad enough when you can't answer the question, but it is really bad when you don't know what the question is.

One time when Jack called upon me, I made a fatal error. As an undergraduate, I had learned that it was sometimes an effective strategy, especially on blue book essay exams, to answer a different, somewhat related question and get some credit for winging it. You could demonstrate that at least you knew something, hopefully somewhere around the penumbra of the original question. I tried this strategy on Jack, and I had barely finished my answer before he began booing me from the lectern. For what seemed like a minute, each boo louder than the one before, Jack bellowed like a cow, his voice resounding through the classroom, reverberating off the hallway walls outside, and permeating adjacent classrooms.

Some of my fellow students were cowering in fear of becoming the next victim; others were laughing to the point of tears. I swear you could hear the echo of Jack's booming voice throughout the law school. I slunk down in my seat and tried to make myself invisible, like the guy in the 1958 TV series *The Invisible Man*, but to no avail. I was humiliated and there was nowhere to hide. I hadn't been that humiliated in school since a one-armed algebra teacher at Miami University, who'd lost his arm in a corn picker, threw a piece of chalk at me for talking in class.

Just when I thought things couldn't get much worse, they did. Early in the course, Jack decided to give us a practice law exam to see how we were doing. A week after the test, with a grimace on his face, Jack handed back the blue book pages. He explained that out of a possible one hundred points, the class's grade range was from thirty-seven to thirteen, a shocker for most of the students, who had never received less than ninety points on any exam in their entire lives. Pretty soon a buzz started around the classroom: "Who got the thirteen?" I opened my blue book, and there it was, the dreaded number *13* staring me in the face. I started to squirm. But instead of acknowledging my abject failure, I said to the person next to me, with a quizzical look on my face, "Who got the thirteen?"

Jack said that every student who received a grade lower than twenty would have to come in for a private counseling session regarding their future at the law school. At the designated hour, I entered Jack's well-appointed office and sat in a chair in front of his desk. He did not look up when I entered the room. He was slowly thumbing through my blue book, occasionally emitting soft grunts as he hit particularly incoherent answers. I feared I was destined for a public shaming session, where a scarlet *13* would be emblazoned on my chest, and—with a drumbeat—I would be escorted out of the law school, whisked off to an air base, forcibly loaded onto a military plane, and parachuted into Vietnam.

Finally, after several minutes, Jack peered up from his desk and pushed his ridiculously giant oversize glasses (in vogue, back in the day) up on the bridge of his nose. After a long pause, he looked me straight in the eye. Then, with the high-minded countenance of a former editor of the *Harvard Law Review*, he grimly announced the verdict: "Mr. Erxleben, I think you can possibly make it at Stanford Law School, but you will need to study very, very hard. By the way, I don't think you will be on the law review."

What could I say? I couldn't argue with objective facts. I did get the scarlet thirteen, the lowest known exam score ever recorded in the history of Stanford Law School. (For the record, the thirty-seven, the top grade on Jack's practice exam, was received by Bill Reppy, who later was on the law review, graduated first in our class, and served as a US Supreme Court clerk for William O. Douglas, winning the triple crown of early legal accomplishment. To no one's surprise, Reppy later was a visiting law professor at the University of Washington and then became a distinguished professor of law at Duke Law School.)

Our first real exam didn't occur until the end of the first quarter, and some of my classmates who'd had scores of twenty or below on the practice exam started watching television with me as a cure for their blues. Needless to say, when I was anxiously anticipating my grades at the end of the quarter, my pucker factor was sky-high.

Besides my all-time low Stanford class record from Jack, I had other reasons for concern about my academic performance. Not only was I competing against many students from Ivy League schools with LSAT scores much higher than mine, but on top of it all, although I had a photographic memory, it was selective: I couldn't remember names, especially case names—these being a shorthand way to reference a legal principle on a test without fully stating it, and a useful shortcut in a blue book exam. I thought I had some form of selective expressive dysphasia, again self-diagnosed. (A former US vice president and governor of New York, Nelson Rockefeller, was similarly afflicted. He compensated by greeting people whose names he should have known with an enthusiastic and generic "hiya.") But to my relief and surprise, when I received my grades after the quarter ended, I had an equal number of Bs and Cs, with a C+ from Jack. I guess I had finally learned how to think like a lawyer. These grades were respectable, though not outstanding. Jack was right about one thing, however: I wasn't going to make the law review.

Many years later, after graduating from Stanford Law School, my classmate and former roommate Dick Stall, our class correspondent, solicited me for our class reunion donation to the law school. I told Dick that I would give money only if my old nemesis, Professor Jack "Socrates" Friedenthal, apologized for mentally abusing me in violation of the Geneva conventions. Being an enterprising person, Dick wrote to Jack, who was then dean of the law school at George Washington University, and told him what was required of him. In a humorous

letter to Dick, Jack said that his practice exams were designed to make
sure everyone studied for the final. He confessed, "Today I couldn't
get away with that. The psychiatrists would have me up on charges!"
Although he still gives practice exams, he does not assign grades. The
results are the same, he said, "simply by making the practice questions
unanswerable."

The atmosphere in the law school my second year was as different from the first as night is to day. A new law school dean, Bayless
Manning, from the faculty of Yale Law School, had been appointed.
In *Time* magazine, he was described as one of the "shiniest fish in the
sea." But it wasn't clear what kind of fish they had in mind. I wanted
one that didn't devour law students.

With Manning's appointment, Neptune, the Roman god of the sea,
was kind to me. Gone was the law school's boot camp atmosphere. The
revised school mantra was "Look to your left, look to your right; you
are all going to be here, and we are happy to have you."

The new administration was a sea change for me. I learned how to
think like a lawyer and actually started to enjoy law school, although
legal research and writing were dry, dusty bores. Legal writing showed
no respect for the aspirations of a writer's inkwell. The objective, it
seemed, was the planned destruction of whatever writing skills you
may have had. Gone were adjectives, metaphors, similes, analogies,
and humorous asides. They were replaced by cold linear logic and hair-
splitting analysis, carefully reasoned for maximum erudition, with a
bucket of copious long footnotes available for generous insertion. And
there was one other problem: Stanford Law School, like its Ivy League
competitors, was a training ground for big-law-firm corporate lawyers.
Never my cup of tea. I had other ideas for the use of a law degree.

As part of his law school renaissance, Dean Manning weekly
invited groups of fifteen students at a time to his house for a reception
to meet with him and his wife and enjoy refreshments. Stanford takes
good care of its faculty and staff. Homes are available for purchase or
for rent on campus with subsidized terms. Dean Manning had a beautiful home and a beautiful wife. One Friday, it was my turn to attend
the reception. I planned to have a few glasses of beer from the keg

located on Dean Manning's backyard patio, then hit the hors d'oeuvres hard, thus avoiding the need to eat dinner later.

Dressed in a natty yellow checkered sport coat and tie—with a white handkerchief sticking haphazardly out of the coat's front pocket, I cut through the dean's front yard to reach the beer keg located on the patio. After two sixteen-ounce beers in plastic cups, I meandered around the side of the house and stepped inside a door to check out the hors d'oeuvres. Entering the kitchen, I slammed on the brakes when an aromatic scent from a batch of freshly baked chocolate chip cookies, warm from the oven, wafted by. Soon I found a platter of cookies on the kitchen counter, camouflaged under a large piece of tinfoil. I found a mother lode of my favorite cookie. I started to salivate.

She'll never miss a few, I reasoned. It also seemed like an excellent idea to take some back to the dorm for later enjoyment. As I was loading cookies into both side pockets of my now-bulging sport coat, I felt a soft hand tap my shoulder. I turned and a woman, smiling, gently said, "Hello, I'm Mrs. Manning. You don't have to do that. I can get you a bag."

Thoroughly embarrassed, I mumbled, "No, thank you, Mrs. Manning. I think I have enough already."

The next day the word spread around the law school that Bill Erxleben had been caught stealing from the dean's house. Since it was a good story, I didn't really mind the notoriety, but for some reason, I was never invited to Dean Manning's house again.

AMARANTA FIVE

During my second year in law school, I rented a house with four of my classmates—Dave Pender (University of Pennsylvania), Dick Stall (Purdue University), Dan Crawford (College of Wooster), and Darryl Wold (Claremont McKenna College)—on Amaranta Avenue in the city of Mountain View, south of the Stanford campus. We became known as the "Amaranta Five."[1] Gayle, my college sweetheart during my junior and senior years at Miami University, had by then graduated from Northwestern University in a physical therapy program. At my urging, she followed me to California and started work at the Stanford Children's Convalescent Hospital. She became an auxiliary member of the Amaranta Five. We had tentative plans to become engaged at Christmas. I soon discovered that maybe marriage was a good idea: I was a disaster in the kitchen.

The Amaranta Five had a cooking arrangement. Each week, on a rotating basis, one of us would be the designated cook and grocery buyer for the weekday evening meals. Although my dinner-cooking experience was pretty much limited to putting a can of beans directly on the stove, I ended up on the schedule to cook on Thanksgiving of 1964.

I've always believed that if you can read a recipe, cooking is not that hard. I also believed that when it comes to food, more is always better. With these axioms in mind, I purchased the largest turkey I could find—a twenty-eight-pounder. Next—and already in the wrong order—I read the turkey recipe. To my chagrin, I calculated that I would have to get up at five in the morning to put the bird in the oven. Waking at five to my alarm, I went into the kitchen and stuffed the bird with all the bread stuffing I could pack into the two available cavities, tied it tightly shut like a good surgeon, and placed it in a deep aluminum baking pan that I'd purchased with the turkey. The bird barely fit in the pan. I then muscled the fowl into the oven and went back to bed.

The recipe said to baste the bird several times while cooking. I stayed home to tend the turkey while my roommates were out and about. As I pulled the bird from the oven to baste it for the first time, the juices and grease from this big boy slushed over the baking pan, igniting an oven fire that shot up through the four burners on top of the electric range. Remembering my Boy Scout training to "never put a grease fire out with water," I reached for the nearest available flame retardant: a five-pound sack of flour that was on the kitchen counter in preparation for making gravy. I threw half of the sack of flour at the fire, first on the stove top and then on the turkey. It worked like a charm and put the fire out, but now I had an albino turkey and a mess on the stove. I found several old rags to wash the bird with, and forty-five minutes later, the turkey was no longer white, the oven was spotless, and all evidence of my culinary crime had vanished.

I cooked the turkey a few hours longer than the recipe said because I didn't want to give my roommates trichinosis, or whatever it was you got from a bird not fully cooked. By dinnertime, it was dark outside, and I vowed I was not going to have another major grease spill in the kitchen. *This bird will have to be carved outside, in front of our house, on the sidewalk, under a streetlight,* I reasoned. I carefully carried the bird outside in the baking pan—filled again with another two inches of grease—and placed it on the sidewalk. Then, with scissors, I cut the string holding the stuffing in the main cavity of the turkey.

I couldn't believe what happened next. Like a cannon, the stuffing blew out of the turkey's cavity, squirting almost a full yard down the sidewalk. I guessed that I had packed it too tightly or something. Quickly, I scooped up the stuffing from the sidewalk with my hands and dropped it into a serving dish. As I cleaned the remaining stuffing out of the smaller front cavity, my hands felt a plastic bag that upon close examination proved to contain the neck and giblets. I'd been wondering where those were.

Now it was time to carve the bird.

I stuck the carving knife into the turkey's breast, and the bird deflated like a basketball with a big leak. Apparently, I had cooked the bird too long; it became a real softy. There was no need any longer to use a carving knife. I was easily able to pull the bird apart with my hands and arrange the meat neatly on the serving platter.

At eight o'clock that night, with fresh cranberries, mashed potatoes, and gravy on the table (we didn't believe in vegetables), I called everyone to join the feast. My roommates thought the stuffing was a little gritty, but otherwise the meal was delicious, they said. "Where did you ever learn to cook a turkey?" Dan said, eager to know.

"Hell, all you have to do is follow the recipe," I responded with a straight face.

***

Gayle and I became engaged at Christmas. The decision to get married at this time was fraught with risk. The Vietnam War was rapidly escalating, and the draft deferment for married men was under review. If the law changed, I would be subject to the draft upon graduation and would likely be shipped overseas to Vietnam for a year's tour of duty. *This may not be a good way to start a marriage,* I thought.

Gayle began to wonder whether "till death do us part" would occur before the marriage when I decided with a few of my classmates, including my Amaranta roommates, Dave and Dan, to jump out of a decrepit plane in Castro, California, because we were bored with law school. With minimal instruction on what to do, we drove to Castro, strapped on WWII surplus military parachutes, climbed into an old crop-duster plane, and jumped. Everyone landed safely.

Left to right: Dan Crawford, John Dudley, Bill, and Nick Folley.

In August, between my second and third year of law school, Gayle and I were married in Louisville, Kentucky, and as a honeymoon took an extended grand American road trip from the heartland of the country to the breadbasket states through the Rocky Mountains and on to the Pacific coast. Without the benefit of smartphones and GPS, with paper maps, we easily navigated westward, occasionally passing faux wood-sided station wagons crammed with luggage and kids. Through vast corn and wheat fields, down the Grand Canyon and up Pikes Peak, through deserts and over snowcapped mountains, we drove. The world was our oyster. Months earlier, Old Blue had been retired to a junkyard graveyard; now with the top down and the wind whipping through our hair, in our new white Plymouth convertible, we returned to Stanford, via Palm Drive, in style.

Marriage wasn't quite what I thought it would be: Gayle didn't know how to cook either. It seemed her mother hadn't allowed her into the kitchen at home because she made too big a mess. In her first culinary exposure to someone other than me since we married, for a potluck dinner she fixed a mac-and-cheese casserole, swimming in generous portions of melted Velveeta cheese. Both of us nervously watched to see if anyone would eat it, but it was quickly gone, and someone even asked Gayle for the recipe. Later, through trial and error, Gayle became an excellent cook.

My skills never really improved. My second, and last, attempt to cook a turkey was also a disaster. I tried to barbecue the bird this time, but it seemed the temperature gauge on the barbecue wasn't very accurate, and the bird was cooking at a lower temperature than indicated. With a table full of guests yelling, "Where's the bird?" we ended up having Thanksgiving dinner at ten o'clock at night. I was then summarily banned from cooking the turkey again. Like Uncle Remus's Br'er Rabbit, I feigned disappointment about being thrown out of the kitchen and into the briar patch.

***

In retrospect, and in spite of all my misgivings, I gained a great deal from my three years at Stanford Law School, besides a wife. The law school over the years has continued to gain prominence, and I benefited from the brand. It has long ranked as one of the top law schools in the nation. My professors were outstanding;[2] my classmates were engaging, eclectic, and talented; and I formed lifelong friendships with many of them. The Socratic method toughened me up for a life in the arena. Most importantly, I learned to honor the rule of law—the legal principle that a nation should be governed by laws, as opposed to being governed by arbitrary decisions of government officials. I also became aware of the fragility of the might of the rule of law and the need to diligently defend it against those who would subvert it. And I came to understand and value the role of lawyers in preserving our fundamental freedoms. As Alexis de Tocqueville noted in *Democracy in America*, lawyers perform an intermediary role between individuals and the state, representing a "form of public responsibility and accountability that would help preserve the blessings of democracy without allowing its untrammeled vices."

I graduated from Stanford Law School in June 1966 with 142 other students who made it to the finish line, including five women. Academically I ended up smack-dab in the middle of my class and with an LLB, or bachelor of law—which really wasn't too bad considering my enthusiasm for the endeavor. The accepted wisdom was that the A students became law professors, the B students became judges, and the C students made all the money. With my grade average between the two lower rankings, I reasoned that, best case, I was destined to become a rich judge.[3]

My mother came to California to attend my law school graduation ceremony. For her, it was a special time of joy and satisfaction, the culmination of a struggle to carry on after the death of my father a decade earlier and see her children succeed. The week before my graduation, she had attended my older brother Walter's graduation from the University of Michigan Medical School, which had been my father's school. She now had a doctor and a lawyer as offspring; she could not have been prouder.

CHAPTER FOUR

A UNIQUE AND UNUSUAL AIRMAN

It was early August 1965, the summer after my second year in law school, just three days before Gayle and I were to be married. I was ironing the white shirt to my tuxedo while listening to the radio news. The announcer said, "Effective today, President Johnson said that married men of draft age will no longer receive a draft deferment."

The best-laid plans of mice and men . . . , I thought.

The Vietnam War was the defining experience of my generation. Under five successive presidents, America was drawn into the vortex of a war that ended up destroying for many young people the notion that our country and its national government were always a force for good in the world and would not knowingly risk the nation's seed corn— its youth—in misadventures abroad. The mournful lyrics of balladeer Pete Seeger's song "Where Have All the Flowers Gone?" was a sad reminder to many of my friends of the price the country paid in a war that cost fifty-eight thousand American lives. The burden of the war was not equally shared. Black men disproportionately served and died in Vietnam. Many of the wealthy, the connected, and the educated managed to avoid the war entirely. Out of 2.5 million enlisted men who served in Vietnam during the official Vietnam War era (1964–75),

80 percent came from poor or working-class families, and the same ratio had only a high school education.

But it was the Vietnamese who paid the real price in human casualties. As many as 2 million civilians and 850,000 North Vietnamese and Viet Cong and 250,000 South Vietnamese soldiers also died. To compound the carnage, in an environmental disaster, US planes sprayed nineteen million gallons of Agent Orange defoliant on South Vietnam and Cambodia in an effort to deny the enemy forces jungle cover and food.

Aeschylus, an ancient Greek tragic dramatist, said, "In war, truth is the first casualty." And so it was regarding the Vietnam War. The Pentagon Papers revealed the serial mendacity of the US government's involvement in Vietnam from 1945 to 1967. This secret Pentagon study was purloined by Daniel Ellsberg and released for publication to the *New York Times* and the *Washington Post* in 1971. It revealed that from the very beginning, the US government had lied about the war. Presidents Kennedy, Johnson, and Nixon privately confided that the war could not be won, yet publicly pretended otherwise. Artificially inflated enemy body counts were regularly released by the US Army in an effort to convince the public that we were winning the war when we were actually losing it. The mass media was also complicit in the cover-up by parroting the government propaganda, hypocrisy, and untruths. I was dismayed and depressed by it all.

I calculated that my chances of being drafted into the army, when my educational deferment ended upon graduation from law school, were very high. The war in Vietnam was rapidly escalating. Student protests were convulsing the campuses at Stanford and at Berkeley. President Johnson proclaimed, "America wins the wars she undertakes. Make no mistake about it." I guess President Johnson conveniently forgot that his home state of Texas was a member of the Confederacy that lost the Civil War. And it turned out that the North Vietnamese were no ragtag army. They could do a lot with a little. They had better generals, and their troops, armed by Russia and China, had a greater will to fight. After all, it was their country.

As the Kennedy administration had done when it started the war, the Johnson administration ignored the history of Vietnam. The

French colonizers who had ruled Vietnam for more than eighty years had been soundly defeated by the Vietnamese a decade earlier and fled the country in 1954. In 1965 the Vietnam War was primarily a civil war and had little to do with international communist expansion. The historical enemies of the Vietnamese were the Chinese, who had occupied Vietnam for a thousand years and had incorporated it into the Han Empire. The Vietnamese wanted to be free of any foreign domination, but who would control the country precipitated a civil war after the defeat of the French. Ho Chi Minh had actually reached out to the United States earlier to avoid US intervention in the civil war. In a series of letters to President Truman following World War II, Ho Chi Minh denounced French colonialism and clearly stated, "Our goal is full independence and full cooperation with the United States." Regrettably, his letters were ignored.

I knew I would really have to scramble to avoid ending up as cannon fodder in Vietnam. Should I enlist in the Judge Advocate General's Corps (JAG Corps), where at least I could practice law in a noncombat position? But since so many law students were applying for JAG Corps, the military was able to extract a five-year military commitment for the privilege. Five years of military discipline? No thanks. Scratch that option.

Two of my Amaranta Five roommates, Dave Pender and Dan Crawford, successfully applied to the FBI to become special agents, a draft-deferred position with a three-year commitment. This sounded like the perfect answer. I applied to the FBI, qualified for a security clearance, and was fingerprinted. (This was my first big step down a slippery slope to the loss of personal anonymity and privacy, which was a luxury of the pre-Internet social media and DNA testing era.) Then I took the FBI physical exam, but I did not pass. I had elevated systolic blood pressure. It seems I had psyched myself up too much about avoiding the draft and was not relaxed at the time of the examination. One month after I failed the FBI physical, I was summoned for my military draft physical, and as fate would have it, I passed with flying colors.

Which branch of the military should I join? My options were narrowing. The army was eliminated because I wanted to live; and the navy was eliminated because I didn't want to get seasick again. By the spring of my third year in law school, with only one option left, I decided to enlist in the US Air Force as an officer, even though it required a four-year commitment, two more years than the commitment of an army draftee. I selected the air force's Office of Special Investigations—the OSI—their military version of the FBI, where my law degree would have some value. After three months of officer training school, I would be commissioned a second lieutenant.

***

After I graduated from law school, Gayle returned to Kentucky to stay with her mother while I flew from San Francisco to San Antonio, Texas, to the nearby United States Air Force's Officer Training School (OTS) at the sprawling Lackland Air Force Base (AFB). The weather in November in Texas was gray and overcast, cold, in the low forties. I thought the weather would be sunny and balmy this far south. Fooled me. I'd called that wrong and was only barely off the plane—not a good omen.

I was soon processed into military life. Issued the standard uniform and sporting a closely shaved head, I was assigned to a two-person room and awarded the rank of staff sergeant for pay purposes. I had to measure and precisely fold all my clothing, spit shine my black leather shoes—until I could see my reflection—and make sure my bed was so tightly made that a quarter would bounce off it. During room inspection, I had to grovel appropriately before my higher-ranking betters with a feigned enthusiastic "Yes, sir." The unstated goal in this training was to exorcise your individual identity and reduce you to a faceless common denominator, subject to command and with unquestioned obedience to authority. I hated it.

Our first training movie was on how to avoid venereal disease—something I was sure all officers should be well versed in as they headed out for a tour of duty in Asia. But after two weeks of indoctrination, I was still dispirited and wondering how I was going to get through four more years of such a controlled existence. Then, at the end of a lecture on military protocol, the instructor, a captain, growled and offered a

Kmart "Blue Light Special": "If any of you officer trainees don't like it here, you can leave OTS and become an enlisted man with a two-year commitment." A light bulb went off in my head. I ran up to the officer as the class ended and said breathlessly: "Dear Captain, sir, tell me more about this two-year special deal."

The little-known and unpublicized "two-year deal" was called Self-Induced Elimination, or SIE, the captain explained: "After you eliminate from OTS, you will transfer to basic training as an airman, with a two-year active-duty military obligation." Although the SIE program sounded like a self-administered rectal laxative suppository, it would cut the time I would spend in the military by half. As a huge bonus, after three months of basic training, I would not have the two-year remaining service time that was required under air force regulations for an overseas assignment (i.e., the steamy, snake-infested jungles of Vietnam).

***

Joseph Heller's personal experiences in World War II influenced him when he wrote *Catch-22*. This book, published in 1961, is considered one of the greatest literary works of the twentieth century. An outrageous and satirical black comedy, the book profoundly influenced my views about the folly of war and the absurdity of some military regulations. Trapped in a war he did not believe in, the protagonist, Yossarian, the lead bombardier in a squadron of airplanes, sought to avoid almost certain death as he continued to be assigned to high-casualty bombing missions in the European theater. Whenever Yossarian flew enough combat missions to be sent home, his commander raised the limit. Thus, a catch-22 is a situation where it is impossible to obtain the desired outcome because of a set of inherently illogical rules. Faced often with nonsensical orders, Yossarian sought to survive in a world gone mad.

I thought America had gone mad too. This time it was in Vietnam. I felt like my country had lost its moral core. I didn't recognize it anymore. I was no conscientious objector, but I did have a choice: I would serve, but I would not lead; I would not kill. I would minimize my participation in the carnage. With a stroke of the pen, I self-eliminated and was transferred from OTS to airman basic training. It was a matter of conscience and self-preservation.

My next two months in basic training, sleeping with sixty snoring men in an open barracks, are best described as being in jail. My life was totally controlled twenty-four hours a day. As recruits, we were reborn, part of a cohesive unit, subject to command and unquestioned obedience, supposedly trained to kill.

The US Air Force was not very good at producing trained killers, except from the air. We marched around a lot with rifles that we shot only once. Our drill instructor (DI) was a senior master sergeant that didn't like the way I marched. The spring in my step—probably a holdover from some ill-fated dancing lessons my mother had enrolled me in as a child in Chicago—irritated him because I stood out: a no-no in military precision marching. To emphasize his displeasure—when he thought no officer was watching—he would walk up beside me, scowl, and give me an elbow in the ribs.

To educate us on the proper nomenclature for our weapon, we would march as the DI, marching alongside us, would call the cadence—with his right hand balancing his rifle on his right shoulder and his left hand grabbing his crotch:

> DI: This is my rifle. This is my gun.
> Response: This is my rifle. This is my gun.
> DI: One is for killing. The other's for fun.
> Response: One is for killing. The other's for fun.
> DI: Sound off, one, two . . .

One day we were told to obtain our dog tags, which were particularly important for identification that allows the military to notify your family after you have been killed, we were told. Part of the information required on the metal tag was a line for religion. *This might be a problem*, I thought, since I didn't have one. The conversation between the officer filling out the information for the dog tags and me went something like this:

"Religion?"

"I don't have one, sir."

"You have to have one."

Catch-22. "OK, Unitarian, sir."

And that's how I became a Unitarian Universalist without ever having attended a Unitarian church or having even known a Unitarian.

Since air force marksmanship is an oxymoron, the one time my training flight went to the rifle range was a token exercise. After ten minutes of safety instruction, we were given M16 rifles—the standard rifle issued during the Vietnam War—and issued sixty rounds of ammunition to try to hit a small paper target. An instructor said that a high score would qualify for a marksman ribbon, seldom awarded in the air force because most airmen couldn't even hit the target, let alone the bull's-eye.

After we fired off our sixty rounds of ammunition, the instructors commanded us to cease firing and retrieve our targets for scoring. When I reached my target, I saw that I had only six bullet holes in the scoring zone. Then I noticed the airman next to me punching holes in his target with a pencil.

"What are you doing?" I asked, obviously intrigued.

"Qualifying for a marksman ribbon, doofus," he answered.

"Could I borrow your pencil when you're done?" I said, only half joking.

When I left basic training after three months, I had a single row of ribbons on my uniform, and I hadn't even left Lackland AFB. In the air force you were awarded a ribbon as a Vietnam-era volunteer, a ribbon showing the participation of your unit in past wars, and a couple of other ribbons for occasions that I can't remember. But they didn't require any bravery—or even my presence.

With one week of training left, we were told that our assigned specialty would be determined as follows: If you had a master's degree or higher, you could choose your specialty. Otherwise, the air force would do it for you. This was great news because with a Stanford law degree, I was probably the most overqualified basic recruit at Lackland AFB and should have a wide choice. Here's how that conversation went:

"Sir, I want to choose my specialty."

"What's your advanced degree, Airman?"

"Law degree from Stanford, sir."

"Is that a master's degree?"

"No, sir, it's an LLB, a bachelor of law degree."

"That's not a master's degree. That's a bachelor's degree. You don't get to choose."

Joseph Heller was right. Catch-22.

(Many law schools, including Stanford, later eliminated this flagrant discrimination by the military against law school graduates by awarding JD, or doctor of jurisprudence, degrees retroactively, but it was too late for me.)

I soon learned my fate, assigned randomly by a computer. I was assigned to the 341st Combat Support Group at Malmstrom AFB in Great Falls, Montana, as an audiovisual specialist. Whatever that was. I figured I was probably the projectionist at the base movie theater. *I like movies; I can do that,* I convinced myself.

During my time at Lackland, a twenty-year-old recruit from Texas named Trevon had been my best barracks buddy. He regaled me with good-old-boy redneck Texas humor. Whenever you asked him what he considered to be a dumb question with an obvious answer, he would respond with a pithy, sarcastic aphorism, like "Do the big bear shit in the woods?" Or "Is the White House green?" Or "Do Pinocchio have a wooden dick?"

Our last week at Lackland was spent preparing for our first deployment. Two days before the end of basic training, our flight was given an eight-hour leave. We took a military bus to nearby San Antonio and visited the Alamo and cruised some bars, bumping into other recruits on leave. Trevon collared me and said, "Can I borrow twenty bucks? I'm running low."

"Yeah," I said, "if you pay me back."

"C'mon," he said. "Is the pope Catholic?"

I laughed and lent him the money. But I guess the pope is only Catholic when money is not involved. After we returned to the base that evening, I never saw Trevon or my money again.

***

Malmstrom AFB is a small base located just outside of Great Falls, Montana—a midsize town around forty-five thousand in population at the time. It is the missile base headquarters for the 341st Missile Wing, Strategic Air Command (SAC). It maintained and operated 150 Minuteman intercontinental ballistic missiles armed with nuclear warheads in remote underground sites scattered throughout north-central Montana and targeted on our perceived communist adversaries at the time—the Soviet Union, China, North Korea, and Vietnam. In the 1960s, the base had the firepower to become the Bhagavad Gita's "Death, the destroyer of worlds."

Landing in Great Falls, Montana, to report for duty in February 1967 was a bit of a shock. It was twenty-five degrees below zero with two feet of snow on the ground, but a day later, it was forty degrees above zero. A warm Chinook wind, people said. The second shock occurred when I reported to the base and found out that my assignment as an audiovisual specialist was not in the base theater, but at the base maintenance shop. I was expected to maintain, repair, and manage the entire inventory of several hundred 16-millimeter movie and slide projectors. Since I had scored in the bottom 10 percent of all airmen on a mechanical- and spatial-ability test given in basic training, I knew this wasn't going to work out very well. Better put, this had all the earmarks of an impending disaster.

I needed a plan B. I immediately applied for a transfer to the base judge advocate general's office for a law clerk's position, where I surmised they would be happy to have me and my law degree. During the interview, I was asked how many words a minute I could type. I put on a brave face and explained that I was very familiar with the functions of a typewriter after having taken (and almost failed) two typing courses in high school. The interviewer asked again, more sternly.

"How many words a minute?"

"Fifteen, maybe," I answered meekly.

"Fifteen? You've got to be kidding. It takes sixty words a minute to qualify as a law clerk."

Catch-22.

Working my way down the alphabet, I tried plan C. I went to the base education office, figuring with my educational background, I might qualify for something. Bingo. Mr. Mattfeld, the director of the education office, a grade GS-15 civil servant and a retired school superintendent, immediately recognized my potential. Like a general manager in professional sports, he sought to acquire me with a trade. Since the base education office was in a different division from the audiovisual support services, he engineered a trade between the two division commanders involved. The base education office would acquire me in exchange for a training group consisting of one lieutenant and two sergeants. I was now an education specialist, and apparently a hot property at that.

As an airman (one stripe), my salary was only a pittance. But Gayle soon joined me and acquired a well-paying job as a physical therapist at the hospital of Great Falls. Along with my military housing and spousal allowance, and family medical coverage, we would live comfortably, if modestly. For seventy-five dollars a month, we rented a small house near the base; acquired a golden retriever puppy, Flame; and had a very normal life. Gayle and I each worked a forty-hour week, and the rest of the time, for the most part, was our own, with ample seasonal opportunities for downhill skiing an hour away at Kings Hill or Big Sky Resort in the winter, fishing on the Missouri River for iridescent rainbow and huge spotted brown trout, and trips to spectacular settings in Glacier National Park in the summer.

The city of Great Falls is a nondescript town located in the center of Montana on the northern Great Plains under the huge dome of a big sky, nothing remarkable except for the Missouri River and a series of five waterfalls located in close proximity to each other and close to the city. For the Lewis and Clark Expedition, the beauty of the falls—now partially harnessed by a hydroelectric dam—was contrasted by a hazardous and grueling ten-mile portage around the falls. Ill-tempered grizzly bears, upset with the expedition's intrusion into their prime fishing grounds, constantly menaced them.

Life was pleasant in our four-person base education office. In addition to Mr. Mattfeld and me, the office consisted of Senior Master Sergeant Givens and another young airman—who didn't last long before he was arrested for passing forged checks and cashiered out of the air force. But Sergeant Givens was a go-getter. During the previous

year, under his initiative, the office had started an on-base undergraduate continuing-education program with the local Great Falls College
(now the University of Providence), and the program now had sixty
students enrolled. The office had also recently formed an alliance with
the Institute of Aerospace Management at the University of Southern
California (USC) to offer an on-base master's degree program. It had
fifteen students enrolled.

Shortly after I arrived, Sergeant Givens left to attend OTS. After
ten years as an enlisted man, and having earned a college degree
while on duty, he had a chance to become an officer, an offer he felt
he couldn't turn down. I inherited Sergeant Givens's handiwork and
was designated Malmstrom's on-base director for both the College of
Great Falls and USC. This was a great opportunity for me, and financial manna from heaven, as it turned out.

Since I counseled officers and enlisted men on educational opportunities, every new person entering the base had to have an interview
with me. Of course, I recommended that they enroll in one of the programs I supervised. Along with a little added off-duty publicity and
marketing, I was able to greatly expand both programs. Within six
months, I had increased the College of Great Falls' on-base enrollment
from 60 to 350 students, and USC's enrollment from 15 to 60 students.
The base commander was very pleased with both programs and later
cited them as examples of his significant accomplishments during his
tenure at Malmstrom.

My relationship with the College of Great Falls was warm and
symbiotic. The financially strapped, small Catholic college, run by the
Sisters of Providence in Spokane, Washington, saw me as a money
machine. The on-base courses were almost pure profit for the college.
Since I managed the program, including the selection of instructors
from qualified officers on the base, the only expense to the college
was the instructors' salaries. My selection of the officer instructors
allowed me to accumulate a bank of favors owed, which from time
to time I would call in. I also taught business law in the college program, which was a pleasant diversion and provided some fun money
for Gayle and me.

One night I lectured in one of the war rooms—temporarily a college classroom—about the doubtful legality of the Vietnam War under the United Nations Charter to a class composed of missile silo officers. Behind my lectern, white lights were flashing on a missile target map. The scene was positively surreal. But my students were quite receptive to my anti–Vietnam War legal arguments. Rather surprising, I thought, given that at their fingertips in the missile silos, they had the ability to blow a good part of the world to smithereens.

The real moneymaker for me, though, was the USC program. Every two months, USC flew in a new professor from their campus to teach an intensive course. The student officers would take courses on base for two weeks while off duty from their missile silos, and then spend two weeks in their missile silos in the vast Montana countryside—in the middle of nowhere—with their study assignments. Since the air force paid in full for each student's cost for the USC program, and provided the facilities, it worked out perfectly for everyone, especially me. USC paid me as the director of the program fifty dollars per student for every two-month course. Pretty soon I was making as much money as my boss, Mr. Mattfeld, and much more than I would have made in the JAG Corps or OSI programs. Things were going so well that my division commander wanted to recommend me for a Good Conduct Medal for "exemplary accomplishments." I politely demurred. Like Milo Minderbinder, the entrepreneur extraordinaire in Heller's *Catch-22*, I didn't want to draw too much official scrutiny to my extracurricular activities that upon official review might cause eyebrows to rise, but since I was the golden goose for base educational activities, I wasn't too concerned.

At Malmstrom AFB there was very little of the military discipline—such as marching in parades, or physical deprivation— that is common in the army and marine corps. After all, this was the air force. Whenever someone called me out for not respecting military protocol—for instance, by saluting an officer with my right hand while my left hand was in my pocket—I would do my best Beetle Bailey impression and thank the officer for reminding me of the proper military etiquette. I remember on one occasion we were lined up for an inspection—two hundred enlisted men standing at attention in a straight line along the edge of the base airfield—facing the blinding morning sun. I immediately put on my cool aviator sunglasses to avoid the glare. When the inspecting officer passed me, he suddenly stopped and spun around with a quick left face and said sarcastically, "Step forward, Airman. Do you have any idea why you are the only person on this flight line wearing sunglasses?"

"No, sir. Maybe the other airmen forgot to bring them? Sir."

With a big eye roll, the officer said, "Take those damn glasses off and step back in line."

Like I said, I wasn't a very good airman. For some reason or other, while the military is great at logistics and teaching leadership skills, it doesn't seem to celebrate individualism.

Given my personality, it was no surprise that after a time I became bored with my routine at the base and thought it was time to liven things up. I remembered reading somewhere that if you were a really good athlete, you could be released from normal military duty and transferred to temporary duty assignment while pursuing your sport. Since I wasn't good enough at any individual sport, I needed a new angle: a team sport. Sport competitions between the air bases in the SAC were strongly encouraged as a means of fostering esprit de corps among the men. Since Malmstrom AFB was a small base, it was not well represented in the competitions. I learned that it didn't have a base volleyball team, and that spelled opportunity.

With the help of my division's first sergeant—and wisely including that first sergeant—I began to recruit a volleyball team. Two of the recruits were from Southern California and had played beach volleyball before they joined the air force. They were terrific ball spikers and anchored the team. The rest of the team members, including me, were pretty good, but not outstanding. We needed to practice hard if we were to become competitive.

My division commander—a lieutenant colonel who I regularly played handball with and let win most of the games—was absolutely delighted to have a volleyball team from the base in the SAC competition. Since we were the only team on base, the base commander, upon the recommendation of my division commander, immediately declared us the base champions. Then the entire team was given a temporary duty assignment to play volleyball and was released from all military duties in preparation for the 1968 SAC Volleyball Championship games, to be held in a few months at Plattsburgh AFB in New York.

For two months we practiced volleyball every day and traveled around the country by hitchhiking on air force planes to play teams from other SAC bases. I loved the experience. On a good day, when I jumped to spike the volleyball, I felt weightless, levitating, like I was flying through the air. And at night, after we played a game, the day was capped off with the camaraderie of my teammates as we celebrated at a local watering hole, win or lose.

We were on a roll and won the Area 4 Volleyball Championship title at Minot AFB in North Dakota. A week later we finished a respectable third out of seven teams in the SAC championship games in New York. Returning home to Malmstrom AFB after the tournament, we were feted as conquering heroes who had represented the base well.

***

Military life at Malmstrom AFB provided a pleasant sanctuary for me while a "dirty little war" raged in Asia. Others were not so lucky.

War is hell, they say; yet it has been a near constant in human history. Humans are one of the few species that prey en masse on their own kind. Lucky is the generation that manages to avoid the cruel costs of war.

All three of my brothers were swept up in the Vietnam War. My oldest brother, Walter, spent four years in the army as a medical doctor, including a one-year tour in Vietnam, and was later discharged as a major. My younger brother, Dick, served as a supply officer in the army for two years in the Panama Canal Zone and was discharged as a lieutenant. My youngest sibling, Terry, was the unlucky one. He paid the greatest price in our family for his service to his country.

At age nineteen, Terry dropped out of college and enlisted in the army infantry. I was saddened and shocked by his decision and feared for his safety. *At six foot five with red hair, he will be an easy target,* I worried. I tried to dissuade him, but he said it was too late. He had already signed up. Perhaps he saw it as an adventure, a chance to be a

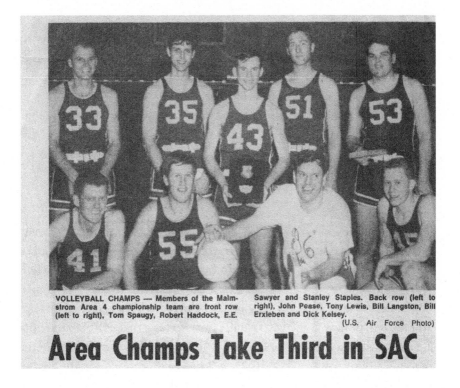

VOLLEYBALL CHAMPS — Members of the Malmstrom Area 4 championship team are front row (left to right), Tom Spaugy, Robert Haddock, E.E. Sawyer and Stanley Staples. Back row (left to right), John Pease, Tony Lewis, Bill Langston, Bill Erxleben and Dick Kelsey.
(U.S. Air Force Photo)

Area Champs Take Third in SAC

hero, to make friends and family proud. When you are nineteen and male and have the risk profile of a teenager, you tend to believe you are invincible, but he was not.

After six weeks in Vietnam, while on a night-ambush patrol, he was shot three times, in the stomach, in the hand, and in the foot, in an act of fratricide—defined euphemistically by the army as unintentional death or injury to friendly forces by friendly fire. He survived his wounds and convalesced in several hospitals for over a year. In recognition of his wounds, he was awarded the Purple Heart, declared 100 percent disabled, and retired from military service. Later, after many years and countless surgeries, his foot was amputated.

The Vietnam War was a vale of tears for so many. Good people paid in sorrow and blood, sent to their graves or subjected to grievous wounds that no amount of compensation could repair. The experiences my brothers and I had, some for better and some for worse, underlined the randomness of life and the capriciousness of fate in war. As foretold in the Bible (King James Version), in Ecclesiastes 9:11: "I returned,

and saw under the sun, that the race is not to the swift, nor the battle
to the strong, neither yet bread to the wise, nor yet riches to men of
understanding, nor yet favour to men of skill, but time and chance
happeneth to them all."

For me it was now time to look forward, beyond the war. I had
important decisions to make about my professional career and the
future of our family.

***

To practice law, you must pass a rigorous legal examination in each
state in which you wish to practice. To practice in the federal courts,
you must be a member of at least one state bar and be admitted to federal practice as well. Each state exam is different and requires knowledge of local law. There is very little reciprocity between the states: if
you move to a new state, you usually have to take that state's bar exam.
As a consequence, for most lawyers, the state where they first take the
bar exam determines where they will live and practice for the rest of
their lives. It was a big decision for us to make.

Over the years, like most professions, the legal profession has
sought to limit competition by restricting either the number of lawyers, the prices they can charge, or the ways they can advertise. The
state bar exam is one such rule. When I was in Montana, for example, out-of-state applicants were required to take the bar examination, but graduates of the only law school in Montana, the University
of Montana School of Law, were admitted to practice merely on the
motion of the state's attorney general. Graduates of law schools other
than the University of Montana were further disadvantaged because
there was no bar review course to help alert one to the peculiarities of
Montana law; this made it difficult to pass the exam. A catch-22.

In spite of the expected difficulty in passing the bar exam, I thought
about staying in "God's country": beautiful Montana, whose unofficial
state motto is "The Last Best Place." John Steinbeck wrote, "For other
states I have admiration, respect, recognition, even some affection. But
with Montana it is love." But the lure of making it in a bigger pond—
and Gayle's aversion to living so far from a large city with greater

cultural advantages—eventually eliminated Montana from consideration. We also eliminated California's Bay Area, which had too much traffic, too-expensive housing, and too much competition in the legal market for an outsider like me without connections. I wanted to live in a beautiful place with ample opportunities for outdoor recreation and an informal lifestyle, a place open to opportunity in the legal profession. Our list of states finally narrowed to Oregon and Washington. Both states possessed world-class beauty.

Gayle was game for an adventure. She had never traveled to Washington or Oregon. But as long as the climate was mild and there was a big city nearby, she was open to suggestions. While Oregon's magnificent ocean beaches and laid-back lifestyle were alluring, my wonderful experience in the Puget Sound area during the Seattle World's Fair—and the fact that I had two cousins in the Seattle area—put Washington State in first place. There I would become part of the Midwest diaspora who were drawn to the state by the 1962 Seattle World's Fair and later came back to seek their fortunes.

Now I had to figure out a way to make Washington State my home. My strategy was to take two months of accumulated leave from the air force to take the bar review course and the bar examination and hunt for a job in Seattle. Fortunately for me, Boeing was booming and Seattle law firms were hiring.

Critics called Seattle a one-horse town—more accurately, it was a one-plane town—since the Boeing Company was by far the area's largest employer. Seattle was far from stylish. The restaurant scene was largely a barren wasteland: there was a Chinatown (now called the International District) with a few good restaurants, like Tai Tung, and an expensive steak house called Canlis, populated mostly by Boeing executives and their customers, along with a fawning retinue of suppliers seeking contracts; and for the tourists, there was the locally famous Ivar's Acres of Clams on the downtown waterfront at Pier 54, where the main culinary claim, other than the mountainous white Baked Alaska (cake, ice cream, and meringue), was the aphrodisiac qualities of Ivar's clam nectar—"allowing only one serving per customer, unless you have a note from your wife." Besides these restaurants, not much else was notable, except for the iconic Space Needle, a symbol of

Seattle's future as a center of science and technology, where the great view from the revolving restaurant distracted you from the mediocre food on your plate.

Because of the Boeing boom, Seattle law firms might as well have had barkers with shepherd crooks standing out on the sidewalk to snag promising talent to meet their demand for lawyers. Within a few weeks, I had offers to start as an associate at two of the major law firms in the city, but I was not very enthusiastic about joining a large law firm. For one thing, you start off as an associate, an indentured servant, and spend five to eight years working long hours against the clock, expected to bill between eighteen hundred and twenty-two hundred hours a year, kowtowing to partners in hopes of attaining the golden wedding ring of partnership status, which includes lifetime job security, prestige, and entry into the top income percentile for professional service providers. I say *golden wedding ring* because in the 1960s, joining a law firm was like a marriage: you were expected to stay "until death do you part." I really didn't know enough about these firms and the people in them to marry them, let alone have them bury me too.

There were other things that bothered me then as well. All the partners' names were listed on the firm's letterhead in order of seniority. Then as you retire, or die, you are excised from the letterhead. I could see my life flash before me by just looking at a law firm's letterhead, realizing that just as one gets closer to the top, it is curtains. It was too predictable a journey for my taste. Finally, the work at these law firms was mainly corporate work, which didn't excite me. (Actually, it doesn't excite most lawyers who do corporate work, but it pays pretty well.) Public sector law for me looked far more attractive.

Ambitious lawyers from the top law schools usually look down on public law because it doesn't pay nearly as well as private practice and it often attracts lawyers who couldn't land jobs at the major firms. But to my way of thinking, it was more important work, and it meshed with my desire to use my legal skills to pursue the public interest. I decided I would again take the path less traveled: I would not be a Stanford-branded lawyer following the Stanford-branded corporate-lawyer path. I would practice law in the public sector. Very few of my Stanford classmates made the same choice.

While taking the bar exam, I applied for a position as a Washington State assistant attorney general, headquartered at the state capitol in Olympia. The attorney general's office was the largest law office in Washington State at the time, with 110 lawyers. My application was approved in record time, after only one interview with the chief deputy attorney general. With a starting salary of $7,200 a year—almost four times my salary in the air force—I was assigned to work in the Department of Natural Resources, an independent state agency located in Olympia. The department was charged with managing 1.8 million acres of land—mostly timber, and state-owned tidelands and shorelands. I was passionate about the environment and the sustainability of natural resources. It looked like a good fit.

Now it was time to plot an early escape from the air force. Afflicted with an earworm—the 1965 song "We Gotta Get Out of This Place," by the Animals, which was immensely popular during the Vietnam War—I was propelled into action. Using my lawyer's training, I researched the subject and petitioned the Air Force Command at Lackland AFB for an early discharge. The only category I potentially qualified for under military regulations was a discharge for "unique and unusual reasons," but only if my value to the country far outweighed my value to the military. With only a two-stripe chevron on my arm, I thought I had a shot at it.

To my amazement, only forty-eight hours after I submitted my application, an airman delivered a telegram to me at my desk at work. I immediately tore open the envelope and read: "A2C William C. Erxleben, for unique and unusual reasons, you are released from the United States Air Force at 12:00 a.m. tonight with an honorable discharge to become a Washington State assistant attorney general."

"Oh my God, I'm free," I exclaimed aloud to the wonderment of my office mates, whose mouths gaped when they heard that, after only nineteen months of service, during the height of the Vietnam War's Tet Offensive, I was released from active duty.

I whistled "zip-a-dee-doo-dah, zip-a-dee-ay," clicked my heels, and with a newfound spring in my step and an ebullient mood, bounded out of the office. I was free and safe at last. Yossarian and Milo are proud of me; I know it to be true.

***

Why did so many intelligent and knowledgeable people in the US government continue to double down and pursue a failing war strategy in Vietnam? The most serious miscalculations began in the Kennedy administration with the Whiz Kids—brilliant leaders of academia and industry, many of whom continued on with the Johnson administration, including Robert McNamara as secretary of defense. David Halberstam's revelatory book, *The Best and the Brightest*, traced the origins of the Vietnam War to these individuals, who suffered from a combination of hubris and groupthink—a desire for harmony and conformity within the group that results in irrational and dysfunctional decision-making. In my experience, high intelligence is no substitute for judgment and critical thinking, in war or in life.

The United States is the unquestioned military world superpower. But its military hegemony is fading. Over the last fifty years, all of its chosen major military interventions into other countries have been impotent. Our military is great at conventional warfare: leadership, logistics, and lethality, but poor at fighting asymmetrical warfare, where guerilla tactics dominate. Our military can destroy, but it cannot build nations where it is not wanted and where sectarian hatred and religious passion trump reason. In Iraq, we intervened and occupied, but to no avail; as many as 500,000 were killed, and Iran was the main winner. In Libya, we intervened but did not occupy, and 5,000 people were killed and the country remains in disarray. In Syria, we neither intervened nor occupied, and as many as 470,000 people were killed and 12 million displaced. In a stalemated proxy war in Yemen between Saudi Arabia and Iran, which the United Nations calls the world's worst humanitarian crisis in the poorest country in the Arab world, we provide logistics, bombs, and other support for Saudi air strikes. Now we find ourselves facing possible complicity in war crimes for the indiscriminate bombing of civilians, with 5,000 children dead and 400,000 malnourished, as 3 million have fled their homes. In Afghanistan—the graveyard of so many empires—the war in 2019 has now surpassed its eighteenth year, becoming the longest war actively fought in US history. Since the US involvement in Afghanistan started, more than 2,300 Americans have died and over 23,000 have been wounded. An estimated 111,000 Afghans have been killed. And $718 billion of the nation's treasury has managed to produce only a stalemate in the conflict. As Sun Tzu taught us centuries ago in *The Art of War,* "There is no instance of a country having benefited from prolonged warfare."

The carnage from our history of failed military ventures over the past fifty years is both mind-numbing and morally reprehensible and would seem to call for a fundamental reevaluation of our military strategy. But unfortunately, our collective memory of past military mistakes lasts only about ten years, and then the trumpets sound, people cheer, the media gets giddy, and off we go to war again. George Santayana was right when he said in *The Life of Reason* (1905), "Those who cannot remember the past are condemned to repeat it." Or, as put more plainly by Warren Buffett, "What we learn from history is that people don't learn from history."

PART II

IN PURSUIT OF THE COMMON GOOD

1968–1979

There is an opportunity to do work that is infused with moral purpose. . . . The sidelines are not where you want to live your life. The world needs you in the arena. There are problems that need to be solved, injustices that need to be ended.

—Tim Cook, Apple CEO

CHAPTER FIVE

MAKING MY BONES AS A LAWYER

Serendipity can play an important role in launching any career. In my first job as a lawyer, all the stars aligned.

In the fall of 1968, Gayle and I arrived in the Washington State capital, Olympia, located on the Puget Sound, sixty miles due south of Seattle. The beautiful capitol buildings that stood atop a high hill overlooking Capitol Lake and Budd Inlet really impressed me. The neoclassical Legislative Building is one of the largest self-supporting masonry domes in the world, surpassed only by Saint Peter's Basilica in Rome. An icon of state government, it is reputed to be one of the finest examples of state architecture in the United States.

Shortly after we moved to Olympia, our son, David, was born with red hair. David didn't really have much of a chance of being anything but a redhead; genetically afflicted by his maternal grandmother and me, his hair color didn't fall too far from the ancestral tree. And Gayle, after a year working as a physical therapist in Olympia, took on a new job: she was now a young mother.

At the time, I was the only attorney from my 1966 Stanford graduating class to have come to Washington State. Curiously, I hadn't met the man who hired me, Attorney General John J. O'Connell, a Democrat, who was both near the end of his second term and near the conclusion of a gubernatorial campaign against Dan Evans, the Republican incumbent governor. Finally, at a reception in Tacoma for newly hired attorneys, I met the attorney general. A likeable, ruddy-faced, redheaded Irishman from Tacoma, O'Connell was a popular two-term attorney general with a distinguished record as a liberal activist. Most importantly, in 1961, he helped enact the landmark state Consumer Protection and Antitrust Act, which offered an opportunity to dramatically increase the public profile and public reach of the attorney general's office.

In November 1969, John O'Connell lost the governor's election to Dan Evans and returned to private practice. Later, in 1970, the State of Washington brought a civil suit against O'Connell for, while in office as attorney general, splitting a $2.3 million private practice legal fee with Joseph Alioto, a prominent antitrust attorney, then mayor of San Francisco. In 1971, O'Connell was also indicted by a federal grand jury on bribery charges because of the way the legal fees were awarded. O'Connell prevailed in both suits, but his reputation was badly tarnished.

Slade Gorton, a Republican, succeeded O'Connell as Washington State attorney general in 1969. Gorton, born in Chicago—part of the

Back row, third from left, attorney general Slade Gorton; front row third from left, Ted Torve, and, second from right, Bill.

Chicago diaspora now on the West Coast—had gone to Dartmouth College and Columbia Law School and, in search of a political career, came to Seattle in 1953. Seattle looked to him like the land of opportunity for a budding politician. Gorton had the air of an Ivy League patrician and, like Richard Nixon, was socially stiff—he was not a politician particularly comfortable around people. But he had other attributes that more than compensated for any social awkwardness. He was a natural political animal, a brilliant tactician, and an outstanding lawyer driven to succeed, with a clear path to the top of politics in mind. We played on the attorney general's office basketball team together and shared pizzas after each game.

**

The Department of Natural Resources (DNR) had its own building, conveniently located in the center of the Capitol Campus, adjacent to the Legislative Building, and a stone's throw from the state library and the governor's mansion. Washington's 1889 constitution required the DNR to log its forest resources to help pay for K–12 schools and universities. Until the 1980s, DNR's timber revenues—from millions of acres of state-owned forestlands—funded more than 60 percent of school-construction costs. The DNR interpreted the state constitution as mandate to maximize the revenue on the trust lands consistent with the long-run sustainability of its forests.

Bert Cole, a Democrat, former small-time logger, junior high school principal, and county politician, was the independently elected commissioner of public lands in charge of the DNR. His major accomplishment while in office from 1957 to 1981 was to consolidate the state's division of forestry into the DNR.

The attorney general, as the legal advisor to all state agencies, staffed a DNR satellite office in the DNR building that consisted of three attorneys: a chief counsel, Ted Torve, and two brand-new attorneys, including me. Shortly after I started work, the bar results were announced. I passed; sadly, my office mate didn't and had to leave the attorney general's office.

Our satellite office was considered a backwater, a low-visibility assignment. Our job was to give legal opinions to the commissioner—but only when requested to do so—and to defend the commissioner in legal disputes. Most of the work was office work, involving administrative law and legislative bill drafting. From time to time we would make an appearance in a state administrative hearing when the DNR was involved.

The workload was not strenuous, and with coffee and long lunch breaks, it was usually a forty-hour week, sometimes less. I found the history and economics of the timber industry fascinating and used any extra time to familiarize myself with the financial operations of the trust lands and the history of the department. I rode my bicycle to work most days, the start of a lifelong love of bicycling that later led Gayle and I to participate in the Seattle to Portland ride, held annually, and to tour on bicycles in countries around the world.

One day, to my surprise, I discovered that the DNR for a long period held non-interest-bearing cash balances in various bank checking accounts—totaling more than $20 million—from timber sales. This was money not required for working capital. It was a curious situation, because at the time, you could earn 4 percent or more by placing money in federally insured interest-bearing bank savings accounts. By my calculation, the trust was losing about $1 million a year by failing to transfer its cash to interest-bearing accounts, and this was arguably in violation of its constitutional duty to maximize trust income for schools. Because the banks that held these accounts could use the money without paying interest, it was also a financial boon for them.

Two weeks before Christmas in 1969, as I was headed downtown for lunch, I was asked by a secretary in the commissioner's office to pick up a package at the Olympia branch of the Seattle First National Bank. At the bank, a vice president gave me a case of whiskey wrapped with a red ribbon—a Christmas present for the commissioner, I was told. Being of a fairly cynical nature—especially involving politics—I tried to put two and two together. When I discovered that the banks doing business with the DNR had been significant contributors to Cole's campaigns for commissioner, I wondered: Was there a relationship between the failure to earn interest on the cash surpluses deposited in the banks and the campaign contributions? The situation didn't pass my initial smell test.

Proving that campaign contributions are a quid pro quo for a particular benefit to a contributor is impossible in most cases. Generally, it is very difficult to prove there was a quo for the quid. The contributor and the politician seldom leave a well-marked trail allowing the dots to be connected with the required certainty. *What should I do?* I wondered. Tell Attorney General Slade Gorton or Ted Torve, my bosses? Technically, Cole was my client; he was billed for the attorney general's office's legal services. Since I couldn't prove anything nefarious—even though my gut told me it was there—I concluded that the best course of action would be to try a low-profile effort to benefit the trust by getting the money invested.

Then, should I give the commissioner my legal analysis, thus raising the issue? The rule in the satellite attorney general's offices was that you didn't give legal opinions to your client unless you were asked—particularly on questions with political implications. And I hadn't been asked. Finally, I decided on a subterfuge. On an unrelated legal memorandum to the commissioner, I threw in as an aside, "I noticed recently that the DNR has large cash balances in non-interest-bearing accounts. You may want to check on that because it may be a violation of the commissioner's constitutional duty to maximize income on trust monies."

Cole never acknowledged my legal aside, but one month later, over $20 million was quietly placed in interest-bearing accounts, at a benefit to the school trust of more than $1 million a year. *This is a pretty amazing result*, I thought, *but I can't tell anyone.*

***

After a year and a half in the attorney general's office, I felt I was at a decision point. Olympia was a nice town with a newly established innovative small college, Evergreen State. Our two-bedroom Puget Sound waterfront rental cottage on Sunrise Beach, Eld Inlet, ten miles outside Olympia, was positively idyllic. Living on salt water is a unique experience—the invigorating smell of the sea; the ever-changing ebb and flow of the tides; the abundance of seabirds, ranging in size from bald eagles and herons to coots; the flying wing formations of migrating long-necked Canadian geese honking hello to the denizens below; sea otters competing with humans for the clams, oysters, and crabs ready to be plucked for an evening's repast; an errant pod of orcas circling Chinook salmon to form a giant fishnet; a small colony of barking harbor seals lazily basking in the sun on a log raft—these sights, these sounds, these smells could not be replicated if we moved away from the waterfront. Also, I enjoyed the people at the attorney general's office. They were smart, dedicated public servants. But professionally, I was at a dead end. Longer term, the pay as an assistant attorney general was not very attractive, and my skill set as a lawyer was not being fully developed. I lacked pretrial motion and trial experience.

A strange thing about law school: it doesn't train you to be ready to practice law in a courtroom. Since learning trial and pretrial legal skills was considered on-the-job training, the practice skills learned in law school by graduation qualified you to be somewhat competent as a non-trial appellate lawyer or a high-class law clerk, but not a courtroom lawyer. Young attorneys' fear of the courtroom was ever present; it was like contemplating being thrown off a dock into the sea without swimming lessons, with sharks waiting to eat you alive. Normally, the best place to get trial experience is a county prosecutor's office, often by doing criminal cases. Because many assistant attorney generals in Olympia had the same idea as me, there weren't many openings in the local Thurston County prosecutor's office. I would have to look elsewhere. The city of Bellingham, in Whatcom County, looked like an attractive possibility.

Twice the size of Olympia, Bellingham is on the Puget Sound and is anchored by Western Washington University. It also had three other attributes Olympia didn't have: It had close access to the beautiful San Juan Islands. It had nearby skiing at Mount Baker. And it was only twenty-seven miles from Canada—a bonus should I ever have to make a run for the border. There was one downside, though: depending on the wind direction, downtown Bellingham often had a sickly-sweet smell from the emissions of a big Georgia-Pacific pulp mill located on the city's waterfront.

I decided to explore any available deputy prosecutor positions in Bellingham with the Whatcom County prosecutor, Stan Pitkin. Serendipitously, at the same time, the attorney general's office posted a notice for any interested assistant attorney generals to participate in forums around the state to explain a new state educational law. I volunteered to represent the attorney general's office on a panel scheduled for September 1969 in Bellingham.

As luck would have it, Stan Pitkin was also on the panel, and we hit it off. Neither one of us was particularly well versed on education law, but we were both quick on our feet. We actually sounded like we knew what we were talking about. At the end of the forum, I asked him about job possibilities in his office. He told me to stop by and talk to him tomorrow.

During our interview the next day, we found we had much in common. Physically, we were about the same size and build. Like me, he had a bit of small-town lack of sophistication and a midwestern set of values: justice, fairness, and standing up for the underdog, which allowed both of us to recognize a kindred spirit. We had both rejected staying in the Midwest and opted for the more open-minded West Coast and the outdoor splendor of Washington State. Originally from California, Stan had attended Vanderbilt Law School in Tennessee and married a Tennessee girl, a published poet, then headed west to seek his fortune. After a brief stint in private practice, to get his name around town, he ran in 1966 for prosecuting attorney in Whatcom County as a Republican. To his surprise, he was elected and became the youngest prosecuting attorney in the state at age thirty.

In the 1968 gubernatorial race, Stan agreed to be incumbent governor Dan Evans's campaign chairman for Whatcom County. Identified as a rising young star in the Republican Party, with a potential for higher elective office (possibly to challenge the incumbent US congressperson, Democrat Lloyd Meeds, in the First Congressional District), Stan was ripe for a promotion to the Class AAA league of the Republican farm team. Although largely apolitical, he described himself as a moderate Republican in the Evans wing of the Republican Party. Stan professed to being ambivalent about a run for Congress: "The idea of being in Washington, DC, separated from your family during the week and taking the red-eye home to Seattle on weekends, is not very appealing," he told me. He then said that newly reelected Governor Evans planned to ask President Nixon to nominate him for the position of US attorney in Seattle. "That sounds better, doesn't it?" he said. "I don't have any deputy positions open here, but if I become the US attorney, come see me in Seattle." Stan fit the classic profile of the typical US attorney: aggressive, outspoken, and not without ambition to ascend to high political office. He never inquired about my political affiliation, although if he had, I would have told him I was an independent.

A position as an assistant US attorney in the Western District of Washington, the busiest federal law enforcement office in the Northwest, was the most coveted and prestigious public sector job for a young attorney in western Washington—and the office had a reputation for apolitical hiring, which was to my liking. It was also the best place to get your ticket punched for trial experience. The cases were bigger, the judges were often smarter and more experienced, the pay was better, and along with a host of federal agencies that helped in investigations, you had the Justice Department's extensive resources in Washington, DC, backing you up. *This is where I want to be. Maybe I can pull this off,* I thought.

THE HARBOR LINE THAT WENT MISSING

When the Washington State Constitution was adopted in 1889, the state declared ownership of thousands of miles of the beds and shores of all navigable waters in the state, up to the line of ordinary high tide in salt water or ordinary high water in fresh water. To regulate development in harbor areas and protect navigation, the state constitution created a Harbor Line Commission that was directed to draw harbor lines in the navigable waters of all harbor areas within a city. Interpreting the constitution, the commission proceeded to draw two harbor lines: an inner harbor line that reserved an area only for shore structures related to navigation, and an outer harbor line beyond which no structures were permitted. Between the inner and outer harbor line, the state was free to lease land for certain commercial purposes.

In 1969 the Flo Villa Corporation and the Floating Homes Association, a houseboat development on Lake Union in Seattle, sought an injunction to stop the construction of two Lake Union apartment buildings to be built on platforms extending out over the water from the shore. The King County Superior Court judge presiding over the case, Lloyd Shorett, a highly respected longtime jurist, was perplexed because the harbor map showed only one line drawn along the shore around the lake. Was it an inner harbor line, an outer harbor line, or something else? How should a court determine which structures were permitted over the water? Why hadn't the State Harbor Line Commission done its job and drawn two harbor lines? The judge ordered the State of Washington to join the action and appear in court the next day to explain this glaring omission.

Since the Harbor Line Commission, one of the miscellaneous groups under the jurisdiction of the DNR, was assigned to me as one of my clients, my phone rang. Because the commission had been dormant in recent years, I had not performed any legal work on their behalf and had no idea even who the commissioners were. On the surface, it looked like the Harbor Line Commission had not performed its constitutional function. Could I save the day for a client I hadn't even met?

I had less than a half day to familiarize myself with the legal issues and prepare my presentation before I was due in court. There was also the little problem of my confidence. I had never represented a client in front of a superior court judge before, let alone in a high-profile case likely to be filled with critics of my performance. I was about to jump off the proverbial dock into the water without a swimming lesson. My brain told me that I was at risk in these uncharted waters. *But if my law school training kicks in, maybe I can swim,* I told myself.

It wasn't all bad news. I wasn't totally unprepared. When I was initially assigned the Harbor Line Commission as a client, I took the assignment seriously and reviewed the commission's history and legal authority. With that background already under my belt, I spent the rest of the day gathering my research and outlining the presentation that I planned to make the following day to Judge Shorett in Seattle.

The wags of the court system say that if you have a bad complex argument, you want a dumb judge. If you have a good complex argument, you want a smart judge. Before his election in 1948 as a King County Superior Court judge, Judge Shorett had been an assistant state attorney general, later elected as the King County prosecuting attorney. He had also been in private practice with a former Washington State governor, Al Rossellini. Judge Shorett was an intellectually curious, smart judge and an experienced lawyer well versed in land-use law in the Seattle area from his twenty years on the bench. Lucky for me, because I had a plausible but complicated argument to vindicate the Harbor Line Commission and get the State dismissed from the case. I really wanted an intellectually curious, smart judge.

Since this was a high-profile case with significant commercial ramifications, when I arrived at the courtroom the next day, it was very crowded—as expected—with a legion of interested land-use attorneys and the press. As the case began, Judge Shorett peered over his elevated bench at me, standing at the attorney's lectern, and asked me to address the legal issues on behalf of the Harbor Line Commission.

I began my oral argument slowly, tracing the history of waterfront development in Seattle and the work of the Harbor Line Commission. Few judges allow single-party oral arguments to exceed thirty minutes, but when I noticed the judge listening with rapt attention to my every word, I decided to go all out and give him the legal full monty. Then the most amazing thing happened! The judge appeared spellbound and let me argue on and on and on . . . I was on a roll. For the next day and a half, I spoke, the words flowing out of my mouth in a measured cadence, mostly a soliloquy, supplemented with references to dusty historical documents and maps, with the judge always alert, but only occasionally interrupting with a question.

In a very oversimplified nutshell, my rather novel argument was this: The Harbor Line Commission had done its duty, and the single line drawn on the map had a dual purpose. It was both an inner harbor and an outer harbor line, restricting development in the area in between. The judge, although not totally swayed, thought the issue was far too complicated for court resolution. Better guidelines were needed to clarify the matter, he said, because of the impact on statewide waterfront usage in places where other single harbor lines existed. I agreed and suggested that a legislative commission develop such guidelines. The judge adopted my suggestion for a legislative commission and said that since the case was more political than judicial, he would dismiss all parties from the suit, including the state.

Before the court adjourned, several of the attorneys representing parties in the case complimented my presentation on the court record. Bob Graham, a pillar of the Seattle bar—from the venerable old Seattle law firm of Bogle and Gates, the second-largest law firm in the city— who represented the Port of Seattle, said:

> *Certainly as an old-timer at the bar and I think perhaps thirty years do permit me to reminisce a little bit. I want to state this has been one of the finest and best presentations if I may say so, Judge, from both sides of the podium.*
>
> *. . . I have watched the judicial process with a great deal of interest. It has been a delightful experience to participate in this, with some restraint on my part wrestling with these problems for some twenty years on behalf of the Port of Seattle.*
>
> *I am amazed at the amount of learning and comprehension that has been put in Your Honor's lap in a short time and your comprehension thereof.*

Then Judge Shorett chimed in:

> *It certainly is a compliment to Mr. Erxleben that he was able to hold not only my attention but also the attention of lawyers, whose attention is not easily held for over a day and a half. I doubt it has been my lot very many times to hear a more profound argument than we heard here. Certainly he didn't repeat himself either unless he thought something had been missed along the way, like the (harbor) line, which is a very good way to put it. I am sure he will be heard many times in this state.*

My legal appearance in the *Flo Villa* case had legs. The *Seattle Times* ran a story on the court decision the following day, noting that

I had recommended a legislative commission to develop guidelines to resolve the legal issues. The story continued, quoting the judge: "Judge Shorett said the assistant attorney general should be a part of any such commission because of his knowledge of the complex issues involved." I knew Slade Gorton assiduously read the *Seattle Times* every day, and this unusual reference by a judge to an assistant attorney general would come to his attention, giving my legal ability some visibility in the central attorney general's office for the first time.

As said in some television commercials, "But wait, there's more!" Judge Shorett soon became a one-man band trumpeting my legal skills enthusiastically across the state. Four days after the conclusion of the trial, he wrote a letter to Attorney General Slade Gorton:

> *Your assistant, William C. Erxleben, recently represented your office in a case involving Lake Union shorelands. His presentation was positively brilliant and deserves the highest commendation. You should know that you have as an assistant a man who is surely destined to become one of the finest lawyers ever produced in this state. Without going into too much detail, it is sufficient to say that Mr. Erxleben's exposition of the history of the shorelands of Lake Union encompassed every relevant detail from the time of statehood to date. His remarks were so well organized that at the conclusion of the case several of the older attorneys interested in the case rose and profusely complimented Mr. Erxleben on his study and knowledge of the problems and his articulate explanation thereof. Indeed, I think you are fortunate to have such a man on your staff.*

But wait, wait! There's still more.

Because of the importance of the case involving waterfront usage, attorneys from across the state were requesting copies of the legal briefs filed in the case. Richard Jeffers, an attorney from Wenatchee, Washington—whom I had never met—forwarded me a copy of one such letter sent four months after the trial by Judge Shorett. It said:

> *You may not be aware that after the arguments in the case I asked the Attorney General to present an argument on certain constitutional*

features. Mr. William Erxleben, Assistant Attorney General, appeared for the State, and gave one of the most thorough, detailed, and perceptive analyses of the constitutional requirements that it has ever been the pleasure of these old ears to listen to. If the question in your case involves any constitutional considerations, I suggest you contact Mr. Erxleben who possesses such detailed knowledge of the history of the constitutional provisions relating to navigable waters, that I believe he could tell you whether or not any delegate to the Constitutional Convention wore a long-tailed coat or had his shoes shined. He was most impressive.

Thus I hit the jackpot early in my legal career. Every young lawyer fears his or her first appearance before a judge in court on a major issue will be a disaster. Success is usually measured by surviving the experience without embarrassing yourself. In my first courtroom experience, time, chance, and curiosity about an arcane area of the law vaulted me to the front of the pack of promising young lawyers. I also received a needed boost of confidence about my potential as a lawyer. *The easiest way to become a legal expert is to know a lot about a subject that nobody else knows much about,* I concluded. I was lucky, but I saw that often luck is not totally random; it is more complicated, more nuanced. Pure good luck is winning the lottery; pure bad luck is being struck by lightning. What we call *luck* is often a combination of random chance, hard work, opportunity recognition, and talent—an important lesson for those in pursuit of Lady Luck.

I was now a made man in the law, with a prominent superior court judge in Seattle as my unpaid publicist.

CHAPTER SIX

CROOKED COPS

In late fall 1969, President Nixon appointed Stan Pitkin the US attorney for the Western District of Washington. It was time for me to pay Stan another visit.

I met Stan in his capacious office on the tenth floor, the top floor of the original US District courthouse in downtown Seattle, between Fifth and Sixth Avenues and Spring and Madison Streets, now occupied by the Ninth Circuit Court of Appeals. The courthouse, a ten-story neoclassical building with art deco accents and an expansive lawn, is one of the few spots of greenery in the densely developed central downtown district. But the block-shaped building by itself to me looked like a fortress or a prison.

Stan's office was designed to impress and convey the majesty and power of the federal legal system. His office was dark, and the rug had seen better days, but it had a massive wooden desk in a space the size of a handball court, flanked by the United States and Washington State flags. Stan said that he had only one open position in the seven-attorney office. He leaned back in his oversize, high-backed brown leather chair, and after a long, teasing, and pregnant pause, broke into a wide grin and said, "Bill, how soon can you start?" I told him I would need some time to arrange my affairs and for the FBI to complete its background investigation to reinstate my security clearance from the military. We agreed that I would start in February 1970.

"C'mon, I'll show you where your office is. Of course, it's a bit smaller than mine," he joked.

Tell me something I don't know, I thought.

In search of a vocation committed to justice and the common good, I had found an appropriately named white horse to sally forth on: the United States Department of Justice. I was thrilled.

I sent my letter of resignation as an assistant state attorney general to Slade Gorton. He responded with a very kind letter that said: "Everyone who has dealt with you has expressed the opinion that you were one of the outstanding young lawyers of your class and in our office."

I left the attorney general's office after only one and a half years, but I left on a high note, after I'd made what I thought was a significant contribution, and I thanked Lady Luck for the jump start to my legal career.

It really was paradise lost when Gayle and I and our four-month-old son, David, came to Seattle. We went from our storybook cottage on Sunrise Beach in Olympia to a nondescript, but newer, rental house in north Seattle, which faced Meridian Avenue North, a busy thoroughfare, on one side, and fronted a dead-end street whose main destination was the Shoreline Transfer Station near the I-5 freeway, two blocks away. Rather than the singing of birds and the smell of sea air in the morning, we were serenaded by the sounds and smells of garbage trucks hauling the detritus of Seattle to a temporary repose before being trucked backed down our dead-end street again to its final graveyard in a landfill. But the rent was what we could afford in an area that had good access to the downtown federal courthouse.

The Soaring '60s were over for the Boeing Company in 1970: the bottom had fallen out of the market for commercial aircraft because of high interest rates, oversupply, and the canceling of the supersonic transport program for supersonic jets. Employment at Boeing fell from a 1968 high of 100,000 to a low of about 33,000 in 1971. The local economy was in a free fall. People were exiting the state in what became known as the "Boeing Bust" to find work elsewhere. Two real estate agents put up a billboard near the airport: "Will the *last person* leaving SEATTLE—*Turn out the lights*." Had I made a mistake coming to Seattle?[1] I was starting to have second thoughts about leaving Olympia. *This job better be as exciting as I've been led to believe,* I worried.

Just as I was beginning my new job as an assistant US attorney, I was assigned a raft of smaller matters called *in rem* actions. In these actions, the government sues an inanimate object rather than a person, usually resulting in a forfeiture or fine. After a couple of cases involving railcars full of grain, which the government sued to destroy the grain because its rodent fecal content was above the FDA minimum allowed, I quit eating cereal. Who knew there was an allowable rodent fecal content in our grain?

Run-of-the-mill bank robberies were also assigned to me. The cases often sadly followed an unfair stereotype: Two black teenagers rob a federally chartered bank in Seattle's Rainier Valley, triggering a silent alarm that rings in the local FBI office; the robbers flee on foot; they fail to cover their faces and are now clearly identifiable on the bank's cameras; they are given marked bills for easy evidentiary proof of guilt; they take the bait money, which explodes, covering them in red dye, and soon after the caper, they are captured by the FBI five blocks from the bank. Easily identifiable by the red dye and the security camera footage, the teens plead guilty to the charges and are sentenced to prison, where they refine their criminal skills before being released. Then, a short time later, older but not much wiser, the teens, now in their twenties, are rearrested for additional criminal activity and, through a continuously revolving door, return to prison.

I was deeply troubled by the criminal justice system's handling of minorities. Was it just to recycle a never-ending stream of poor, primarily black males to and from prison? For sure, some violent offenders need to be warehoused, but the prison system must be, I believed, about more than warehousing repeat offenders. It should be about rehabilitation and addressing underlying social conditions whenever possible. The economic cost and suffering caused by long-term confinement didn't make sense if there was a better approach. It was my first introduction to the futility and waste of economic and human resources in America's outmoded and broken criminal justice system.

Any change, however, would require a political solution, and the current frame of mind in the body politic favored punishment, not rehabilitation and the alleviation of causative economic and environmental conditions in the inner cities.

I did have my scruples regarding some criminal matters. I refused to take drug cases. I told Stan not to assign them to me. I believed the federal drug laws were far too harsh on nonviolent offenders, particularly small-time dealers and recreational growers of marijuana. Stan didn't argue with me; he assigned drug cases to other attorneys in the office. I soon learned he had bigger plans for my time.

Shortly after I began work, Stan asked me to come down to his office. With a look of concern on his face, he said, "We're about to blow the lid off public corruption in Seattle. I really need your help."

"What's up? What are you planning to do?" I asked.

"I am going to ask the grand jury to indict M. E. 'Buzz' Cook, an assistant chief of police in Seattle, for perjury. We are going to try and destroy the tolerance policy that has corrupted this city for decades."

As the newbie in the office without a full caseload yet, I was the prime candidate to be drafted for special duty. What was the tolerance policy? What was I in for? I had thought by coming to a young city like Seattle, I had left behind the public corruption of older cities, like my birthplace, Chicago. (Morris "Mo" Udall, US Representative from Arizona from 1961 to 1999, was a congressional wit who once said that he wanted to be buried in Chicago so he could continue to vote and remain "active in politics.") Now I discovered that Seattle had a pervasive payoff system involving its police officers. Seattle was a city with its own extraordinary history of vice and public corruption.

***

Payoffs to cops are like candy to babies: once they acquire a taste for it, they become hooked on the sugar, and it's hard to resist the temptation to take some more. Seattle was no exception.

Bribery of law enforcement officials was nothing new. It had existed since laws were first carved on stone. Port cities on the West Coast—Seattle, San Francisco, and Vancouver, BC—all had notorious twentieth-century histories of vice and payoffs to police and politicians. Seattle managed to lead the pack handily, however, being distinguished by the ubiquity of its public corruption.

Seattle's reputation as a wide-open frontier town goes back to the gold rush of 1897 and the boom times of two world wars. Soldiers and adventurers mostly wanted booze, gambling, and prostitutes. Seattle happily supplied all three. The city also was considered a friendly town for gay men serving in the military during World War II. Areas of the downtown were so open to hedonistic pursuit that it became too much even for the US Army, which declared certain areas off-limits to soldiers.

Although, as of 1970, gambling had been illegal in Washington State for decades, there were almost six thousand pinball and other illegal gambling devices in the state. To give an aura of permissibility to illegal gambling, the Seattle City Council went one step further than the rest of the state by passing an ordinance, in 1954, licensing illegal card rooms. This tolerance policy toward gambling in card rooms provided the wedge to allow other illegal activities to flourish. As long as the conduct involved was consensual and nonviolent—including prostitution and homosexual activity in gay bathhouses—it was fair game to fall under the protective umbrella of Seattle's tolerance policy. The official rationale was that by limiting most of the illegal activities to the Central District—including Skid Road, Chinatown–International District, and portions of Capitol Hill—these minor offenses, "victimless crimes," could be better controlled.

The tolerance policy offered the Seattle Police Department the allure of easy money. It was a made-to-order opportunity for beat cops on the street to supplement their incomes by extorting protection bribes from people and businesses engaged in consensual criminal activity. Otherwise, the offenders would face the threat of harassment or business license revocations. It was pay to play. If you wanted to do business under the tolerance policy without getting wet, you had to pay the men in blue for an umbrella.

I soon learned that patrol officers and members of the Seattle Police Department's vice squad extracted regular monthly payments from the denizens of the Central District, keeping half of the money and passing the rest up the chain of command in one-on-one transfers. Some beat cops pocketed a share worth as much as $800 a month. Particularly hard hit were tavern operators and bathhouses with gay and lesbian clientele. How far up the chain of command did the other half of the money go? It was rumored that the money went up the chain of command in an inverted pyramid all the way to the police chief's office, and beyond the police department to city and county politicians, including even to the longtime King County prosecutor, whose jurisdiction encompassed Seattle: Charles O. Carroll.

Over the years, there were periodic exposés of graft and corruption in the Seattle Police Department. Invariably, the defenders of the status quo described the problems as due to a few "bad apples," rather than a systemic problem. With only temporary crackdowns to discipline the bad apples, the payoff system continued to prosper and grow. While most police officers were not involved in the payoff system, many were, particularly those officers who patrolled the Central District or served on the vice squad.

To clean up the city for the 1962 Seattle World's Fair, Mayor Gordon Clinton had ordered a crackdown on the illegal activity permitted under the tolerance policy. But the crackdown didn't last. In 1964 the next mayor, J. D. Braman, reinstituted the tolerance policy, and once again, illegal activities flourished.

In 1967 the *Seattle Times* ran a series of articles that exposed the corrupt system of police bribery. In response to public pressure, Mayor Braman impaneled a four-person blue-ribbon commission to investigate the charges. The commission consisted of Seattle luminaries, including Bill Boeing Jr., scion of the founder of the Boeing Company and a staunch Republican conservative, and Richard Auerbach, special agent in charge of the Seattle office of the FBI. Dominated by supporters of Charles O. Carroll, the commission reviewed the evidence uncovered by the *Seattle Times*, but concluded there was no widespread criminal activity or basis for criminal prosecution. Assistant Seattle police chief Buzz Cook, as a special liaison from the police department, testified before the commission, but the commission failed to question him specifically about payoffs.

Charles O. Carroll, the King County prosecutor—a local hero sometimes referred to as "Football Charlie" to distinguish him from Charles M. Carroll, "Streetcar Charlie," who was a longtime member of the Seattle City Council—had been a legendary football player at the University of Washington. An All-American running back in 1927 and 1928 and a National Football Foundation Hall of Fame inductee in 1964, he was one of three Huskies to have his number retired by the university. He had served as a Republican King County prosecutor from 1948 to 1970, across the heyday of the police department payoff system. As the unquestioned political kingpin in King County, he called the shots on the appointment of judges and was the arbiter of who was prosecuted and who was wiretapped. The police reported to him, and Carroll kept files on the personal indiscretions of politicians and judges—much like the FBI's J. Edgar Hoover.

Hoover was an acknowledged master at using incriminating dossiers—particularly of a sexual nature—to get what he wanted from a US congressperson or president. No one in Washington dared hold J. Edgar Hoover accountable. No one in Seattle, it seemed, dared hold Charles O. Carroll accountable either.

Carroll wasn't about to shut down the tolerance policy. He was proud of the fact that organized crime run by the Mafia was not a problem in the county. But organized crime was a problem, and many thought the cops and the politicians, not the Mafia, controlled the rackets. After the 1967 *Seattle Times* story, Seattle-based KING-TV followed up with an investigation suggesting a strong connection between Carroll and gambling interests. It seemed the biggest gambling operators in the county were regular visitors to Prosecutor Carroll's home.

By October 1969, the payoff system was starting to show signs of unraveling. When President Nixon appointed Seattle's Republican mayor Braman as an assistant secretary of transportation, interim mayor Floyd Miller replaced him for the last nine months of Braman's term. Soon thereafter, three assistant police chiefs, in an internal palace revolt, objected to the mayor about the police chief's interference in a gambling investigation that exposed local corruption. As a result, Mayor Miller forced the police chief, Frank Ramon, into retirement.

As US attorney, Stan Pitkin faced huge challenges in filing any criminal cases against local police officers and politicians for bribery and corruption. Absent a relevant federal statute, there was no federal jurisdiction that would allow him to indict police and politicians for local corruption. The US attorney could investigate for potential federal violations, but without a federal statutory nexus, he could not prosecute. Local corruption was the province of the local prosecutor—Charles O. Carroll. Stan would have to find another way.

Criminal jurisdiction wasn't Stan's only problem. The FBI refused to investigate local corruption. At first, Stan had two FBI agents, assigned by the Seattle FBI office, to assist us in the police corruption investigation, but word came down from J. Edgar Hoover that the agents were not permitted to interview current or former Seattle police officers. We were told that Hoover believed the FBI should only cooperate with local police, not investigate them. With the absence of any federal investigations by the FBI or the US attorney's office, it became increasingly clear to us how the Seattle police and the King County prosecutor had been able to control the narrative on police corruption for decades.

Without the FBI, Stan was stymied. He needed street investigators to gather evidence, interview people, and feed the federal grand jury with a slew of witnesses to uncover the scope of the payoff system. Without investigators to find targets, he could not use the powerful investigatory tools of the grand jury to investigate local corruption.

***

In February 1970, upon Stan's recommendation and following the testimony of several police officers and affected businesses, the grand jury issued an indictment against Assistant Chief of Police Buzz Cook. Cook was the powerful head of the patrol division, which included the Central District—the hot spot of police corruption. The indictment for perjury was based on this exchange between Pitkin and Cook:

> *Pitkin (Q): Do you have any knowledge of law enforcement officers being paid by operators of gambling establishments?*

Cook (A): No, I do not.

Q: Have you any knowledge of anybody currently on the force who participated in shakedowns?

A: I do not.

Q: You don't have any knowledge of anybody currently on the force that participated in shakedowns?

A: No.

Q: Have you at any time received any money, property, or things of value from any person, directly or indirectly, who has been involved in gambling activities?

A: No.

Stan Pitkin had found a back door for federal jurisdiction to indict local Seattle police officials: lying to the grand jury. The perjury trial against the assistant chief of police would be the vehicle to publicly expose corruption in the Seattle Police Department, but an unindicted and unnamed codefendant in the case in reality would be the tolerance policy itself.

No more routine criminal cases for me. I wanted excitement, but little did I realize I was about to jump into a crucible of fire.

CHAPTER SEVEN

CLEANING HOUSE

Two days after Buzz Cook's secret indictment by federal grand jury, and barely thirty days after I joined the office, thirty-three-year-old US Attorney Stan Pitkin assembled his three-person trial team. Stan was the lead counsel; he had tried a few short civil and criminal jury trials but had no federal trial experience. The second member of the team was Assistant US Attorney Dick McBroom, an obviously intelligent, even-tempered twenty-eight-year-old Columbia Law School graduate with a dry sense of humor, who had participated in several long civil trials when he worked for the civil rights division of the Justice Department in Washington, DC, but had no criminal trial experience. And then there was me, the youngest: twenty-seven years old and with no trial experience whatsoever. There was no way to sugarcoat it—given the stakes in the trial, we were a highly unseasoned team.

We divided up the work. Stan would orchestrate the continuing investigation with the grand jury; Dick would concentrate on pretrial motions and assist with the grand jury; and I would hit the streets to take over for the two FBI agents who had been directed by J. Edgar Hoover not to help us. I thought there was a touch of irony there: despite my earlier rejection by the FBI, I was now a replacement for two FBI agents.

***

There is an ebb and flow to corruption in major metropolitan police departments. Many large cities like New York City and Chicago are convulsed by police scandals every twenty years or so. Time passes, the crisis fades, and the cancer of corruption goes into remission. Often a trial occurs and a few are punished, but that's merely collateral damage. The cancer lurks in the recesses of the system, waiting for an opportunity to again metastasize. What would happen in Seattle? Would Seattle be different this time around, with a federal indictment of an assistant chief of police?

Prosecutors, especially federal prosecutors, have enormous power. They only investigate and file cases they deem worthy. Usually it's a process of triage, with only the most important cases filed; the rest are left to languish until the statute of limitations expires: this is called prosecutorial discretion.

Grand juries are designed as a check on abuse of prosecutorial power. A proposed felony indictment by a US attorney must be approved by a federal grand jury, showing probable cause that a crime has been committed. Yet because the US attorney controls the evidence that a grand jury hears, it has been said that a grand jury would indict a ham sandwich if that was what a prosecutor wanted. There's some truth to that, but the other side of the equation is that grand juries represent a powerful investigative tool in the fight against organized crime and political corruption. How ethically a grand jury operates depends heavily on the integrity of the prosecutor.

Immediately on his arrival in Seattle in the fall of 1969 to assume the duties of US attorney, Stan Pitkin ordered the convening of a federal grand jury with broad subpoena powers to look into the scope of corruption in the city. Witnesses who were subpoenaed were faced with a choice: testify truthfully or face the possibility of a perjury indictment. Or assert their Fifth Amendment right to remain silent and possibly be forced to testify, if given immunity. If a witness lied to the grand jury after immunity, he or she could still be prosecuted for perjury.

An appearance before a federal grand jury is definitely a sweaty-palms and racing-heartbeat experience for a subpoenaed witness.

Counsel for the witness is not permitted in the grand jury room, although, following a question, a witness may ask to leave the room to confer with his or her attorney. The prosecutor controls the proceedings and has wide latitude in asking questions. The proceedings are usually supersecret, although witnesses are generally not required to keep their own testimony secret if they do not wish to. My first experience observing a grand jury proceeding made me very glad I wasn't the one subpoenaed. I watched a nervous witness, his hands trembling, as he was led to a well-lighted area at the front of the windowless grand jury room to be seated. Twenty jurors stared in silence from the shadows in the back of the room. Then Stan, the prosecutor, stood eyeing the witness like a piece of meat that he was getting ready to grill, adding to the tension. For a first-time grand jury witness, the experience is intimidating and extremely stressful. It's designed to scare people into telling the truth. If you were a witness, there are few places you would rather not be.

Eager to assess our chances of success at trial, Dick and I queried Stan about the strength of the case. We soon learned that it hinged largely on two witnesses for the prosecution: Dave Jessup, a major in the Seattle Police Department, who would testify that he passed payoff money to Cook, but this testimony was tainted because Jessup had also accepted payoffs; and an assistant chief of police, Eugene Corr, who knew a lot about the payoff system, but most of his information was hearsay or circumstantial evidence.

"Is this it?" Dick and I said, almost in unison, with an air of shock and disbelief.

"Yes, it's all we have now, but I'm sure more witnesses will come forward once the indictment becomes public," Stan said, with a disturbing note of uncertainty.

Dick and I soon realized that Stan was a full-speed-ahead, damn-the-torpedoes kind of guy. To build the case after the indictment seemed reckless or courageous or both—we weren't sure which. *Are we babes in the woods, in over our heads? What did I sign up for?* I thought, decidedly uneasy about our prospects for success. But with the battle now joined, with Cook's indictment, we had nowhere to go except forward.

The trial judge assigned to the *Cook* case was US District Judge William Lindberg, a white-haired jurist with an unusually avuncular personality for a federal judge. Thomas P. Keefe, an experienced and accomplished trial attorney, a former deputy prosecuting attorney for Charles O. Carroll, and at six foot five, a towering figure in the courtroom, led the defense team, supported by his legal partner, Emmet T. Walsh. Keefe and Walsh soon became the attorneys of choice for a large number of the active-duty officers subpoenaed by the grand jury. We viewed this as an apparent attempt to coordinate testimony and keep the defendant, Cook, apprised of any cracks in the notorious blue wall of silence.

Judge Lindberg scheduled a hearing to calendar the case for trial. Stan told me to represent the office at the hearing. There, the defense argued for an early trial—not surprising, because if police officers were vulnerable to being turned to testify against Cook, time was not their client's friend. With as straight a face as I could muster, I told the judge that we welcomed an early trial too, which was really not true, since we had only a few witnesses. But it was important to give the impression that our case was strong, because that would encourage police officers to come forward and cut a deal before the trial rather than go down with the ship. The court set the trial on an accelerated timetable for mid-June, about five months away. To determine the likely duration of the trial, Judge Lindberg asked me, "How many witnesses does the government intend to call?"

Without hesitation, I responded confidently, "About thirty-five, your Honor." This was wildly optimistic, since it was thirty more witnesses than we actually had. When I returned to Stan's office, he asked me what had happened. I told him.

He said approvingly, "Thirty-five? Good number. Where did you come up with that?" I pointed to the ceiling.

I'd thought I was a risk-taker, but Stan, with his damn-the-risks, we-can-do-this attitude, was in a different league altogether. *His strategy is either brilliant or crazy*, I thought. I was now on a train speeding down the tracks, hoping that we would arrive at the station before we derailed.

So began the arduous task of building the case and finding thirty more witnesses. Stan later estimated that the trial team worked twelve-to fourteen-hour days, seven days a week, for five months to develop the case for trial. But we had one respite: most weekday nights, we would gather at the College Club across the street from the federal courthouse to unwind and to coordinate our activities, usually accompanied by snacks and a couple of gin and tonics. At the same time, many of the cops would repair to Vito's—a restaurant and bar and a Seattle institution, on Capitol Hill at Ninth Avenue and Madison; a notorious Italian-style place frequented by many politicians, criminals, cops, celebrities, and gamblers; and a favorite hangout of former governor Al Rossellini. (Vito's was remodeled and reopened in 2010 under a banner: "Behaving Badly Since 1953.")

For exercise and mental clarity, I ran down the waterfront sidewalk on Alaskan Way through Myrtle Edwards Park for a three- to four-mile jaunt at noon many days, weather permitting. Otherwise, I ran on the indoor track or played volleyball at the downtown YMCA. To manage the stress of this high-stakes, fast-paced work environment, I practiced transcendental meditation for twenty minutes most days.

Stan asked for some additional investigative assistance from the Justice Department's criminal division in Washington, DC. Soon I would have a partner: Tim Oliphant, a thirty-year-old lawyer and graduate of the University of Colorado Law School, who, after a stint as an assistant attorney general in the Virgin Islands, had recently joined the Justice Department's organized crime section as a special attorney.

With a full trial team in place, we now had to figure out how to prove to a jury the wide scope and conspiratorial nature of Seattle Police Department shakedowns. We were at ground zero with an actual investigative strategy. We brainstormed with a whiteboard, jotting down ideas, until finally a strategy emerged. After much discussion, we decided that we needed to identify all the officers who had worked in the vice squad or the Central District over the last twenty years and contact as many of them as possible, working from the bottom up through the chain of command. Tim and I were the feet on the street. We worked in tandem as partners. Our job was to get the officers to confess.

Neither Tim nor I had any idea how you got a cop to confess. We weren't trained in interrogation; presumably the cops were, and knew all the tricks of the trade. As an old Norwegian proverb says, "Necessity teaches a naked woman how to knit." Tim and I needed to learn quickly how to knit or we would all soon be naked in court before Judge Lindberg.

To identify potential police officer witnesses, we had help from both the state attorney general's office and from some extralegal resources. A gaggle of investigative reporters, who had chased the Seattle police corruption rumors for years, showed up daily at our office, gleefully funneling tips and information. We couldn't keep them away; nor did we want to—they were critical allies. John Wilson, Marshall Wilson, and Dee Norton from the *Seattle Times*, flamboyant investigative reporter Don McGaffin from KING-TV, and Maribeth Morris from the *Seattle Post-Intelligencer (P-I)* led the scrum of journalists, smelling blood and hoping for a kill. Lou Guzzo, the managing editor of the *Seattle P-I*, was our most enthusiastic editorial cheerleader, determined to break the system open in true Hearst Newspapers muckraker style and sell a few newspapers in the process.

The *Seattle Times* and the *Seattle P-I* were great rivals in a newspaper circulation war, but with different constituencies. The *P-I* was Democrat-leaning and liberal. The *Seattle Times* was Republican-leaning, conservative, and business oriented. The *Times*, editorially, took an antagonistic view toward the indictment and our investigation, which I found rather odd, since they had broken the story on police corruption four years earlier. I later learned the reasons: Ross Cunningham, the longtime editorial page editor, was tight with Charles O. Carroll; they did each other favors. Also, the *Seattle Times* was the newspaper of the Republican business community, and they liked Carroll.

The blue wall of silence, akin to the Mafia's *omertà*—or code of silence—hindered our investigation of on-duty Seattle police officers. The code does not allow one to rat on a fellow police officer. Police forces are insular quasi-military organizations, with their own cultures, worldviews, and conservative political affiliations, and local politicians fear antagonizing them. With the general respect of the public for law enforcement behind them, police unions—the Praetorian Guard of police departments—can throw their weight around in local elections with endorsements, money, and feet on the street. In Seattle's case, the union is called the Police Guild. Defensive, politically powerful, and aligned with conservative King County Republican politicians, the Police Guild was the guardian of the police force's darkest secrets, ready to challenge and intimidate anyone who sought to reveal them.

Our best bet to induce confessions was to try to flip retired police officers. They didn't have jobs to lose by confessing, and they were also far less likely to be prosecuted for past criminal conduct than officers on active duty. Tim and I planned an interrogation tactic based largely on knowledge gleaned from watching *Perry Mason* episodes.

"Do you want to be the good cop or the bad cop?" I asked Tim, suspecting what the answer would be.

"Good cop," Tim said immediately.

"Why?"

"Because you're a better bad cop."

Tim—wiry, slightly built, four inches shorter than me, and wearing glasses—was right. As the six-foot-two-inch 215-pound alpha male, I would make a better bad cop.

We got good at our shtick. Tim was a really funny guy. Our humor was mostly black and improvisational. When we were alone, we laughed our way around the streets of Seattle. While this might seem strange, like black humor in an operating room among surgical staff, it was the perfect antidote to the stress of our mission. And, to our delight and great surprise, our confession-inducing technique started working. Retired police officers eager not to be prosecuted or subpoenaed before the grand jury in the continuing investigation of local organized crime and corruption started confessing left and right. The blue wall of silence now had a crack as big as a crevasse on Mount Rainier.

Sometimes my bad cop act didn't work very well. One sunny afternoon, Tim and I interviewed a retired assistant chief of police at his residence in West Seattle. It was a very nice house with an oversize kidney-shaped swimming pool. The former chief invited us to join him in the lounge chairs poolside and asked if we wanted a drink. We said yes, but it must be nonalcoholic, because we were still on the government clock. After some pleasantries, I decided to get right to the point and said something like, "Let's quit beating around the bush. Tell us about all the payoffs you took while on active duty."

At this point the former assistant chief jumped out of his chair, waving his arms, his face crimson red, and started fuming and screaming at us: "Get out of here, you bastards." Normally we might consider this an affront to our mothers, but this time discretion clearly was the better part of valor. We bounded out of the chaise longues and beat a hasty retreat around the pool and out the gate to our car. I think it was right after this incident that I started—every morning before going to work—lifting the rear engine compartment of my green VW Beetle (bought new in 1969 for $1,700) to see if I could spot any extra wires.

The toniest address that Tim and I visited in our search for Seattle ex-cops was Broadmoor, an exclusive eighty-five-acre gated and walled residential complex with a golf course that borders Lake Washington. Located in the Madison Park area of Seattle, it is a safe, protected haven, for old wealth and arrivistes, sporting a convenient in-city location. It was also the home of Bill Boeing Jr., the conservative Republican and a close friend and political supporter of Charles O. Carroll, the King County prosecutor. A curious stop for us, since Bill Boeing was one of the members of the 1967 blue-ribbon commission that investigated—and whitewashed—charges of Seattle police corruption. But we weren't investigating Bill Boeing. Our target was a former police officer who was reportedly working as Boeing's chauffeur. Unfortunately for us, Boeing's house had to be contacted for permission to enter the gated complex. By the time we arrived at the house, the chauffeur was gone. We never managed to find him.

Our street investigation of former Seattle police officers often took us to neighboring cities and rural areas, like Vashon Island, in pursuit of retired officers. Stan once went as far as Yakutat, Alaska, population 662, to conduct an interview with a retired police captain who participated in payoffs. But it was a trip to the city of Mercer Island, located in the middle of Lake Washington, that particularly stands out in my memory.

Midmorning, Tim and I arrived at the Mercer Island town marshal's station to interview Marshal Wesley Moore, a retired Seattle police lieutenant with twenty-six years of service. When we entered the police station, passing several deputy marshals in the eight-officer department, Moore intercepted us dressed in full uniform. He was a big bear of a man, well over two hundred pounds, with a rather menacing nickel-plated Colt .45-caliber revolver on his hip and a pair of silver handcuffs dangling from his belt. We were unarmed. We identified ourselves. The marshal whispered that he couldn't talk in the station and wanted us to accompany him in his squad car to a discreet location where we would be unobserved.

We climbed into the back seat of the squad car. Marshal Moore drove up a winding road to the top of a hill overlooking the city of Mercer Island and Lake Washington. He stopped in a secluded parking lot behind an apartment building under construction. Then he turned his head to face us in the back of the car and, without much prompting, began to confess his participation in decades of corruption in the Seattle Police Department. We furiously took notes.

"Payoffs to policemen in the Central District and to members of the vice squad were a long-standing practice," he admitted almost matter-of-factly, without a hint of apology. "It is part of the police culture and accepted as a benefit of working the seedy parts of the city." When he was finished, he said, "You young fellas think you're doing the community a favor by exposing corruption in the police department, don't you?"

"Of course," I said, thinking the loftiest thoughts possible. "Public corruption is the worst kind of corruption. It destroys the community's faith in government."

"Did you ever wonder why the Mafia isn't active in Seattle? Why there aren't bodies with cement shoes in Lake Washington or the Puget Sound?" he countered.

"Too many Scandinavians and not enough Italians?" Tim blurted out, in a dry, witty reference to the high concentration of Scandinavian fishermen and their families in Ballard, one of Seattle's largest neighborhoods.

"No, no," Moore said. "It's because the cops run the rackets. We only run the good rackets: no violence, no drugs, and no murders. We tax mostly homos, whores, and gamblers, particularly the Chinese in

Chinatown. You take the cops out of the rackets, and you'll get the Mafia." Although I appreciated his weirdly nuanced explanation of the situation, it did seem to ignore the rule of law.

But at the top of the list for my most bizarre police officer interview was the hospital interrogation of a retired Seattle police captain, Edgar True Corning. (A curious middle name, as it turns out, because he was very reluctant to tell the truth.)

It all began one spring evening in Bothell, Washington, just north of Seattle. It was early May, about nine in the evening. Tim and I were planning to interview Captain Corning at his house about his knowledge of payoffs while he was an active-duty officer. We arrived at his house unannounced. After we identified ourselves, he invited us into his living room to talk. His wife asked graciously if we would like some milk and freshly baked cookies. Never one to refuse a pastry, I said sure. (I was hoping for chocolate chip.) She then left the living room and went to the adjacent kitchen to prepare the refreshments.

Captain Corning was reticent to talk until we offered the usual blue-light special: "Talk to us or talk to the grand jury." He quickly opted to talk to us and began to relate information about his involvement and the scope of the payoff system. Unfortunately for us, his wife overheard our conversation from the kitchen. She ran into the living room without the cookies, grabbed a lamp off a side table, and, with lamp in hand, told her husband to shut up and ordered us to leave the house immediately.

The smell of fresh-baked cookies notwithstanding, we skedaddled out of there, but not without leaving a grand jury subpoena behind ordering Captain Corning to testify.

Just before he was due to testify to the grand jury, Captain Corning was admitted, on the advice of his personal physician, to Swedish Hospital in Seattle because of a "heart condition." After the subpoena expired, Corning was released from the hospital. With time running out before the trial, we subpoenaed him to testify at trial. He then immediately checked back into Swedish Hospital, citing his heart condition again.

This was a little too convenient for our tastes. Stan petitioned Judge Lindberg for permission to take Captain Corning's deposition in the hospital for use at trial. Judge Lindberg said his decision would await the examination of a court-appointed doctor, a Virginia Mason Clinic cardiologist named Robert Paine. (Yes, that really was his name.) Dr. Paine examined Corning and found him healthy enough for a deposition in early June.

"Would you mind doing the interrogation for Corning's deposition?" Stan said to me, with a bit of a sheepish look on his face. He didn't have to tell me why. We really didn't think Captain Corning had a heart problem, but if he did, and he died during the examination, the optics wouldn't bode well for Stan's political aspirations. Convinced Corning was faking, I had no problem doing the interrogation.

Stan and I, and a court reporter, arrived at Swedish Hospital at the appointed time. Corning's personal physician, Dr. Houk, met us at the front door. He said he had just given Corning some drugs; it wasn't clear what drugs. I wondered if this was an attempt to obstruct justice in case Corning talked. His testimony might be excluded in the trial as incompetent, as clouded by the influence of medications.

We arrived at Captain Corning's hospital room and found him on his back in bed, eyes wide open and staring at the ceiling. He was hooked up to a heart monitor that showed the blips of his heartbeat gyrating across a green screen. I sat down in a chair next to Corning's bed and asked the court reporter to give Captain Corning the oath to begin the deposition. But Corning refused to speak; with his lips tightly pinched together, he shook his head no and refused to raise his hand. We ended the deposition, noting his refusal to testify on the record. Corning's ruse prevented us from taking further action to force him to appear at Buzz Cook's perjury trial.[1]

Despite the loss of a witness like Captain Corning, our efforts to round up trial witnesses to expose the corrupt tolerance policy and the police payoffs were looking promising. To my relief, we now had more than thirty-five witnesses prepared to testify.

***

Chiseled into a slab of granite in a courtyard outside the Seattle Police Headquarters was a Bible verse, Proverbs 29:18: "Where there is no

vision, the people perish: but he that keepeth the law, happy is he."
With Buzz Cook's perjury trial looming, there were a whole lot of
Seattle police officers who had failed to "keepeth the law" and were
about to become unhappy.

The trial had an explosive debut. It would be sensational, and everyone knew it. Buzz Cook, an unimposing man, partially bald, with thinning short hair, sat quietly at the defense table with his two defense
attorneys, and Stan, Dick, and I sat across from them at the prosecution
table. But anticipation dripped from the courtroom ceiling as spectators, the media, and courtroom sketch artists entered the courtroom.
The public was eagerly anticipating the scandal the trial would surely
reveal.

The media was out in force: radio, TV, and print journalists all present in the spacious high-ceilinged Seattle federal courtroom of Judge
Lindberg. The major Washington State papers covered the trial daily,
often in front-page headlines. As an unabashed news junkie who liked
living in the moment, I felt an adrenaline rush from the excitement of
being in the arena with foreknowledge of tomorrow's headlines. We
didn't read the news. We were the news.

After the opening day of the trial on June 24, 1970, the *Seattle P-I*
ran a bold banner headline under the front-page masthead: "Six Say
They Made Payoffs to 19 Seattle Policemen." Below the headline, on
the right side of the front page, was a six-inch, full-figure sketch of
Stan Pitkin standing with his arms folded behind his back, looking
downward across the page. On the left side of the front page was a six-
inch, full-figure sketch of Beverly Grove, the very attractive manager of
the Casbah Tavern and Cardroom—in a miniskirt—who had testified
that her life had been threatened by a Seattle police officer when she
resisted further payoffs. From across the page, Stan was clearly looking
at her shapely legs. Tabloid journalism at its best. (You've got to love
the old *P-I*!) Beverly Grove said that one of the officers in a shakedown
told her father, "I'm sure you don't want anything to happen to your
little girl. We can't protect her and the tavern unless we receive certain
little gifts." Refusing to make payoffs, her father closed the Casbah.

The first week of the trial involved a parade of witnesses testify-
ing to their knowledge of widespread criminal activity in the police

BEVERLY GROVE

U.S. ATTORNEY
STAN PITKIN

Courtesy of Seattle Post-Intelligencer.

department. The money trail went all the way back to 1936. After a week of testimony, Judge Lindberg rightly started to get a bit testy, wondering when the name of Buzz Cook would be mentioned. We assured the judge that would happen soon, but we argued first it was necessary to show through circumstantial evidence the pervasiveness of the police corruption, demonstrating that Cook must have been aware of the payoff system.

While our primary objective was to convict Cook, we wanted to get as much as possible on the public record in order to blow the system wide open. Cook provided an instrument for public truth-telling. If we had presented direct testimony about Cook early in the trial, the judge might well have excluded many of our witnesses on the grounds that their testimony was repetitive and unnecessary.

One retired police sergeant, Palmer M. Hughes, testified that he started receiving money from subordinates in 1949. I questioned him:

Q: *Why did patrolmen under you give this money?*

A: *It was something that wasn't talked about. I assumed it came from somebody who wanted a favor or who had received a favor, but we never talked about it . . .*

Q: *Was it automatic, just because you were there?*

A: *Yes, it seemed to be routine.*

Sergeant Hughes estimated that he had received money from or passed money to at least fifty different officers during his police career.

Wesley Moore, the town marshal of Mercer Island, whom Tim and I had interviewed earlier, took the stand and admitted taking multiple bribes during his twenty-six years of duty on the Seattle police force. In later testimony, one of my witnesses, Tony Gustin, an assistant chief of police involved in the overthrow of Police Chief Frank Ramon the year before, testified that he once replaced the entire vice squad because he didn't trust any of its members. One vice squad member who had been replaced was now a sitting Seattle City Council member, Wayne Larkin. Assistant Chief Gustin also testified that early in 1970, Marshal Wesley Moore agreed with his request to meet with the newly elected Seattle mayor Wes Uhlman, but they ended up meeting with Deputy Mayor Robert Lavoie instead. Marshal Moore told the deputy mayor about the payoff system.

"Did anything come of this?" I asked.

"No, nothing happened," Gustin said.

The star witness for the prosecution was Major David Jessup, who had been trying for years to gather evidence to expose corruption in the police department. Jessup, tall, fit, and articulate, with a chiseled chin, could easily pass as a look-alike for Clint Eastwood in a *Dirty Harry* film. He was an impressive witness who could have come right out of Central Casting. On direct examination by Stan Pitkin, he said that he had known about the payoff system since 1955 and began taking money in 1965. Jessup said that in 1967, he told Seattle's deputy mayor Ed Devine; Robert Lavoie, then administrative aide to Mayor Dorm Braman; and Police Chief Frank Ramon about the payoff system. In response to these revelations, Jessup was named head of the Seattle Police Department's internal investigations unit and was asked by Devine and Lavoie to infiltrate the system with the assurance that his job would be protected. Jessup testified that from 1966 to 1967, he both received and passed payoff money to the defendant, Buzz Cook.

During his three and a half hours of testimony, Jessup implicated himself and a score of other high-ranking officers, including former chiefs of police. He testified—and was corroborated by former deputy mayor Ed Devine—that despite widespread knowledge of impropriety, there was a total lack of action against police shakedowns by top city and police officials and the Federal Bureau of Investigation.

After two weeks of testimony and more than forty witnesses for the prosecution, more than one hundred former or active-duty police officers were implicated in receiving or passing payoffs. Now it was time for the defense case.

Although there was a string of defense witnesses, mostly character witnesses and testimony of some officers who said they knew nothing about the payoff system, the defense case didn't amount to much. Buzz Cook did not testify. During my cross-examination, Major Neil Moloney, the head of the Seattle Police Department's criminal investigations division, related an "indirect" bribe from Captain Corning, but he said he took no money himself. Moloney also testified that Cook had "the very best reputation" as an administrator.

There was one surprise defense witness: Wes Uhlman, the Democratic mayor of the City of Seattle, elected only seven months earlier in 1969; he was the first Democratic mayor of Seattle in thirty years. Born in Cashmere, Washington, the son of Pentecostal preachers, at thirty-four, Uhlman was Seattle's youngest mayor and a boy wonder in politics: as a twenty-three-year-old law student, he had been elected the youngest member of the Washington State House of Representatives.

An extremely bizarre episode involving Mayor Uhlman occurred just prior to the start of the trial. One morning, under the door at the

Courtesy of Seattle Post-Intelligencer.

entrance to our offices in the federal courthouse, we found a large manila envelope containing about thirty well-written, copiously documented, single-spaced typewritten pages meticulously detailing the murder of a prostitute by the mayor and her subsequent burial by him in the scablands of eastern Washington. We dismissed the report with an air of disbelief as a probable political dirty trick. The *Seattle Times*—who like many in the press had no love for Uhlman, reportedly received a copy of the same report but took a different tack. In 2006 an essay by Emily Leib, a professor of history at Seattle University, revealed that the *Times* sent a reporter, Don Duncan, to eastern Washington in a wild-goose chase to "dig up" the body of the woman Mayor Uhlman was rumored to have murdered.

From the start of the grand jury investigation, Mayor Uhlman had been antagonistic to the federal probe of the Seattle Police Department. Some thought it was an attempt to embarrass him and his police department in retribution for his action in February 1970, when he had blocked a planned federal raid on the Seattle offices of the Black Panther Party, earning national headlines and the enmity of the Nixon administration. Before the trial, Mayor Uhlman stated that he would take no action against Seattle police officers until the trial was over, but he would fire all officers who admitted to participating in payoffs. "I'm not going to permit a few officers on the force of thirteen hundred to destroy the integrity of the entire group," he told the press. Of course, this put a damper on any active-duty officer's willingness to admit in a public courtroom to accepting bribes.

Mayor Uhlman testified at trial that he once rejected an offer of information about police payoffs because the informant, an assistant Seattle police chief, demanded that the source of the information be withheld. Uhlman's attitude struck me as an example of the three wise monkeys: "See no evil, hear no evil, speak no evil," a refusal to acknowledge impropriety by feigning ignorance.

***

At the conclusion of the trial, exhausted and nervous about the outcome, Stan, Dick, and I, now joined by Tim, who had been observing the trial, retreated to our offices four floors above the courtroom to await the verdict. *We are either going to be heroes or villains when this is over,* I felt, hoping for the former.

The jury didn't deliberate long. After a few days, on July 9, 1970, in a hushed courtroom jam-packed with spectators and the press, a jury of seven women and five men found former assistant chief of police Buzz Cook guilty of perjury for lying to a federal grand jury. On August 12, 1970, Judge Lindberg sentenced Buzz Cook to three years in prison at the McNeil Island Penitentiary.

Stan, Dick, and I were ecstatic. We jumped up from our seats behind the counsel table and embraced each other. We had accomplished what five months earlier we'd thought was a shot in the dark. For the US attorney's office, hard work, preparation, and strategy had triumphed over inexperience—but most of all, we had the facts, and truth and justice prevailed.

Stan Pitkin picked up a raft of enemies after the *Cook* trial. Because of the broad scope of the evidence of widespread corruption presented, some accused Stan of grandstanding to the press. Stan would unabashedly say, "If informing the public about corruption is grandstanding, grandstanding is a virtue, not a vice."

Many individuals deserve credit for bringing down the tolerance policy in Seattle and the corruption that flourished under it. But Stan Pitkin, on a riverboat gamble, through a backdoor criminal case against Buzz Cook for perjury, was clearly the catalyst that exposed three decades of police corruption for all to see and finally propelled its downfall. He was courageous. He made a real difference and helped to recapture good government in Seattle.

***

Seattle police corruption was now dormant, but was it stamped out? History was not encouraging. Mayor Wes Uhlman soon brought in Charles Gain, Oakland California's chief of police—who had a reputation for honesty and toughness—on a temporary appointment as SPD chief to stabilize the department and begin reforms. Gain wasn't sanguine about Seattle's long-term prospects for a clean department free of widespread corruption. "In most cities, the corrupt element waits out the investigator and the reform effort dies; the system is too overwhelming," he said. In 1971 the *Wall Street Journal* published a long retrospective on the *Cook* trial and police corruption in Seattle. It quoted a tough-minded Seattle cab driver, who said cynically, "The cops have been getting paid off since the beginning of time, and they always will."

To the surprise of many observers, the SPD has proved to be an exception to the rule that you can't stamp out payoffs for long. As the *Seattle Times* said in a 2005 editorial on the death of Gene Corr, a former assistant chief of police and witness for the prosecution in the *Cook* case, who came forward to testify despite anger and death threats from some of his colleagues: "The struggle to clean up the Seattle Police Department was one of the high points of Seattle's history. It made the police force better and the city better."[2]

***

Shortly after the trial, Dick McBroom, my trial partner in the *Cook* case, left the US attorney's office to head up the continuing grand jury investigation of the Seattle Police Department by the newly elected King County Prosecutor Chris Bayley. Dick died—at age thirty—soon after he left the US attorney's office, of a rare blood disease. He left a wife, Maureen, and two young children.

CHAPTER EIGHT

REVOLUTION!

The year 1970 did not start out well for the city of Seattle. A major police corruption case and a dramatic downturn in Boeing employment called into question both the integrity of city government and the prospects for the region's economy. They say bad news comes in threes. In this case they were right. Adding to the city's troubles, laid-back Seattle also convulsed with a series of violent demonstrations and bombings.

The Vietnam War was the catalyst for the reemergence of radical leftist movements in Seattle. From February to July 1970, more than ninety incendiary devices exploded around the city. In fact, Seattle ranked number one in the nation for the number of protest bombings per capita. Demonstrators repeatedly shut down buildings at the University of Washington, jammed downtown streets, and occupied the freeways, sometimes spilling over onto the federal courthouse lawn.

While Seattle was being roiled by demonstrations and violence, the Seattle US attorney's office was a relatively passive bystander. Local police and the FBI were investigating the violence while Stan Pitkin, Dick McBroom, and I were totally consumed with the upcoming trial of Buzz Cook. Meanwhile, the newly elected president, Richard

Nixon, and his attorney general, John Mitchell, were on the warpath, absolutely incensed by the anti–Vietnam War demonstrations taking place across the country. Some of the demonstrators were suspected of bombings, break-ins, and rioting. They also were perceived as communist sympathizers, as undermining the conduct of the Vietnam War, and as a threat to the internal security of the United States. The highly publicized protests were politically embarrassing to President Nixon both domestically and internationally. At Nixon's direction, indicting the leaders of violent anti-war protests became a national strategy for the US Department of Justice.

***

The form of law which I propose would be as follows: In a state which is desirous of being saved from the greatest of all plagues . . . there should exist among the citizens neither extreme poverty, nor, again excessive wealth, for both are productive of great evil.
                    —Plato (427–347 BC)

Washington State has a seldom-discussed radical, violent, and anti-capitalist past. In times past, many working-class people in Seattle and other cities in Washington State were far from docile and accepting of what was seen as the unequal distribution of wealth and the exploitation of the working class.[1] Capitalism was overtly challenged by labor. The working class sought to revolt. The battle: between capitalism and labor for the fruits of production.

In the first part of the twentieth century, many Washington workers widely embraced a Marxist share-the-wealth philosophy.[2] A lingering reminder of that past occurs in the annual May Day parades held in Seattle and other western Washington cities. Originally intended to honor workers, annual parades sponsored by unions celebrating labor and showcasing workers' rights and other social issues have in recent years often been hijacked by anarchists, hate groups, and petty criminals, who come out of hibernation once a year to rail against capitalism and destroy commercial property. (At least, this was true until 2012, when Washington State legalized recreational marijuana that mellowed the marchers.)

Radical labor history in Seattle and Washington State goes back a hundred years. Mirroring Soviet Union strikes in 1917, the Seattle General Strike of 1919 was the first citywide labor action in the United States to be called a general strike. The police and vigilantes rounded up the "Reds," and federal agents shut down the labor-owned daily newspaper in Seattle. When the strike ended after only a week, headlines across the country screamed that Seattle had been saved from Bolshevism. Big Jim Farley, President Roosevelt's postmaster general, later famously toasted: "To the forty-seven states and the Soviet of Washington."

Washington State was also a hotbed for the Industrial Workers of the World (IWW), a militant union whose members were known as the Wobblies. They believed that the employing class unfairly exploited union workers. Their agitation led to the bloodiest battle in Pacific Northwest labor history. As many as fifteen people were killed and fifty wounded in what became known as the Everett Massacre of 1916. Three years later, in 1919, during a parade celebrating the first anniversary of Armistice Day following World War I, a clash between the IWW and the local American Legion left six people dead and many wounded in Centralia, Washington.

By the mid-1930s, Washington State had garnered such a reputation for being friendly to leftist radical causes that it was the target of a colonization attempt by the socialist leader Eugene Debs. He persuaded thousands of his followers to migrate to the state with the goal of creating a leftist state.

Following a period of quietude after World War II, a multitude of events converged to provide fertile ground for a new radical social uprising in the 1960s. Young people, rather than union workers, were the primary protagonists. From 1963 onward, race riots erupted in cities across the country, leaving over one hundred dead, thousands wounded, and more than a billion dollars in property damaged. Brutality against those fighting for civil rights was endemic in the South. The murders of John F. Kennedy, Robert Kennedy, and Martin Luther King Jr. shocked the country. The killing of unarmed students at Kent State, and the dreadful carnage of the Vietnam War, made the notion of President Johnson's 1964–65 "Great Society" a mirage.

By the late 1960s, in a country at war with itself, and hope in the future rapidly fading, I was not surprised that some would turn to violence. Disillusioned with their government and the politics of the day, thousands of young people took to the streets demanding a reordering of the nation's priorities and a stop to the Vietnam War. Like Humpty Dumpty, America had fallen and broken into pieces, and no one quite knew how to put it back together again.

***

Students for a Democratic Society (SDS)—a national political movement fueled by civil rights and anti-war protests, infused with a Marxist set of guiding principles—arose out of the political chaos in the mid-1960s to become one of the principal representatives of the New Left on college campuses. Among its most prominent leaders were its first president, Tom Hayden, and later, Bernardine Dohrn and Bill Ayers. Ayers, the son of a prominent Chicago business executive, was the head of an SDS regional group called the Jesse James Gang.

At its last convention in 1969, the SDS collapsed over a dispute regarding its future direction, creating a leadership vacuum between students and radical organizations in the United States. In 1970 two groups formed from the remnants of the SDS to fill the political void in Seattle: the Seattle Liberation Front and a Seattle branch of the Weather Underground Organization, a militant left-wing group colloquially known as the Weathermen.

With revolutionary positions supporting black power and opposition to the Vietnam War, the Weathermen's goal was the violent overthrow of the US government. The 1969 founding document of the Weathermen called for radical movements to achieve "the destruction of US imperialism and achieve a classless world: world communism." Bernardine Dohrn declared: "Protests and marches don't do it. Revolutionary violence is the only way." She would become the best-known national face of the Weathermen.

I met Dohrn for the first time sometime around September of 1970. Looking disoriented and somber, she was handcuffed in a federal courtroom in Seattle. In transit, as I recall, to be arraigned in Chicago on charges related to a federal grand jury indictment. She needed an immediate bail hearing that afternoon. Stan Pitkin told me to represent the government at the hearing that day, with instructions from the Justice Department to oppose bail. I thought, *This is no big deal. Just another bail hearing.*

I knew Dohrn was one of the leaders of the national Weathermen group, but I didn't know a lot more. She was a law school graduate. Although she had been arrested and indicted several times, none of her cases had come to trial, and she hadn't been in jail before. Based solely upon her outstanding charges, I made an argument to the court that she was a flight risk and bail should be denied. The judge gave my argument short shrift and granted bail. Female defendants are unusual in federal criminal proceedings, and in addition, Dohrn was exceptionally attractive. Perhaps my argument would have been more persuasive had I not been distracted by her looks.

When I entered Stan's office to report on the bail hearing, he asked, "How did it go?"

"I freed Bernardine Dohrn," I answered. "She made bail." Stan chuckled. No one had thought bail would be denied.

A true femme fatale, Dohrn was beautiful and stylish. Her good looks, a black leather jacket with an upturned collar, and oversize chic sunglasses made her the center of attention in leftist circles. Peter Collier and David Horowitz wrote about Dohrn's first arrival in New York City in 1967 in their 2005 book, *Destructive Generation: Second Thoughts about the Sixties*:

> *With her tight miniskirt and knee-high Italian leather boots, she created a sensation among males in Movement circles. Even SDS president Greg Calvert was astonished. "I'll never forget the first time I saw Bernardine," he said. "She was wearing an orange sweater and purple skirt, and while everyone else had on Stop the War buttons, hers said Cunnilingus is Cool, Fellatio is Fun. She had a boyfriend . . . but like others buoyed by the new air of sexual freedom, she had relationships*

with men who interested her." J. Edgar Hoover later nicknamed her
"La Pasionaria of the Lunatic Left."

Dohrn was born in 1942 as Bernardine Ohrnstein in an upper-middle-class suburban family in Milwaukee, Wisconsin. Her father was Jewish and her mother was Swedish. When Dohrn was in high school, the family surname was changed to Dohrn.

I later learned Dohrn attended Miami University at the same time I was a student there. In her sophomore year she was a counselor in a first-year women's dorm, Wells Hall, at the same time that my wife, Gayle, resided in that dorm as a freshman. Dohrn left Miami after two years, after the "Tri-Delt" sorority, Delta Delta Delta, reportedly blackballed her because she was half-Jewish. She then transferred to the University of Chicago, where she received both a bachelor's degree and a law degree.

It wasn't long after she was released on bail in Seattle that Dohrn, rather than face trial, disappeared into the hidden shadows of the Weather Underground with Bill Ayers. The judge should have listened to me and not granted her bail, but maybe Dohrn's appearance distracted him too.

In October of 1970, Bernardine Dohrn was placed, along with Bill Ayers, on the FBI's most-wanted list, where she remained for the next three years. She was only the fourth woman in FBI history to make the list. Some called Bernardine the "most dangerous woman in America." Her most-wanted poster said: "Dohrn reportedly may resist arrest, has been associated with persons who advocate use of explosives and may have acquired firearms. Consider dangerous."

Bernardine Dohrn, Bill Ayers, and the Weathermen weren't the only players in the violence that would eventually lead to a conspiracy trial of the Seattle Seven in 1970. To understand what precipitated the trial in Seattle, you had to understand the violence that happened in Chicago in 1968 and 1969, which resulted in the trial of the Chicago Seven a few months earlier.

THE CHICAGO SEVEN

The August 1968 Democratic National Convention was held in Chicago during a period of violence and civil unrest in more than a hundred cities—unrest fueled by a list of grievances including the Vietnam War. Over five days and nights, thousands of protesters marched in the streets during the Democratic convention. Marchers and police officers battled, and hundreds of people, including at least nineteen police officers, one hundred protesters, and several members of the media, were injured. Protesters threw rocks and bottles and were teargassed by the police. Police officers arrested 589 people. It was absolute chaos in downtown Chicago.

Following the Chicago convention riot, a federal grand jury heard some two hundred witnesses. President Johnson's attorney general, Ramsey Clark, was hesitant to indict the protest leaders. He believed that the police had primarily caused the violence. But after Richard Nixon took office in 1969 and John Mitchell was named attorney general, a Chicago grand jury on March 20, 1969, returned indictments against eight people prominently involved in the demonstrations. With more than a touch of irony, they were charged primarily with a conspiracy to violate the anti-riot provisions of the Civil Rights Act of 1968, which were designed to protect protesters from violence from hate groups.

The best known of the original eight Chicago defendants were Bobby Seale, a Black Panther Party activist; Tom Hayden, a former SDS president; Rennie Davis, a national organizer for the SDS; and Jerry Rubin and Abbie Hoffman, the Yippies—members of the Youth International Party or YIP, a theatrical protest group described as anti-authoritarian and anarchist. Known for their street theater pranks, the Yippies were once described as Groucho Marxists. To mock the social status quo, they advanced a pig ("Pigasus the Immortal") as a 1968 candidate for president.

The Chicago trial, or Chicago circus as it was also sometimes called, began on September 24, 1969. The trial involved a variety of antics and political theater by the defendants. One day Abbie Hoffman and Jerry Rubin mocked courtroom decorum by appearing in court wearing judicial robes. The judge, Julius Hoffman, ordered them to remove the robes. They complied, only to reveal Chicago police uniforms underneath. On another occasion, Bobby Seale called Judge Hoffman a honky, a pig, a fascist dog, and a racist. When Seale refused to be silent, the judge ordered him bound and gagged in the courtroom. Judge Hoffman eventually severed Seale from the case and sentenced him to four years in prison for contempt of court. The Chicago Eight then became the Chicago Seven.

The Chicago trial lasted for five months. After the jury deliberated, all defendants plus their lawyers were sentenced, on multiple counts of contempt of court, to prison sentences ranging from two months to four years. The jury found two of the defendants not guilty of a conspiracy to cross state lines with the intent to start a riot, but convicted the other five on that charge, including Hayden, Hoffman, and Rubin, and sentenced them to five years in prison. Eighteen months later, the substantive convictions were reversed by the United States Seventh Circuit Court of Appeals on the grounds that Judge Hoffman was biased in his refusal to permit defense attorneys to screen prospective jurors for cultural and racial bias and that he had exhibited a "deprecatory and often antagonistic attitude toward the defense." None of the defendants served time, and most of the contempt charges were also dropped. Tom Hayden went on to marry actress Jane Fonda and became a prominent liberal politician in California.

THE DAY AFTER

The Seattle Liberation Front (SLF) issued a call to join a nationwide demonstration on February 17, 1970. Often referred to as "The Day After," or TDA, this was a national protest timed to immediately follow the verdict in the Chicago Seven trial. The Seattle event was to be held at the federal courthouse with an objective to shut the courthouse down.

On TDA, the demonstrators, two thousand strong, marched through the downtown streets of Seattle to arrive at the federal courthouse. I had just started my employment at the US attorney's office, and I watched with amazement from the safety of my west-side tenth-floor office window in the courthouse as the protest turned into a large-scale, violent riot.

I could not believe my eyes! The courthouse was under attack. Protesters were pelting the building and the police with paint bombs and rocks. Federal marshals quickly manned the courthouse entry doors to prevent rioters from breaching the building. The pungent odor of tear gas drifted into the courthouse from the street. By the time the melee was over, twenty people had been injured and eighty-nine arrested, and over $75,000 in damages were inflicted on federal property. Seattle's acting police chief, Frank Moore, told the news media, "The demonstrators came prepared for war . . . they were armed with pipes, clubs, chains, paint, and tear gas . . . and they used them all."

The Nixon administration, under Attorney General Mitchell, sprang into action. Guy Goodwin, the chief of the Justice Department's internal security division was dispatched from Washington, DC, to Seattle to secure indictments from a federal grand jury against TDA demonstration leaders.

Newspaper columnists Jack Anderson and Les Whitten, in their nationally syndicated articles, referred to Guy Goodwin as the "Witch-Finder General." Goodwin, a graduate of the University of Kansas and its law school, was a bit of a fop. A small, fine-featured, soft-spoken man, and an immaculate dresser with a full head of prematurely graying, well-styled hair, he appeared to care greatly about his appearance. At first glance, he seemed an incongruous selection to be the point man of the Nixon administration in charge of subduing the radical left.

Goodwin was also extremely secretive. We in the Seattle US attorney's office had no idea what was happening in Goodwin's Seattle federal grand jury investigation of the TDA riot. Goodwin refused to say. My suspicion of his being up to no good was so strong that at one point I seriously thought of rifling his briefcase to find out what he was doing. Stan and I didn't like Goodwin and didn't trust him. But then, we felt the same way about Attorney General John Mitchell.

One month after arriving in Seattle, on April 16, 1970, Goodwin obtained an indictment from the grand jury against eight members of the SLF on charges of inciting the TDA riot on February 17, 1970. They were charged with damaging federal property and, like the Chicago Seven defendants, under the anti-riot provisions of the 1968 Civil Rights Act, which made it a federal crime to cross state lines to incite a riot. The indictment named SLF members Michael Lerner, Susan Stern, Charles "Chip" Marshall III, Michael Abeles, Jeffrey Dowd, Joseph Kelly, Roger Lippman, and Michael Justesen as defendants.

Before the trial began, defendant Justesen disappeared into the Weather Underground.[3] Originally the Seattle Eight, the defendants were now dubbed the Seattle Seven after the recent infamous trial of the Chicago Seven.

THE SEATTLE SEVEN

The 1970 trial of the Seattle Seven began as the West Coast's reincarnation of the year-earlier trial of the Chicago Seven. Although the Seattle Seven defendants, compared to the Chicago Seven, were younger and sometimes less polished in their antics, the two trials bore an uncanny resemblance to each other—almost mirror images. Only the defendants' names were different.

Back in 1969, as the Students for a Democratic Society disintegrated into various factions, four of the Seattle Seven defendants—Chip Marshall, age twenty-five; Jeff Dowd, age twenty; Joe Kelly, age twenty-four; and Mike Abeles, age nineteen, all former SDS members from Ithaca, New York, who became known as the Ithaca Four—saw Seattle as a counterculture-friendly environment and came west as the Seattle Sundance Collective, a living and political affinity group named after Butch Cassidy and the Sundance Kid, outlaws on the run from the law.

Two of three remaining defendants, Susan Stern and Roger Lippman, besides their membership in the SLF, also were Weathermen. The Weathermen took their name from Bob Dylan's 1965 song "Subterranean Homesick Blues": "You don't need a weatherman to know which way the wind blows." Stern, age twenty-seven, was well educated, with advanced degrees from the University of Washington. From a wealthy New York family that owned a Brooklyn textile company, she was an off-and-on member of the Sundance Collective and worked part-time as a topless dancer. An ardent admirer and aco-lyte of Weathermen leader Bernardine Dohrn, she joined the Seattle collective of the Weathermen in early 1970. The other Weatherman defendant, Roger Lippman, age twenty-three, also well educated, attended Reed College in Oregon. He joined the Seattle Weathermen collective around the same time as Stern.

The seventh defendant was an intellectual leader in the Seattle protest movement: Michael Lerner, age twenty-seven, had received his undergraduate degree from Columbia and was doing his graduate work at the University of California, Berkeley, where he later received a doctorate in Marxist philosophy in 1972. At Berkeley he was a leader in the Free Speech Movement, and he had been chair of the Berkeley chapter of SDS from 1966 to 1968. In 1969, while still working toward his doctorate, Lerner, a self-described Marxist, became an assistant professor of philosophy at the University of Washington. He opposed the violent orientation of the Weathermen and organized a loose col-lection of radicals and collectives in January 1970 to form the SLF to carry out further protest activities in Seattle.

I knew virtually nothing about the Seattle defendants when they were indicted. I was too preoccupied with the grand jury investigation of Buzz Cook. Besides, this wasn't a case our office would be handling: it was a DC-based Justice Department internal security case. But I didn't like the smell of it. President Nixon had a long history of red-baiting when it was politically convenient. Who were these defendants? Were they just anti-war demonstrators caught up in an unjustified crack-down by the Nixon administration? Were they Marxist-Leninist rev-olutionaries espousing the violent overthrow of the US government? Were they oppressed minorities or the working poor? Were they indicted for something the government could actually prove they did? What was their agenda? As Butch said to the Sundance Kid in the epic movie *Butch Cassidy and the Sundance Kid*, "Who are those guys?" I had no idea.

The early 1960s, with the hippie culture joined at the hip (sorry) with a vibe of peace, was known as the age of sex, drugs, and rock 'n' roll. From 1966 to 1970, many politically active protest groups formed,

fueled by the Vietnam War. But a new crop of radical leftist collectives
had broadened the political agenda. The Seattle collectives had a much
broader range of objectives than sex and drugs, including women's
liberation, black power, anti-war protest demonstrations, hatred for
the police ("the pigs"), hatred for President Nixon, revolution, and, for
some, violence. Che Guevara and Ho Chi Minh were idolized. Mao's
"Little Red Book," which advocated the overthrow of capitalism as one
of its main tenets, was pocketed as the ornament of the day, de rigueur
for the fashionable revolutionary. These self-styled revolutionaries
were for the most part white, male, well-educated offspring of middle-
to upper-class families: children of privilege.

Susan Stern, in her over-the-top, racy, tell-all memoir *With the
Weathermen*, published in 1975, left no doubt that Weathermen hated
police and celebrated violence. "Kill the pigs" was a common refrain
directed against the police. Commenting on her participation in the
"Days of Rage" demonstration in Chicago in October 1969, organized
by the Weathermen, where dozens of officers and protesters were
injured and 280 members of the Weathermen, including Stern herself,
were arrested, she wrote: "The reports from Chicago were good. We
had done hundreds of thousands of dollars' worth of damage. We had
injured hundreds of pigs. Greatest of all, one of Richard Daley's [the
Chicago mayor's] chief counsels, Richard Elrod, was paralyzed from
the waist down. I had the right to walk with my head held high; I had
done my share."

The relationship between the Seattle Weathermen and the SLF
was unclear. They had severe philosophical differences regarding personal relationships. Weathermen wanted no distractions from the revolution, including any interference from family or marital bonds, but
destroying monogamy and cutting off family ties was not an SLF philosophy. And while both groups shared political objectives, including
revolution, they differed on the acceptable degree of violence to attain
it. Attorney General Slade Gorton expressed his concern that the SLF
represented a threat to Washington State when he told business leaders
in Walla Walla, Washington, on May 4, 1970, in comments reported
statewide, "the Seattle Liberation Front is totally indistinguishable
from fascism and Nazism."

I found the idea of a successful violent leftist revolution in the United States, a nation armed to the teeth, with weapons in half of its houses, hard to imagine. The liberal values of tolerance and respect for the rule of law underpin our society. Peaceful protests are fine and protected by the First Amendment, but violent protests with indiscriminate violence to persons and property cannot go unanswered or anarchy will rule the streets. Be careful what you wish for. Revolution is easy, but governance is hard. Revolutionary movements too often revert to mob rule. In a representative democracy I firmly believed in grabbing the levers of political power through the ballot box, not by revolution. The history of revolution is seldom a happy one.

THE PROSECUTION

The Seattle Seven case was scheduled for trial on November 6, 1970, in Tacoma, Washington, but that was not Stan Pitkin's worry: a team of attorneys from Washington, DC, headed by Guy Goodwin, were scheduled to try the case.

Since achieving the verdict in the *Cook* trial in July, Stan and I had continued to work closely together, and we were now immersed in prosecuting major industrial pollution suits involving unlawful discharges into the Puget Sound. In October 1970 a surprise was dropped on us: Guy Goodwin and his team would not try the case. Goodwin supposedly was needed in other parts of the country to conduct grand jury investigations into other violent, militant anti-war protests. With only five weeks left to prepare a case he knew nothing about, Stan was directed by the Justice Department to try the case with his Seattle office resources, without help from the internal security division in DC. Stan's euphoria over the successful outcome of the *Cook* trial thus proved to be distressingly short-lived: He was now flying blind into another big case. Could he pull the office's reputation out of the hat twice?

Stan was shocked and visibly depressed by the situation. He suspected that the case, hurriedly prepared, was badly flawed and Goodwin wanted to dump it and get out of town, leaving the Seattle US attorney's office holding the bag. He had few options: he could ask for a trial postponement—which was not likely to be granted since the case was fast-tracked—or resign from office in protest. Resignation wasn't really a viable option for him either. Because of the Boeing downturn, few law partner positions were available in private practice. And he didn't want to leave office on a down note after his big victory in the *Cook* case.

With a young family and a big mortgage on an apartment building he had bought upon moving to Seattle, Stan was in too precarious a financial position to walk away after only a year in office. The prospect of the adrenaline rush of being back in the arena—in the limelight—in what promised to be a headline-grabbing case with national implications also seduced him, I think. Stan was a talented attorney and a risk-taker. He would make the best of it.

Stan chose Charles "Chuck" Billinghurst, a competent, low-key, twenty-year journeyman veteran of the US attorney's office stationed at the old 1910 satellite federal courthouse in Tacoma, as the second member of the trial team. As an experienced trial attorney, Chuck Billinghurst knew the courthouse and, most importantly, the idiosyncrasies of George Boldt, the Tacoma federal judge scheduled to try the case.

Four days before the trial was to begin, Stan called me into the office. For the second time that year, I heard a clarion call to enter the arena with him. "I really, really need your help," he said, with more than a hint of desperation in his voice. *What should I do?* I wondered. I had little respect for the Nixon administration's crackdown on antiwar protesters. On the other hand, Seattle had been plagued with bombings and violence. Which side of the fence were these defendants on? I knew Stan didn't want me for my trial skills; others had much more experience. He wanted me for my judgment and strategy. I was like comfort food. He felt better when I was there.

I was conflicted. This case had a bad aroma, but Stan needed my help, and ever since the *Cook* case, we had been foxhole buddies. I'd become a trusted advisor and strategist to help him thread his way through the pickles he managed to get himself into. You have the back of your buddy when he's in danger, don't you? As important, I confess, was indeed the allure of the arena: a desire to have another front-row seat in what might be the most controversial criminal trial to ever hit Washington State. Additionally, and perhaps as a self-serving rationale to overcome my misgivings, I saw an opportunity, as an "objective" insider—at least as objective as one can be in a subjective world—to be a chronicler of events, a fly on the wall, for the truth of the trial in the historical record.

The prosecution's trial team was now set: Stan Pitkin, lead counsel, and Chuck Billinghurst and me, assistant counsels. On the weekend preceding the start of the trial, I interviewed my witnesses for the first time. Shockingly, I would learn what the case was about only as the trial unfolded.

THE DEFENSE

The Seattle Seven defendants had taken an eclectic approach to assembling their defense lawyers. According to Susan Stern, Michael Lerner wanted a big-shot lawyer like Bill Kunstler, one of the high-profile lawyers in the Chicago Seven trial, on the defense team, while other defendants wanted locals who "could be developed politically" to align their views with those of the defendants. Michael Lerner and Chip Marshall, the defendants' resident intellectuals, decided to appear pro se—representing themselves—which would give them the latitude to inject political issues into the trial and to engage in behaviors that were more likely to be allowed for nonlawyers. The trial judge, George Boldt, agreed. He told Lerner and Marshall that they would be given "a little more leeway than the attorneys."

Four attorneys were retained to represent the defendants loosely as a group, but for the record they were assigned one or more of the defendants. Jeff Steinborn, twenty-six years old, a Yale graduate, a member of a prestigious liberal Seattle law firm, and a young, inexperienced attorney who had a reputation for defending draft cases and drug defendants, was hired to represent Susan Stern. Also retained was Lee Holley, thirty-five years old, a liberal activist who worked with draft resisters and defended alleged communists; Holley was hired to represent Michael Abeles. And then there was Carl Maxey, a University of Gonzaga Law School graduate, who would act as designated co-lead counsel and represent Joe Kelly. Maxey, fifty-four, a liberal civil rights attorney from Spokane and a big, distinguished-looking man with a full head of graying hair, glasses, and a calm demeanor, had a sterling reputation in the bar. He had just lost the Democratic primary race for a US Senate seat, running as an anti-war candidate against the Vietnam War hawk and "senator from Boeing" Henry "Scoop" Jackson. In her book, Susan Stern described Maxey as an inspired choice because "he was the most respected lawyer in the state of Washington, and he was black." He would try, ultimately unsuccessfully, to provide some adult supervision to the presentation of the defense case. As he would soon find out, the defendants were uncontrollable.

Along with Carl Maxey, Michael Tigar was retained as the other co-lead counsel to represent Jeff Dowd and Roger Lippman. Tigar, brash, egotistical, theatrical, self-righteous, and full of himself, was a courtroom showman, although he had very little actual jury trial experience. Defendant Michael Lerner had wanted "flash" in an attorney, Susan Stern wrote, and a compromise choice was Tigar, who was then teaching at the UCLA School of Law. Tigar had done some work on the Chicago Seven trial and had had a brief stint with the Williams & Connolly law firm in Washington, DC, a small, well-known and politically connected criminal defense firm.

Tigar was one year older than me, and we were alike in some respects. Like me, he was a big man, big-boned and over six feet tall with short-cropped hair. Like me, his father died at age forty-nine, and Tigar was driven by the thought that he might not have a long life. Like me, he graduated from law school in 1966 in Northern California. Like me, he opposed the Vietnam War. But he went one step further than me in his opposition to the war. After four years as an undergraduate in Naval ROTC (Reserve Officers' Training Corps), and accepting the benefits, he managed to get himself declared a conscientious objector and avoided military service altogether. Unlike a true conscientious objector, I didn't object to all wars—just ill-considered, unjust wars of choice, like the Vietnam War. Machiavelli had it about right, I think, when he famously said, "War is just when it is necessary; arms are permissible when there is no hope except in arms."

Unlike me, Tigar, earlier in his career, had had a shot at the triple crown, but right at the finish line, he lost by a nose.

At Boalt Hall Law School, at the University of California, Berkeley, Tigar had been a brilliant student: the editor in chief of the law review and first in his class at graduation. After law school, Justice William J. Brennan Jr. of the US Supreme Court hired him as a law clerk. When Tigar arrived with his family in Washington, DC, to assume his clerkship, however, Justice Brennan immediately fired him. Conservatives, including J. Edgar Hoover, had objected to Tigar's leftist politics and his association with left-wing groups. His attendance as a leader of the American contingent at the Helsinki Youth Festival in 1962, prominently participated in by the Soviet Union, was cited as a reason for concern.

But, for the defendants, leftist political persecution by J. Edgar Hoover was not a disqualification; it was a badge of honor. Tigar was hired as co-lead defense counsel.

THE JUDGE

George Hugo Boldt, born in Chicago, was sixty-seven years old when he drew the short straw and was assigned, randomly, to preside over the Seattle Seven case. A Republican federal district court judge since 1953, appointed by President Eisenhower, he was an experienced jurist, very courtly with old-school manners, politically conservative, and a deeply religious man. He was one of two federal district court judges assigned to the federal courthouse in downtown Tacoma—the smaller of the two federal courthouses in the Western District of Washington.

Judge Boldt, a plainspoken man, was a graduate of the University of Montana and its law school and had served as a lieutenant colonel in the United States Army from 1942 to 1945. Despite his experience as a judge, the case he was about to hear would challenge his ability to maintain any sense of courtroom decorum. But he was determined not to lose control of the courtroom like Judge Julius Hoffman had in the

Chicago Seven trial, where the defendants often openly insulted the judge. Faced with a group of defendants who had little respect for the rule of law, he had his work cut out for him. He was soon to be sorely tested.

CHAPTER NINE

THE TACOMA CIRCUS

If the Chicago Seven trial was a circus, the Seattle Seven defendants were not going to be outdone. In a succession of many acts, the performances by the defendants, and one of their counsel, in the big top of a Tacoma federal courtroom were quite an entertaining spectacle. But in the end, with a loud crack of the whip, the show suddenly stopped, and the judge proved to be the ringmaster in charge.

***

There was room for about a hundred people in the high-ceilinged Tacoma federal courtroom occupying the third floor of the courthouse. The two front rows were filled with reporters from TV stations and local and national press, including the *New York Times*, *Wall Street Journal*, and *Time* magazine. Facing the judge and jury, Stan Pitkin, Chuck Billinghurst, and I sat on the left at the prosecution table. To the right of the judge, twelve jurors and four alternates sat on chairs in the jury box in front of us, backed against the courtroom wall.

Seven defendants and four defense attorneys sat to our immediate right at the defense table. Mostly prospective jurors and the news media filled the seats in the courtroom. There were only about forty seats remaining for spectators to sit on the church-like wooden pews behind the counsel tables; these spectators were primarily supporters of the defendants, several hundred of whom journeyed the thirty miles from Seattle day after day.

Framed on one side by a large American flag, Judge Boldt, wearing his flowing black robe, was like a wise raven overseeing his domain. The judge ordered tight security for the trial. Every person entering the courthouse was searched.

On November 23, 1970, the trial began, after a three-week postponement, requested by defendant Susan Stern for what the press reported as an operation of a "private nature." The operation, she later wrote, was an abortion that Carl Maxey tried to talk her out of by telling her in a fatherly manner, "It will look good in the courtroom to have you come in glowing and pregnant, maybe with some knitting." But Stern wanted none of that and had her abortion.

It was a miserable trip each day from Seattle to Tacoma, for all concerned. Overhead the sky was an inky black, and a stiff wind blew off Puget Sound. November and December are dreadful weather months in the Puget Sound area, the worst months of the year if you discount January. "Gloomy" best describes the typical weather, and this year was no exception: It often rains in a gray cloud of mist every day; the sun becomes a distant memory; and there may not be any natural vitamin D produced by your body until February. At 47 degrees latitude, one's circadian rhythms, the "body clock," get thrown out of whack. Most everyone becomes a bit depressed, and many get cranky. And if you were already in a bad mood, it can get worse.

To amp up the national media attention in advance of the trial, Michael Tigar appeared on the *Dick Cavett Show* with Donald Sutherland to discuss the case. As the trial progressed, the media attention would accelerate, until the case made headlines all over the country.

Before the jury was selected—before the trial even started—the antics of the defendants began. Possessing a big lumbering frame, a big head, and a big Afro hairstyle, Jeff Dowd, son of a Cornell University economics professor, slovenly dressed, immature and outrageous, often funny, and a bit of a goofball, opened the first act of courtroom political theater.

In the early morning, prior to the first day of trial, a deputy marshal complained to Judge Boldt that Dowd was putting posters on the interior walls of the courthouse. When the marshal ordered Dowd to stop, Dowd gave the marshal the finger. The judge, in response to the marshal's complaint, ordered Dowd's attorney, Michael Tigar, into chambers and asked Tigar to control Dowd's behavior. Tigar told the judge that he had no responsibility to control his client's behavior other than to defend him if he was cited for contempt of court. Dowd and Tigar had set the tone for the battle to come.

Stan Pitkin began the voir dire—the questioning of prospective jurors—for the prosecution. Any exercise of a preemptory challenge to exclude a prospective juror by Stan brought howls of protest from the defendants and the spectators, especially if the prospective juror was under age twenty-five. Many spectators were then ejected from the courtroom, and the defendants were cautioned about their disruptive behavior. At one point, an exasperated Judge Boldt declared that all the defendants except Stern were in contempt of court for "shouting and violent gestures." Boldt later relented and let the defendants off with a warning, making clear that he, as the judge, held the power of contempt. Contempt citations—with a possible jail sentencing—would be issued if the defendants' disruptive behavior continued, he warned. Finally, twelve jurors and six alternates were empaneled.

Carl Maxey, co-lead defense counsel, was taken aback by the defendants' actions. In a conference in the judge's chambers that day, Maxey expressed his frustration with the defendants' unruly conduct, something he had never seen in a trial before and something he was powerless to control. He was not sure what he had signed up for.

"What do you think the jury thinks of these crazy antics by the defendants?" I asked Stan during a lunch break.

"I'm not sure the defendants care what the jury thinks. Their agenda is political," Stan responded. "I think most jurors think the high jinks are disrespectful of the court and the judge, but it only takes one ringer who shares the defendants' views to hang the jury."

After a recess for Thanksgiving, Stan outlined the government's case for the jury: he would call forty-five witnesses over the next ten days, he said. Then, to the laughter of the spectators, defendant Chip Marshall suddenly interrupted him and demanded the court's attention: "I would like to draw attention to the continual harassment people here face at the door by Mr. Robinson [Chief District US marshal] and Mr. Lurch, the big marshal. I would like that these people be given a more fitting post, like guarding the city dump." Chip Marshall's reference to "Mr. Lurch" was based on the tall, shambling, gloomy butler portrayed in the television series *The Addams Family*, a character that bears an uncanny resemblance to Frankenstein's monster. Time will show that taunting the US marshals, particularly big "Mr. Lurch," is not a good idea. The marshal lies patiently in wait and will eventually exact his revenge.

Stan Pitkin continued with his opening, stating what the evidence would show. He said that the defendants either urged violence at meetings for the TDA demonstration on February 11 and 17 at the University of Washington or were photographed or seen in alleged acts of violence at the courthouse demonstration, or both. In his narrative, he said that defendants Abeles, Lippman, Stern, Marshall, and Lerner led the Seattle TDA demonstration onto the courthouse lawn. A black man representing the group of almost exclusively white protesters asked to be admitted to the courthouse to read a petition to the presiding judge. The man was admitted to the courthouse, and while he was being escorted to the elevator, all hell broke loose outside. Marshall and Lerner led the crowd of two thousand with bullhorns. Marshall then jumped up on the courthouse steps and said to the crowd: "The doors are locked. They won't let us in. Let's take it."

Courthouse windows and doors were smashed, paint bombs were thrown, and a tear-gas canister was thrown into the courthouse, gassing the marshals, the police, and the black protester inside. A full-scale riot was on. Lippman was seen throwing rocks at police officers. Marshall was seen breaking a police car window as he and Dowd led the rioters down the hill to the Federal Building, where more damage ensued, Stan told the jury.

Carl Maxey, Michael Lerner, Chip Marshall, and Michael Tigar made opening statements for the defense, while Jeff Steinborn and Lee Holley chose to reserve their openings until the end of the prosecution's case. Maxey emphasized that the defendants were being prosecuted "not for what they did, but for what they think." He also stated that the prosecution couldn't prove that any of the defendants entered the state of Washington with the intention of starting a riot.

Lerner was next up. He started to address the court with a red telephone dangling around his neck. He said that he should wear the telephone since his conspiracy charge for use of interstate commerce is based upon a self-taped recording of a telephone call by Lerner, in Seattle, to Rennie Davis, one of the Chicago Seven defendants, in Chicago. In that recording, Lerner allegedly said in reference to the TDA demonstration, "Our only choice is to go down there and shut down the judicial system, by any means necessary." Judge Boldt ordered Lerner to remove the phone before Lerner could continue to address the jury.

Last to make an opening statement, Michael Tigar told the jury that this was a political trial. His client, Jeffrey Dowd, didn't travel from New York to Seattle to incite a riot: Dowd was induced to come to Seattle because it was politically friendly. The city had a long history of the "most militant and active organizations of trade unions this country has ever seen—a strong labor town, Seattle," Tigar quoted Dowd as saying.

The pranks and disruptions by the defendants and their supporters, attending the trial as spectators, continued throughout the trial both inside and outside the courtroom.

On many days, the spectators would cause a disruption in the courtroom, timed like clockwork most afternoons for TV evening news coverage, requiring the judge to admonish the spectators or have them be removed by the marshals from the courtroom.

"What time do you think the show will begin today," I whispered to Stan and Chuck at the counsel table.

"I'll put a buck on three p.m.," Chuck responded.

"I'll raise you a buck and say two thirty," Stan countered.

"No, it'll be at two," I said, calling the bet. "The weather is terrible today. With the traffic slowdown, the TV reporters need extra time to get back to Seattle to prepare for the five o'clock news."

I won the bet.

At the prosecution table, we sat back, looked at our watches, and waited to see who would win our daily wagers on the timing of the next "spontaneous" afternoon courtroom disruption. I was amazed at how willing the media was to be manipulated. The unvarnished truth is that the media too often is in the business of selling the news; objective journalism sometimes runs a poor second. The media welcomed the timely courtroom disruptions because they conveniently packaged the next day's newspaper headlines and television lead stories.

On one occasion, Stan, Chuck, and I had just entered the courthouse elevator when all seven defendants piled in in front of us, forcing us up against the back wall of the elevator. It wasn't long before the pungent, skunk-like smell of marijuana, emanating from the defendants' clothing, filled the small space. (Most of the defendants regularly smoked dope in the defense room.) I thought about saying something, but my better judgment restrained me. The defendants just laughed, considering it a joke. We didn't think it was funny.

On another occasion, upon entering the courtroom, we noticed that the water pitcher on our counsel table had a reddish tinge. Were the defendants and their supporters bent on infusing the water with some of their recreational drugs, or poisoning us? The FBI lab analyzed the water. It was nontoxic. Stern later confessed in her memoir that she spiked it one day with grape Kool-Aid, and on another day with wine. She also acknowledged placing a piece of rubber made to look like a pile of dog crap by Stan's chair. The judge ordered it removed. Neither Stan nor the judge was amused.

On the fourth day of the trial, the prosecution presented its first witnesses. Chuck Billinghurst questioned two of the early foundational witnesses, and I questioned three. Nothing dramatic happened that day until Chip Marshall complained to the court about alleged rough handling of Dowd and several court spectators by US marshals: "I would just like to state for the record that unless you do something to stop and get Marshal Robinson, who has earned the name 'Pig'—and

I don't use that name in any kind of way; I have tried to say 'officer of the law'—but if he isn't removed from this court, and if he does not stop this kind of harassment, the next time he touches somebody, he is going to get death, man."

"Your remarks constitute contempt of court. Your language, your threat of violence in the courtroom is grossly improper," Judge Boldt admonished him. Boldt later said that he would not cite Marshall for contempt at this time—it would await a hearing later. *The trial is taking an ugly turn toward violence*, I thought. *This is no longer funny. The battle for control of the courtroom is reaching a new and dangerous level.*

RED PARKER

The next prosecution witness, to be questioned by Stan, was the bombshell and star witness in the trial. Horace "Red" Parker—a thirty-three-year-old paint-store sales manager—was an acquaintance of Susan Stern and her ex-husband Robert "Robby" Stern. Robby Stern was a founder and leader of the Seattle branch of the SDS and was believed by the FBI to be a Weatherman. Stan and I had spent the previous evening in a Tacoma hotel room going over Parker's testimony with him. He was calm and poised and seemed credible.

Red Parker attended Lewis & Clark College in Portland for three years before dropping out. He was a US Army veteran, having served in the early 1960s. Now a Burien, Washington, resident, married for ten years with one child, he appeared stable and rather conventional. As Parker took the stand that morning, a look of shock and disbelief came over the defendants as they realized that the FBI had a confidential, paid undercover informer in their intimate circle!

Red Parker testified that in July 1969, he had contacted Robby Stern—Susan Stern's husband at the time—and expressed his aversion to the Vietnam War. Robby Stern invited him to become a member of the Seattle chapter of the SDS. As part of Parker's indoctrination, Robby Stern gave him reading material by Karl Marx and "some little red books by Chairman Mao Tse-tung." Concerned that he had stumbled upon a dangerous group of people, Parker initially contacted the CIA, who told him it was a domestic matter within the jurisdiction of the FBI, not the CIA. Parker then met with the FBI and told them that his experience with SDS led him to believe that the people in SDS "were communist revolutionaries rather than American revolutionaries." The FBI asked Parker to infiltrate the Seattle SDS and stay close to the SDS offshoot, the Weathermen. Parker accepted the offer and became an undercover informer.

I knew the FBI loved to use undercover informers, sometimes to the point of overkill, to penetrate radical organizations. We would joke, in the US attorney's office, that there were more FBI undercover informers in some radical groups than there were real members. But that wasn't the case with the secretive and close-knit Weathermen. Their organization seemed impenetrable. Although not a Weatherman, Parker testified that he was able to get close to them. Beginning in March 1970, he lived off and on for three months with Susan and Robby Stern and Michael Justesen, at the Fortress, or Fort, a Weathermen collective. Parker testified that the Fort was so named because it was fortified to withstand bullets and was heavily armed with rifles, pistols, and tear-gas canisters.

Parker said that the price of admission to the Fort was to leave his family. He was told, "A monogamous relationship will hold you back from being a better revolutionary." He added, "People did give up their children and their homes."

Parker testified that there were two organizational meetings for the Seattle TDA demonstration, each meeting attended by around two hundred people and held at the Husky Union Building theater at the University of Washington. The first meeting, attended by all the defendants except Joe Kelly, was held on February 11, 1970. It was designed by the SLF to outline the strategy for TDA demonstrators. Defendants Marshall and Abeles made the most provocative comments at the meeting, according to Parker. Marshall, who chaired the meeting with Lerner, is quoted as saying: "We are going to shut the whole fucking judicial system down by any means necessary."

Abeles then amped up the rhetoric in his speech to the assemblage, saying, according to Parker, "I don't give a fuck if you know

who Chairman Mao is or how much Marx you've read or how much
Chairman Mao you've read, or even if you know who Chairman Mao's
grandma is, it doesn't make a goddamn bit of difference unless you do
something about it. Now, we're going to go down to the courthouse,
and we're going to shut that fucking place down, and if these pigs try
and stop us, kill them."

A woman who identified herself as a member of the SLF tactical
committee is quoted by Parker as saying: "I can't tell you which window to throw your firebomb in, which window to throw your tear-gas
canister in, or your rock in this window or that window. All I can tell
you is when you get down there, you be ready, and you'll know what
to do."

Parker testified that the FBI instructed him to do "whatever was
necessary to protect his credibility." Participating fully in the lifestyle
of the radical collectives, Parker admitted to drug use, including the
use of LSD, marijuana, speed, and cocaine. He also testified that he was
arrested with others in December 1969 for trashing several University
of Washington campus buildings, which contained the air force and
army ROTC offices.

During Parker's testimony, the court was frequently interrupted by
the defendants' objections to the removal of disruptive spectators from
the courtroom. Many of the defendants claimed Judge Boldt wrong-
fully singled out the demonstrators. Dowd objected by insulting the
judge: "This morning you are blind, or something or other."

But bizarre and disruptive conduct was not the exclusive province
of the defendants. At one point, during a lull in Parker's testimony,
Susan Stern accused Parker of using hand signals to communicate
from the witness stand to someone in the audience. She explained that
Weathermen and prisoners sometimes employ sign language when
they did not want to be overheard. Out of the presence of the jury,
Judge Boldt asked Parker to explain what was going on. He said that
one of the defendant's supporters, Marjorie Ellsworth, was in the audience and hand signaled him: *I hate you. Fuck you.* He replied: *Hi, trai-
tor.* The judge admonished Parker and the courtroom spectators not to
engage in future hand signaling.

Paid informers are always highly problematic for the prosecution, and Parker was no exception. However, I thought that overall, his direct testimony went well, much better than I had thought it would. I asked Stan after court if he felt as I did, that the testimony of Parker was credible and tied the case together, at least for some of the defendants. (The conspiracy case binding all seven defendants together had yet to be made.)

"I think Red Parker is very believable," Stan said. "He showed clearly that many of the defendants were not innocent protesters. These self-styled revolutionaries had a violent agenda and made a mockery of peaceful protest."

Before we could really tell how well Parker's testimony would stand up, he would have to survive a vigorous cross-examination by the defendants and their counsels. Would his testimony show that he was a patriot, or a misguided and overzealous informer for the federal government trying to entrap the defendants? Or, perhaps, a little bit of both?

When the defense began its cross-examination, it quickly became apparent that Red Parker was no angel.

The defense counsel's cross-examination slowly chipped away at Parker's credibility and motivation. Parker was portrayed as an agent provocateur who falsely implicated the defendants of partaking in illegal acts; a paid FBI informer receiving $500 a month, plus expenses, who was accustomed to lying. Most tellingly, Parker testified under cross-examination by Chip Marshall (Marshall proved to be a better cross-examiner than the attorneys) that he would go "to any length to bring the defendants to justice, including lying."

Parker admitted that he played the role of a radical revolutionary to the hilt: he had once commented that an individual suspected of being an informer should be "offed" before the trial; he had delivered spray paint from his store to individuals, knowing that they would use the paint to deface buildings; he had supplied drugs to the defendants and others; and he had taken individual radicals out for target practice with guns. The defendants and their counsel rejoiced, believing that they had permanently damaged Parker's credibility.

At times, the cross-examination provided some humorous commentary on Seattle's reputation for radicalism, given that the city was a virtually all-white, rather staid middle-class community. At one point, Chip Marshall asked Parker to relate what Marshall had said at a January 19 organizational meeting of the SLF. Parker quoted Marshall, explaining to the audience his and Jeff Dowd's motivation for moving to Seattle in December 1969:

> *We've been watching the Seattle scene. We watched it on the* Huntley-Brinkley Report, *we saw you at the Sea-Tac Airport slugging it out with your black brothers, and we thought this looks like a place to make things happen, so we thought it over for a couple of days, and we came out here, and you know what? This is the deadest goddamn town we have ever been in. Can't even find the ghetto.*

***

The trial was now slowed by the voluminous production required of the prosecution under the Jencks Act. After a government witness testifies on direct examination, the Jencks Act requires the prosecution to give the defendants all relevant statements and writings of the witness in the possession of the government. Red Parker, who once aspired to be a writer, wrote long summaries of his activities and furnished them to the FBI. The summaries had to be reviewed and redacted because they included comments about individuals who were still under investigation, but unconnected to the defendants. The prosecution believed it had given the defense all relevant information in possession of the government.

On cross-examination by Michael Tigar on Tuesday, December 8, Parker revealed that he kept a personal diary, which he referenced before writing his reports to the FBI. The court ordered that the diary be produced immediately for an "in camera review" by the judge to determine what portion of the diary was personal and unconnected to the case and what portion, if any, should be released to the defense. Pitkin told the court he had never seen the diary and had no idea where it was. The court directed the FBI to locate the diary and deliver it to his law clerk, and the judge would ascertain any material relevant to the case that should be released. The FBI learned Parker had possession of his diary. He had never turned it over to the FBI.

The court ordered that further cross-examination of Parker be postponed until all relevant portions of the diary were released simultaneously to the defendants and the prosecution at least a day prior to Parker being recalled to the stand. In the meantime, the judge instructed the prosecution to examine other witnesses, but none were currently available, Pitkin explained.

Because she was to undergo a minor medical procedure, Susan Stern asked to be excused from appearing in court until the following Monday, December 14. The court granted her request. Since no court was scheduled on Friday, Thursday would be the last day of court. Judge Boldt asked Pitkin, "How many more trial days does the government need before the prosecution rests?" Stan said only a portion of the government's case had been presented and he needed about nine more trial days to complete his case with additional witnesses.

On Wednesday, December 9, the court convened without the jury, and all the defendants and their counsel were present except Stern. Judge Boldt indicated that Parker's diary was now in his possession, and it required close scrutiny by him before it could be redacted and released. After the court recessed for the day, as I was leaving the Tacoma courthouse, I passed Judge Boldt's chambers and ran into Stan, who had just exited the judge's chambers and said he had been conferring with Boldt. Curious about this unusual meeting, I asked, "What was that all about?" In a quick hallway exchange, he gave me an update.

"Judge Boldt asked me to stop by to discuss security measures in the courtroom," Stan explained. "During the meeting, he volunteered that although he had not completed his review, Red Parker's diary contained a number of statements relevant to the defense." Then, with worry etched on his face, he continued, "Judge Boldt let me know that the redacted diary will be released very soon to the defense for their use in the continuing cross-examination of Red Parker. We won't see the material until the judge releases it."

I thought it strange and objectionable that Judge Boldt would give Stan a heads-up about his in camera review of Parker's diary off the record, without all counsel present. But since the material would soon be released to both sides, I felt the judge's disclosure was harmless. It might not bode well, however, for the credibility of Parker on continued cross-examination by the defense. *What is in that diary? Is the prosecution's case in for trouble?* I wondered.

***

The next day, Thursday, was another bone-chilling cold, pelting-rain day, with wind blowing in gusts off Commencement Bay, filling my nostrils with intermittent whiffs of the pungent smell from the pulp mill to the north of the city. Before the morning court session convened, defendant Jeff Dowd raced down the courthouse hallway and started pounding on the door to Judge Boldt's chambers, demanding that the spectators left outside in the rain be admitted to the courthouse hallway. For his behavior, Dowd earned the first contempt citation of the day. It was the first in a series of escalating acts by the defendants that would turn out to be a badly flawed strategy undermining their entire opportunity to present their defense.

At 9:00 a.m., with Judge Boldt, the jury, and all counsel present in the courtroom, the judge asked why the defendants—except Stern, who had been excused until Monday—were not present in the courtroom. Defense counsel Carl Maxey said that they were still in the defense counsel room. Maxey told the judge that he had asked his client, Joe Kelly, to be present in court. The judge ordered the three other defense attorneys to go to the defense counsel room and instruct their clients also to appear in court immediately. At that point, the defendants brazenly ignored their counsels' instructions and refused to come to court. Boldt then ordered his bailiff to go to the defense counsel room and again instruct the defendants to immediately appear in court. Despite the bailiff's instruction, the defendants still refused to come. Then the defendants locked themselves inside the defense counsel room.

Still awaiting the arrival of the defendants, at 9:50 a.m. an exasperated and angry Judge Boldt said he would go personally down the hall to speak to the defendants. After hearing the judge order them to appear, the defendants, accompanied by their counsel, began walking back to the courtroom. But before Judge Boldt could reenter the courtroom, defendant Chip Marshall started to address the jury, complaining that spectators were being left out in the rain. Judge Boldt then entered the courtroom and ordered Marshall to stop this unpermitted communication with the jury, a serious breach of court protocol and prejudicial to a fair hearing. But Marshall ignored Judge Boldt's command and continued to address the jury.

Judge Boldt then excused the jury from the courtroom and said that all defendants, except the absent Susan Stern, would be cited for contempt because of "loud and boisterous conduct" including "threatening remarks" to the deputy marshals who had accompanied the judge down the hall for security. An indignant and red-faced Judge Boldt said: "The sum total of all this is one of the most inexcusable and outrageous incidents of contempt of court that I have ever read about or learned of in any way."

But the court went further than just citing the defendants for contempt: "The jury has witnessed contemptuous conduct, and the trial cannot continue with an unbiased jury by reason of misconduct of the defendants," the judge said. To everyone's great surprise, rather than continuing the trial like the Chicago Seven judge had and sentencing the defendants for contempt after the jury's verdict, Boldt declared a mistrial. He also criticized defense counsel—except for Carl Maxey, who had previously instructed his client to come to court—for failing to assist the court in procuring an orderly trial.

Of all the defendants, Michael Lerner—not without some humor—seemed to understand the extreme gravity of the mistrial best.

He pleaded with Judge Boldt: "Now, is there some way we can unmiss this mistrial?"

Judge Boldt: "No."

The judge then explained: "I have been brooding and thinking of this . . . as to what would be the just and proper thing to do, because personally, I think all of you have seriously prejudiced yourselves with the jury."

Lerner: "I feel, and I think most of the other defendants feel, that this is an unfair disaster . . . a disaster."

Judge Boldt then recessed the court until the following Monday to allow himself time to prepare the contempt citations.

The similarities between the Chicago Seven trial and the Seattle Seven trial had come to an abrupt end. The Chicago Seven circus lasted five months before it closed. The Seattle Seven circus had a much shorter run—barely three weeks before the big top was taken down. The prosecution hadn't completed its case, and the defense case was never heard before Judge Boldt declared a mistrial. The trial had careened into anarchy, sorely embarrassing the court and undermining respect for the rule of law. The menagerie of Seattle defendants was about to be shackled and put in cages. But with the national press attention about to end, the defendants had no intention of being caged and silenced without one last outrageous performance in the center arena of the big top, Judge Boldt's federal courtroom.

BEDLAM IN THE COURTROOM

With the jury now dismissed, on Monday, December 14, Judge Boldt entered an order certifying a mistrial and began reading the contempt certificate in open court. He said the trial was over. In a summary proceeding seldom used, the court sentenced the defendants, except Susan Stern, "despite her previous misconduct," to six months' imprisonment.

Exempting Carl Maxey, the court also criticized the defendants' counsel, Tigar, Holley, and Steinborn, for their "refusal to aid or assist in restraining their particular clients or any other defendant for misconduct, however boisterous or serious." Discipline for these attorneys, however, would be the province of the bar association, not the court, Boldt said.

The court then recited the litany of misconduct by the defendants constituting contempt:

The trial judge saw and heard misconduct of the defendants in the courtroom frequently every day for 10 days prior to Thursday, December 10, 1970, consisting of standing, vocal and obviously pre-arranged demonstrations by spectators, sometimes led by one or more of the defendants, and joined in by all; shouting epithets, sometimes threats of violence and profanity, and other improper language accompanied by a variety of disorderly movements and actions.

In a show of defiance, all defendants cited for contempt, except Lerner, angrily tore up their copies of the contempt certificate and threw them up in the air toward the judge's bench.

Straining to show patience and to preserve the record for an almost certain appeal, the court allowed the cited defendants and their counsel an opportunity to address the court for twenty minutes each before sentences were imposed. Carl Maxey was the first to speak, and he emphasized the youth and sincerity of the defendants. He admitted that their singular obsession with the admission of their supporters as spectators to the courtroom, however well intentioned, was misguided. "A prudent counsel would have said, 'You need the spectator gallery in this case like you need a hole in the head.'"

When defendant Michael Lerner addressed the court, he didn't even try to impress the judge. Lerner's intended audience was not the court; he obviously was speaking to the gallery and the press. He read a declaration addressed to him, received a few days earlier from a Hanoi, North Vietnam, government committee: "We strongly protest against the trial of the Seattle Eight conspiracy by the U.S. administration and demand them to cancel it immediately. Please convey our warm regards to the defendants and other militants fighting for peace in Vietnam for the American people's interest. We wish you success."

Not to be outdone by Michael Lerner, Jeff Dowd, in a tandem act with Mike Abeles, spoke next. In a dramatic move reminiscent of the Chicago Seven trial—when defense attorney, William Kunstler, placed a Viet Cong flag on the defense table—Dowd said, to the applause of the spectators: "The thing that disappointed me most is every day coming into this courtroom you [the judge] stand up and you salute that flag . . . That flag was born in revolution and, your Honor, I honestly don't

—P-I Sketches by Bob McCausland.

SUSAN STERN TORE UP A PAPER

Other defendants ripped up contempt citations

Courtesy of Seattle Post-Intelligencer.

think that flag deserves to be up there. The flag that deserves to be up there is this one. The Nazi flag."

Dowd then pulled a Nazi flag from under his shirt and handed it to defendant Abeles, who approached the bench and threw the flag at Judge Boldt, to the further applause of the spectators.

TWO DEFENDANTS HELD UP NAZI FLAG BEFORE JUDGE GEORGE H. BOLDT
Defendant Jeffrey Dowd, in slam at judge, said it should replace American flag in courtroom

Courtesy of Seattle Post-Intelligencer.

Although not previously cited for contempt, Susan Stern then demanded to be heard. The court asked her to be silent and warned her that if she continued to speak, she would be cited for contempt. Stern ignored the judge's admonition and continued with lengthy remarks from the lectern, despite numerous warnings from the court to desist. Stern was then cited for contempt. In response to Stern's contempt citation, other defendants and spectators started shouting and disrupting the court. Judge Boldt then left the bench, ordered the courtroom recessed and cleared of all spectators, and remanded the defendants to the custody of the US marshals.

As Judge Boldt was leaving the bench, Stern shouted, "They will have to drag me off to stop me."

The judge responded, "If that is necessary."

A deputy marshal then grabbed the ninety-eight-pound Stern from behind to restrain her and lifted her off the ground in the air as she kicked and screamed.

Jeff Dowd, out of control, his lumbering hulk rising from his chair, screamed sarcastically at the marshal and the judge: "Come on, let's see it, man, let's see them drag her off, I want to see the sight of those killers dragging off a woman who has just got out of the hospital two days ago, and you old killer, you're so bloody, it's unbelievable." Then Dowd went berserk and started to jump up and down, ranting over and over: "Kill the kid. Kill the kid. Kill the kid. Kill the kid. Kill the kid. Kill the kid. Kill the kid. Kill the kid."

Then the battle was soon fully joined, and all hell broke loose in the courtroom.

A full-scale riot erupted, involving all the defendants except Michael Lerner, who remained seated. In a wild, pitched melee, defendants and spectators battled twenty to thirty deputy marshals and FBI agents, throwing punches and tackling each other. I looked for Chuck and Stan, but I didn't see them. I think they followed Judge Boldt and ran for cover outside the courtroom. To avoid the carnage, I sprung up from my seat behind the prosecution table and headed to a good vantage point from the relative safety of the now-empty jury box, protected by its railings. I vicariously participated in the melee by mentally shadowboxing, bobbing and weaving as the action around me continued to unfold.

Susan Stern offered this version of the event in her memoir: "I was swinging with my arms; Steinborn told me later that I had broken a pig's nose. I saw a hulking marshal grab Joe [Kelly] by the balls and drag him across the courtroom. I saw another slug Abeles and drag him away. Then I got very dizzy and didn't struggle as they pulled me out of the courtroom."

Meanwhile, I thought that some of the deputy marshals, after being oinked at, cursed at, and disparaged throughout the trial, were eagerly anticipating an opportunity to lay hands on the defendants and certain spectators for their disruptive conduct to teach them good manners. Now they had their chance.

The biggest deputy marshal, disparagingly and repeatedly referred to by Chip Marshall as Mr. Lurch, saw his opportunity for an additional redress when Michael Tigar, in an ill-considered move, suddenly decided to join the courtroom riot. Tigar jumped up from the defense counsel table, ran forward, and from behind grabbed the deputy marshal who was restraining Susan Stern at the counsels' lectern. Now at the back end of what in any other circumstance would have been a comical three-decker sandwich, I heard Tigar command, "You can't do that, and she's sick."

The deputy marshal identified by the defendants as "Marshal Lurch" lit up as he at last saw his chance for a fitting reprisal. Lumbering over to join the fray, with a powerful sweep of his arms, he jerked Tigar off the deputy marshal restraining Stern, breaking the three-way embrace. Tigar was manhandled across the courtroom and plastered up against the courtroom wall by the marshal, only three feet from my sanctuary.

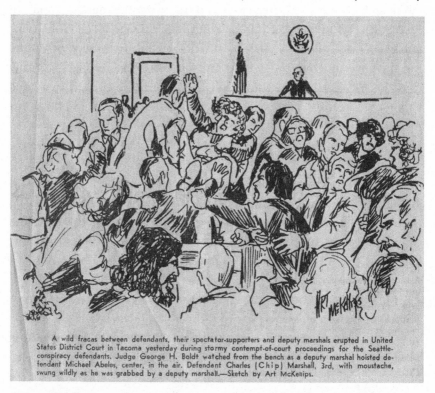

A wild fracas between defendants, their spectator-supporters and deputy marshals erupted in United States District Court in Tacoma yesterday during stormy contempt-of-court proceedings for the Seattle-conspiracy defendants. Judge George H. Boldt watched from the bench as a deputy marshal hoisted defendant Michael Abeles, center, in the air. Defendant Charles (Chip) Marshall, 3rd, with moustache, swung wildly as he was grabbed by a deputy marshal.—Sketch by Art McKellips.

Courtesy of Seattle Post-Intelligencer.

With one hand around Tigar's throat and his other hand on the trigger of a small canister of mace, the marshal sprayed Tigar repeatedly in both eyes. Released from the marshal's grip, a blinded Michael Tigar stumbled around the courtroom, flailing his arms high in the air and screaming, "I can't see! I can't see! I can't see!"

This is otherworldly! I thought in amazement. Momentarily stunned, my heart pounding, I realized I had just witnessed one of the most bizarre courtroom dramas in American history, with a front-row jury-box seat to boot.

In thirty minutes the courtroom was cleared and the defendants were handcuffed and in custody. Fifty demonstrators continued to pro-test outside the courthouse in the rain; ten were arrested and charged with assault.

That afternoon, court resumed with all defendants and counsel present. Because they declined to give assurances that they would behave in court, Marshall and Kelly remained handcuffed. Judge Boldt then issued a second certificate of contempt, applicable to all the defendants including Stern, but excluding Lerner, who had remained seated during the courtroom riot.

Judge Boldt said that his use of a summary contempt proceeding, rather than waiting until the end of the new trial for sentencing, was very unusual, but necessary. "In every disruptive trial in recent times in which defendants were cited for contempt and the penalties there-fore delayed until the end of trial, disruptive conduct did not stop or even diminish." Judge Boldt clearly was not going to tolerate another Chicago Seven trial. Rather, he said, by having the contempt sentences served before a new trial began, "These sentences will give defendants an ample opportunity to reflect on their past misconduct and what it has brought them."

Boldt thought he had found a judicial holy grail, a solution to dis-ruptive trials. As a devoutly religious man, he attributed his insight to God. "I believe Divine Providence may have given the court and others guidance to an effective solution of disruptive trials. I pray it may be so."

Chaos in Court: All Seven Sentenced
                    —Seattle Post-Intelligencer front-page
                              headline, December 15, 1970

The defendants, except Stern, were sentenced to six months in prison on the first contempt citation. On the second contempt citation, the defendants, except Lerner, were sentenced to an additional six months, the sentences to run consecutively. Judge Boldt denied bail, but his ruling was reversed on appeal on January 8, 1971, and the defendants were released from prison after one month after posting $25,000 each in bail. In November 1971, on a second appeal regarding the adequacy of the contempt citations, the appellate court remanded the case because the certificates failed to incorporate factual findings of the actual instances of contempt. After the deficiencies in the citations were corrected, at the direction of the Justice Department, Stan Pitkin refiled the contempt charges. The defendants, exhausted by the ordeal, chastened by their time in prison, pled nolo contendere (no contest) to the contempt charges and were sentenced—excepting Lerner—to additional short prison terms ranging from one to five months. In March 1973, after another year had passed, the Justice Department decided to end the prosecution and quietly dropped all remaining charges against the defendants. The Justice Department, it seemed, had achieved its objectives.

***

In the ensuing years, the defendants and their supporters have spun a narrative in various publications that the real reason the judge declared a mistrial was that the prosecution's case had totally fallen apart after the cross-examination of Red Parker by Chip Marshall. But this narrative itself falls apart upon closer examination. Of course Parker's entire manufactured persona was, by necessity, predicated upon a lie. The ability to lie is qualification number one for an undercover informant to successfully infiltrate a secretive organization. The standard cure for the problem occasioned when an undercover informant's credibility is challenged on cross-examination because of lies told to defendants is to rehabilitate the witness on redirect examination by asking, "As directed by the FBI, you admittedly told lies to gain the confidence of the defendants, but are you lying under oath in this trial?" Parker's answer would have been a resounding no. He would have explained that he had never lied under oath and would not do so now. Also, Pitkin had other prosecution witnesses waiting to testify that could have corroborated much of Parker's testimony that implicated the defendants in various illegal acts.

Defense counsel were well aware of what Red Parker's answer would have been if he had been asked if he was lying under oath during his testimony. That's why the defendants or their counsel did not ask that specific question during the trial. In an inexplicable error and disservice to Mr. Parker and the historical record, defense counsel Michael Tigar, in his memoir, *Fighting Injustice*, asserted that Red Parker had actually admitted at trial a willingness to lie under oath while under cross-examination by the defendant Chip Marshall.

Q: [Marshall] You don't like us at all, do you, Red?

A: [Parker] No, I don't.

Q: You would do anything to see us convicted and sent to jail, wouldn't you?

A: Yes, I would.

Q: *You would even lie under oath, wouldn't you?* [Emphasis supplied.]

A: Yes, I would.[1]

This exchange never took place. The actual relevant exchange between Red Parker and Chip Marshall was recorded as follows in the court transcript:

Q: [Marshall] It's very important to you that people like us be brought to justice, isn't that correct? I mean, you feel very strongly that we are bad people and should be brought to justice?

A: [Parker] That's one way of putting it.

Q: All right. So I mean, you would go to almost, not any length, obviously not killing somebody, but almost any length of trickery to bring us to justice?

A: Yes, any length.

Q: Any length, and for months and months, you took people who you—who thought perhaps that you were their friend, and you were willing to lie to them in order to get us, is that correct?

A: That is absolutely correct.[2]

This testimony is pretty much what one would expect from an informant inserted by the FBI to infiltrate suspected terrorist activities.

***

The Sundance Collective and the rest of the defendants had their Wild West moment. But just like in *Butch Cassidy and the Sundance Kid*, the movie with Paul Newman and Robert Redford, it didn't end well. They fought the law, and the law won. Yes, the Department of Justice won, but was justice served?

Justice, like morality, is not always black-and-white; the scales of Lady Justice do not work perfectly. Like the Puget Sound winter skies, justice displays a palette of many shades of gray. In this case, justice was very opaque and without clear resolution. Unfortunately, neither side was focused on justice. The defendants overplayed their hand, engaging in political theater, mocking the court, whatever the cost and consequences. And, in its haste to clamp down on violent political dissent, the Justice Department cut corners in carefully constructing and properly charging its case. What about the court? Did the judge over-step judicial boundaries and put his thumb on the scale to prematurely end the trial? If the judge set a trap, the defendants raced to the cheese. The defendants prized political theater over winning the case in court. It was a bad decision; there would be no award other than jail for their acting skills. In the end, however, there were no clear-cut heroes or villains in this courtroom drama. *My white horse probably got a little mud on it too,* I thought, pondering my own mea culpa for even getting involved.

How might the trial have ended if Judge Boldt had allowed it to continue to judgment? Of course, one can only speculate. But I think it would have concluded with a mixed verdict; although the conspiracy charges involving interstate commerce to incite a riot were weak, the charges of destruction of federal property would likely have been sustained against most of the defendants and, along with additional convictions for contempt of court, resulted in prison sentences.

When the Justice Department agreed to drop the case, defense counsel Carl Maxey summarized the trial: "I am pleased to see that the government has determined not to re-prosecute. But there are two matters of grave personal concern to me. The defendants' intemperate conduct and the government's bringing this case of dubious merit in the first place. I'm glad it's over." I was too.

***

After only ten months in the US attorney's office in Seattle, I had participated in two of the most celebrated criminal trials in Washington State history. I was now ready to dial back the stress and enjoy a more normal routine as an assistant US attorney. *Perhaps the excitement is over,* I thought. I was wrong about that, as usual.

CHAPTER TEN

SAVING THE SALISH SEA

Say what you will about President Richard Milhous Nixon. He was morally deficient, he was devious, and he was duplicitous and criminal when he engineered the Watergate cover-up. He did many terrible things, including the treasonous way he prolonged the Vietnam War by asking the South Vietnamese government to boycott peace talks until he was elected. Although a trained lawyer, he treated the rule of law with disdain. Nevertheless, despite his badly flawed character, he deserves great credit for opening the door to China, creating the Environmental Protection Agency (EPA), and passing the Clean Air Act. Fittingly, under Nixon, the EPA's first director was Seattle resident William Ruckelshaus, an environmental icon born and raised in Indiana.

Washington State was the first state to take up the mantle of environmentalism—not surprising, given its natural beauty. Several months before the EPA was established in 1970, the Washington State Legislature, with prodding from the newly elected Republican governor, Dan Evans, created the Department of Ecology, the first environmental state agency in the nation.

Seattle was an even earlier believer in protecting the environment. Since the 1900s, untreated sewage had been discharged by surrounding municipalities directly into Lake Washington, the second-largest natural lake in the state of Washington. The lake was once a sapphire-colored liquid jewel separating Seattle and the Eastside, but by the late 1950s, a blue-green algae caused by pollutants noticeably diminished the clarity of the water. Worst of all, the lake began to stink. The *Seattle P-I* once called it "Lake Stinko." A researcher at the University of Washington identified the problem as phosphates from sewage. Fortunately, there was enlightened leadership in Seattle that sparked the beginnings of an environmental awakening that would save the lake.

A citizens group headed by Seattle attorney James Ellis spurred the state legislature in 1958 to form what was then called the King County Metro agency to address the problem. A massive sewer infrastructure capital project began treating the waste and diverting it from Lake Washington into the deep waters of the Puget Sound. It was considered one of the most ambitious and expensive pollution-control efforts in the United States at the time. The results were remarkable, and the lake was restored.

***

When you are young, you think real change is possible merely through the power of persuasion. The truth is, in a democracy like ours—with many checks and balances on government power, and vested interest blocking pathways to reform—you measure progress not by how many mountains you climb, but by how many molehills you surmount. A frontal assault on an issue is seldom successful; it allows vested interests to organize and block any real reform. Smaller steps and stealth often produce better results. There are two important exceptions to these observations: First, it has been said that a crisis is too good to waste. A crisis can present an opportunity for radical reform. And second, a big wave of populist demand can also provide the necessary conditions for disruptive change.

Rachel Carson's 1962 book, *Silent Spring*, ignited the environmental movement with her exposé of the deleterious effects of agricultural pesticides, particularly DDT. She opened a dialogue about the relationship between people and nature and merged the public health and conservation movements.

I observed a huge wave of populist support emerge for environmental protection aimed at corralling pollution in the 1970s, laying the groundwork for aggressive action by federal and state governments to clean up the nation's waterways. Many people credit April 22, 1970, the first Earth Day celebrated by twenty-two million people, as the birth date of the modern environmental movement in the United States. Given my passion for environmental issues, I was delighted to have an opportunity in the US attorney's office to ride this wave and join a state-federal environmental effort to save the Puget Sound.

In the early 1970s, the federal government had very limited power to deal with water pollution in the navigable waters of Puget Sound. A seldom-noticed and little-enforced 1899 federal statute—the Refuse Act, the oldest federal environmental statute in the United States, which declared illegal the dumping of any material into federal waters without a permit from the US Army Corps of Engineers—was seen as a possible vehicle for federal water pollution enforcement. The statute was clear about who was charged with responsibility for enforcement: "It is the duty of U.S. Attorneys to vigorously enforce the Act." A light bulb went off in my head. The planets of change were aligning. *This is an opportunity for meaningful federal environmental action to clean up the Puget Sound,* I thought, excited by the realization. Now we needed a plan.

Working with the Justice Department's civil division, US Attorney Stan Pitkin, Assistant US Attorney Tom Lee—on loan from the US attorney's office in Portland, Oregon—and I developed an enforcement plan to assist the State of Washington and the EPA in corralling illegal industrial discharges into the Puget Sound. Stan asked me to lead the effort in the US attorney's office. I proudly saluted. With substantial aid from the state Department of Ecology and the EPA, we used the 1899 Refuse Act to force compliance from industrial polluters unwilling to enter into state-sanctioned voluntary cleanup plans. From 1970 to 1971, a coalition of federal and Washington State agencies led by our office obtained nationally recognized, landmark federal cleanup agreements against polluters.

LANDMARK ENVIRONMENTAL CASES

The first major federal settlement involved the ITT Rayonier pulp mill in Port Angeles, Washington. ITT Rayonier had been stonewalling the State of Washington for a decade and was the last holdout among the eight Puget Sound–area pulp mills refusing to reach an agreement to control sulfite waste discharges. We filed suit against the company under the Refuse Act, leading to a $20 million settlement. Under the settlement, the pulp mill agreed to prevent 85 percent of its sulfite waste from being discharged into the Strait of Juan de Fuca, which separates Canada and the United States.

The second major settlement involved reducing mercury discharge from the chlorine plants associated with pulp mills. Mercury is one of the most dangerous and toxic chemicals. When ingested by fish and shellfish, it can find its way into the human food chain. Our targets: the Weyerhaeuser Company, for discharging mercury into the Columbia River at its Longview, Washington, pulp mill; and Georgia-Pacific, for discharging mercury into the Puget Sound from its Bellingham, Washington, pulp mill. Under threat of an injunction to stop all production, the two companies entered into agreements that lowered the amount of mercury discharged to the level found in nature.

Our third settlement involved a suit to halt the operations of United Transportation Company, a Seattle-based barge company, and Texaco, Inc. The firms were charged with the spill of over 230,000 gallons of No. 2 diesel fuel into the Puget Sound during a barge-loading operation at the Texaco refinery near Anacortes, Washington. We required the companies to substantially improve their operating procedures, including systematic monitoring and lighting on dock facilities during night petroleum-transfer operations. This was the first case under the Refuse Act to order broad remedial measures for an oil spill.

***

As a port city, Seattle has historically been plagued by industrial pollution from major waterways that front the city and discharge into the Puget Sound. There had previously been no enforcement of the

Refuse Act to mitigate this pollution. Now I had an opportunity to see what our office could do creatively with the 1899 Refuse Act to reduce unlawful discharges from these freshwater tributaries into the Puget Sound.

The Duwamish River, the name of the lower twelve miles of the Green River, Seattle's only freshwater river, was the major Seattle concern. This river is part of a ninety-three-mile-long system that drains 483 square miles of the state's interior and flows into salt water at Elliott Bay, through Seattle. Its industrialized estuary is called the Duwamish Waterway. Divided by man-made Harbor Island, which is constructed from fill material, the river is a big part of the Seattle harbor area. The last 4.6 miles of the river—all located within the city limits of Seattle— is where most of the pollution occurs.

The Duwamish River was not only a working waterfront but also an important fishing and recreational resource in the twentieth century that had been largely destroyed by industrial uses. Unpermitted filling, unpermitted toxic liquid discharges, and refuse dumping plagued the waterway. While it was widely known that the river was in trouble, nobody seemed to be doing anything about it. *Another great opportunity for the Refuse Act,* I thought, eager to start.

I asked my client, the Seattle District US Army Corps of Engineers, to survey the Duwamish River for Refuse Act violations. Based upon their investigation, in a case that made front-page stories in Seattle, we filed a criminal complaint against Farwest Capitol Co., a company that had dumped scrap lumber and metal from a good-size building into the Duwamish River near Harbor Island. The corps—living up to its reputation as a risk-averse bureaucracy focused on industrial development—voiced displeasure with our strict enforcement approach that allowed no free bites of the apple. Colonel Richard McConnell, chief of the northwestern division of the US Army Corps of Engineers, said, "The normal procedure would be to check a supposed violation and then write a warning letter." We pointed out that the traditional warning letter was not part of the law. The law called for "vigorous prosecution" by our office. After the favorable publicity from our successful prosecution of Farwest Capitol, Colonel McConnell recanted: "The corps will act more vigorously in the future," he said.

The Refuse Act was an imperfect tool. I still had two remaining problems. First, the Refuse Act wasn't well designed to deter water pollution violations. Convicting a corporation of a criminal misdemeanor with a small fine really wasn't much of a deterrent. You can't put a corporation in jail. Second, the conservative Army Corps of Engineers, with its affinity for dredging waterways and building levees for flood control—not for environmental protection—was never going to be a very enthusiastic environmental enforcement partner. We needed a bigger net—separate from the corps—to reel in polluters of the area's waterways. What else could we do?

I had an epiphany, or so I thought.

I drew up a plan to enlist the public's help in spotting violations. We would provide detailed checklists for use by the general public that encouraged people to take pictures and pollutant samples, and report suspected violations. The corps would then check to see if discharge permits had been obtained. If no discharge permit had been issued, we would prosecute the miscreant. To provide an incentive for the public's participation in spotting violators, we would recommend to a federal court that up to one-half of any fine obtained be awarded to the private citizen reporting the violation: a bounty program. The maximum fine under the Refuse Act was $2,500 for each violation. If we could convince a court that each discharge was a separate violation, the fine could be substantial. Stan Pitkin, recognizing the potential for greater environmental enforcement, quickly approved my plan.

Stan kicked off our new bounty program on October 29, 1971, at a press conference, with the announcement of a criminal Refuse Act case that held both the corporation and an individual employee of the corporation responsible. The case was against Pan-Alaska Fisheries and the captain of the crab boat *Mercator*, for multiple illegal discharges of substantial amounts of oil into Salmon Bay—the portion of the Lake Washington Ship Canal that empties into Puget Sound's Shilshole Bay. The news received a large front-page, above-the-fold headline in the *Seattle Times*: "Boat owner, captain charged: 'Bounty hunters' urged in pollution fight." Stan emphasized that the bounty program was necessary because he was concerned that the pollution would not be stopped "unless the public acts as information gatherers."

In the first four weeks after the program was announced, we received over nine hundred requests for pollution-reporting kits.[1] In the ensuing weeks—just as the bounty program was beginning to gather steam—the *Seattle Times* opposed the program in a lead editorial, saying it would only encourage citizens to spy on one another. The *Daily Chronicle*, out of Centralia, then chimed in, saying that we were trying to convert Washington citizens into "stool pigeons."

The media backlash was a serious blow to continuing our whistle-blower program. Since public support was critical to making the program work, the loss of media support put the kibosh on private participation, making it appear undemocratic and legally overreaching. We simply couldn't risk our enforcement credibility by further pursuit of a bounty program.[2]

I told Stan not to get discouraged. You run new programs up the flagpole and see who salutes. Unfortunately, we didn't get the critical salute from the area's largest newspaper. Charles Brownson—an American congressman when newspapers were king—illustrated the problem, saying, "One should never quarrel with anyone who buys ink by the barrel." After the pollution bounty program was terminated, our effort to clean up the Duwamish soon languished for lack of reporting of violations.

***

The Army Corps of Engineers had little interest in taking up further Duwamish Waterway pollution control after we terminated the bounty program. Almost a half century passed before the federal government reengaged, and not before the Dungeness crabs, clams, perch, and sole in the lower Duwamish River had become too toxic to eat. In 2001 the Lower Duwamish Waterway was listed as a Superfund site, which is an EPA designation for the nation's worst contaminated land requiring cleanup. After fourteen years of research and planning, the EPA in 2014 announced a $342 million cleanup plan that federal officials claimed would relieve the beleaguered waterway of 90 percent of its pollution. The effort will take the next two decades, with the costs borne by Boeing, King County, the City of Seattle, and the Port of Seattle.

JOE MENTOR

In the summer of 1971 my mother came to Seattle to see her new granddaughter, Jennifer Renee, just four months old. Another redhead. As luck would have it, I had a trial scheduled at the same time of her visit, a high-profile criminal case involving a powerful state politician and an unpermitted landfill in the Puget Sound. Mother wanted to attend the trial to see "Billy Boy" in action. Of course I said yes. What son could refuse?

Landfills on tidelands that create new uplands are highly regulated in the Puget Sound and its estuaries today because of the potential for adverse impacts on marine and bird populations, flood control, and upland erosion of adjacent properties. But there was little concern about the impact of landfills in tidal basins when Seattle was first established in the nineteenth century. The entire topography of the downtown Seattle waterfront and its deepwater port is the product of a series of huge informal regrades. The hills were flattened with huge water cannons, and the soil was washed downhill to fill Elliott Bay tidelands. The original settlement that became Seattle, today's Pioneer Square, was once a low-lying island.

In the 1899 Refuse Act, the federal government put a stop to the informal filling of tidal basins. Now if you wanted to dump fill material into the navigable waters of the United States, you had to first get a permit from the US Army Corps of Engineers. But Joseph Mentor, the defendant in my case, didn't operate that way. A major land developer, builder, and, since 1968, a Washington State Republican representative, Joe Mentor was a big fish in a small county: sparsely populated, mostly rural Kitsap County, located almost entirely on the Kitsap Peninsula, with bays and estuaries flowing directly into the Puget Sound.

Representative Joe Mentor was used to getting his own way. Described by friends as a bull in a china shop, he had a reputation in

Kitsap County for starting projects and—if he had to—getting the governmental permits later.

Among other ventures, Mentor owned a seafood restaurant, the Sandpiper, which fronted Dyes Inlet on the Puget Sound in Silverdale, Washington. He thought his restaurant's parking lot was too small. When Kitsap County Public Works started a road expansion nearby, he found an inexpensive solution to his problem. He asked the county to donate the excess material from the road project and dump it onto the beach in front of his Sandpiper restaurant. The county, seeming ever willing to accommodate its state representative, dumped 175 truckloads of fill material—composed of dirt, gravel, and stone—onto the tidelands. Mentor promptly graded and covered the fill with asphalt, expanding his restaurant's parking area.

When the Army Corps of Engineers got wind of the project, they contacted Mentor. He denied that any of the fill dumped by the county was seaward of the line of mean high tide, the starting point for federal waters. To document a violation and assert federal jurisdiction, the corps commissioned a land survey that showed that most of the fill was below the line of mean high tide, which meant Mentor had illegally filled the tidelands. Based on the survey, which showed that the fill had pushed the tide line seaward nineteen to sixty-seven feet—onto federal tidelands, Mentor was asked to remove the fill. He refused, and hired a lawyer. The corps referred the case to me for an enforcement action. I charged Mentor with a criminal violation of the Refuse Act, with a demand that the fill beyond the line of mean high tide be removed.

The case seemed pretty straightforward, although I was soon to relearn something every experienced attorney knows: you don't really know what kind of case you have until you've heard from the other side. In criminal cases—without the benefit of discovery that you have in most civil cases—you may not hear from the defendants until it's too late to remedy any defects in your case without dismissing and refiling the action. Ten days before the start of this trial, I heard from the other side when Bill Houger, Mentor's attorney, requested a meeting with me.

Bill Houger was a very smart attorney who would later be one of the founders of Houger, Garvey and Schubert, a highly regarded

Seattle maritime law firm. When Houger entered my office, I expected him to be considering pleading his client guilty and wanting to bargain regarding the penalty. Instead, Houger said he wanted the case dismissed. He said the land survey upon which the charge was based was flawed: he explained that one of the critical tidal benchmarks had previously been destroyed, and therefore the corps' survey was unreliable, especially in a criminal case where the burden of proof is beyond a reasonable doubt.

"You are toast," he said with a grin. "Dismiss the case or it's likely to be embarrassing."

Furthermore, Houger informed me, he was a former surveyor, and our surveyors wouldn't survive his withering and knowledgeable cross-examination. I was absolutely gobsmacked, but pretended to be unruffled.

"I'll get back to you," I said, with as much confidence in my voice as I could muster.

But there was no doubt about it: my case was in big trouble.

Immediately I contacted the corps. They reviewed their survey data. A few days later, they sheepishly confirmed what Bill Houger had told me. The survey was flawed. I had filed a high-profile case against a prominent politician, and dismissing the case would be a great embarrassment to the office. And, most importantly, it would seriously undermine the credibility of our environmental protection program. This would be tough to explain to Stan—to say nothing about Mother. It's funny how our parents—besides being irreplaceable sources of affection—are also the most important audiences for our victories and defeats, be they great or small.

Two weeks before trial, Republican Representative Joe Mentor raised the stakes further. When asked by the press if the charges were without substance and "political," he replied, "Well, what do you think?" I thought it was disingenuous to hint that the charges were political, when Stan Pitkin, the US attorney, was also a Republican.

It was time to scramble big-time. I took the problem to my Portland lifeline, Tom Lee, the environmental specialist in the Portland US attorney's office with whom I had worked previously on the pulp mill cases. He had three suggestions to replace the flawed survey. One, we could search for some old-timers who had observed the beach in front of the Sandpiper restaurant over the years and ask them to testify about the location of mean high tide on the property before the fill. Two, we could see if there were any aerial photographs available that might show the location of the mean high tides before the fill. Three, we could contact the National Ocean Service and ask if they could run tests off the remaining tidal benchmarks in Dyes Inlet and locate the former line of mean high tide. I got lucky on all three counts.

We found two old-timers living on Dyes Inlet who, based upon their personal observations, were willing to testify that the landfill spilled seaward of the line of mean high tide. The corps also learned that the National Geodetic Survey had three aerial reconnaissance photographs of the property done in 1951, 1970, and 1971. After reviewing the photographs, the survey said they were willing to supply an expert photogrammetrist who would testify that the area filled was below the line of mean high tide. The National Ocean Service also came through when they said they could triangulate off the surviving survey benchmarks to establish the approximate former line of mean high tide and show the area of illegal fill.

The trial began in a federal courtroom filled with spectators, including friends and family of the defendant and members of the press. And in my corner, there was a cheering section of one: my mother, beaming proudly, as she was sure her son would win. The jury case was presided over by Judge Walter McGovern, who had been appointed to the federal bench by President Nixon in 1971 to replace Judge Lindberg, the judge in the *Cook* case, who had retired.

During the trial, I asked Mentor why he had failed to obtain a permit to dump fill on the tidelands: "Was it so the neighbors would never have a chance to complain at a public hearing?"

"I didn't think I needed one," Mentor retorted.

The case was no slam dunk. We had to prove the location of the line of mean high tide beyond a reasonable doubt in a highly technical case, perhaps incomprehensible to a lay jury. I managed to get the defendant's own surveyor to admit on cross-examination that he could not testify to the prior location of the line of mean high tide and, further, that he could not testify that the fill had not been responsible for relocating the line farther toward the water. Mentor also admitted on cross-examination that he had failed to obtain a permit to divert a creek adjacent to his property.

After a three-day battle of dueling experts, the federal jury composed of eight women and four men retired at 3:00 p.m. and came back with a verdict at 9:40 p.m. In a complex case, this was a remarkably short deliberation for a jury. Their verdict: guilty as charged.

I breathed a sigh of relief. I'd pulled a rabbit out of a hat, or, perhaps more apropos, I'd pulled clams and oysters out of a hat and put them back into the tidelands.

"That sure was an interesting case," Mother said, "I'm glad you were kind to Mrs. Mentor."

Mother was referring to my six-word cross-examination of Mrs. Mentor, who was one of her husband's effusive character witnesses in the trial. "You love your husband, don't you?" I said softly to Mrs. Mentor. "Yes, I do. Very much," she answered.

"Thank you, that is all," I said, and immediately sat down. It seemed to work.

Later, I learned I'd had a secret weapon on the jury. The jury had elected a retired US Navy captain as the jury foreman, and he led the jury through all the nautical terminology and technical detail, cementing the case for me.

Before sentencing by Judge McGovern, Jack Avril, the surveying engineer for the road project, who turned Mentor into the Army Corps of Engineers for illegal dumping, filed a request in court that he receive half of any fine, as provided by the Refuse Act. I joined the request noting that Avril gave the information to the corps "despite a risk to his livelihood." At sentencing, Judge McGovern ordered Mentor to remove all the fill material on the tidelands, but assessed no fine. A few months later, Avril lost his job. His employer, Roats Engineering of Poulsbo, denied that Avril's dismissal was connected with his role as a whistleblower in the Mentor case.

Because of the unique method of proof, the case received extensive review in several federal environmental case reports. It was the first criminal conviction in the country of an individual following a jury trial under the 1899 Refuse Act. It would prove to be a significant precedent to deter unpermitted filling of the tidelands in Puget Sound.

Mother was impressed. I told her it had been an easy case—just another typical day in court for me.

***

Based upon our office's performance and increasing workload, the number of lawyers in the Seattle US attorney's office had more than doubled since I started in 1970, to fifteen people. Stan Pitkin said it was time to reorganize. "Effective June 7, 1971, you are the executive assistant U.S. attorney for the Western District of Washington," the announcement from Washington, DC, stated. The Justice Department had approved a new position created for me by Stan. It included a nice bump in pay and wide supervisory authority. I was now in charge of all administrative matters, all environmental matters, all civil rights and civil disturbance cases, and all organized crime, rackets, and corruption investigations in the federal judicial system's Western District of Washington.

What was not in the job description: I was also Stan's aide-de-camp, his consigliere, his wingman. He wanted me close.

THE ART OF WAR

A highly publicized, major US congressional subcommittee hearing was scheduled at the Seattle Pacific Science Center theater on December 10 and 11, 1971. The center, formerly known as the United States Science Pavilion, is where I had previously worked as an attendant during the Seattle World's Fair. The subject of the hearing, near and dear to my heart: *Protecting America's Estuaries: Puget Sound and the Straits of Georgia and Juan de Fuca.* This geographic designation would later be expanded in 1979 by the State of Washington and the province of British Columbia and called the Salish Sea. It refers to the cross-border ecosystem of Canada and the United States and is considered the most important natural resource in the Pacific Northwest.

Congressman Henry Reuss, a liberal Democrat from Wisconsin, a lawyer and a Harvard Law graduate, chaired the nine-member House Subcommittee on Government Operations holding the hearing. A parade of twenty-eight witnesses, representing all the major state and federal agencies involved in water pollution, plus academics and members of environmental organizations were asked to testify. The hearing would eventually produce a 741-page congressional report. For some strange reason, our office was not invited to speak, although we were one of the main players in the Puget Sound's regional water quality enforcement effort.

The congressional subcommittee was concerned with what many environmental critics claimed was a lack of coordination and slow pace of enforcement by state and federal agencies to address pollution in the Puget Sound, especially the discharges from the twenty-two pulp and paper mills that ringed the sound. A federal task force in 1967 had highlighted the seriousness of the problem, finding that the pulp mills discharged into the Puget Sound the equivalent of four times the amount of raw sewage created by the entire rest of the state.

Two days before the subcommittee was scheduled to hold hearings, Seattle's KING-TV, the politically liberal and Democratic-leaning broadcast station—anticipating the big news peg of a local congressional hearing—began an investigative series on pulp and paper-company pollution in Washington State. The station ran a teaser promising that they would expose a "water pollution tolerance policy" by the federal government. I feared a setup, a political hatchet job to embarrass the Nixon administration and our office. *I'd better attend the hearings to find out what's up,* I concluded.

The congressional hearing, held in the large auditorium at the Pacific Science Center, was packed with about two hundred people: industry representatives and their attorneys, government officials, members of the public, and the Puget Sound–area press. The auditorium fronted an elevated stage with a set of stairs, which led to two tables on either side of the stage, angled to face the audience. On the right-side table sat members of the subcommittee, their legal counsels, and, behind them, their legislative aides. The other table, on the left, was reserved for people scheduled to testify and their retinue of assistants and advisors. Things started off slowly and seemed to be going rather smoothly until the testimony of Marvin Durning, who represented the Sierra Club, a national environmental group that claimed over two thousand members in the Puget Sound area.

Marvin Durning and Attorney General Slade Gorton had been classmates at Dartmouth College. Slade Gorton didn't do too badly in college. He was elected to Phi Beta Kappa at Dartmouth. But his Dartmouth classmate Marvin Durning did him one better. He was the valedictorian of their Dartmouth class, went on to Yale Law School, and became a Rhodes scholar. He left an economics professorship at Yale to come to Seattle in 1959 to practice law. For leading a citizens' drive for land conservation, President Johnson named Durning Conservationist of the Year in 1965.

Durning was a tall, imposing man, forty years old, of medium build, with a mop of curly salt-and-pepper hair that took off in every direction. He was known as an ardent environmental attorney, a passionate conservationist, and a politically ambitious liberal Democrat prone to hyperbolic presentations.

In a booming, authoritative voice, Durning began his testimony at the hearing. He immediately threw down a gauntlet, with a salvo of criticism directed at the federal government, and largely at our office. He said one of the main purposes of his testimony was to make the congressional committee aware of the inadequate water-pollution-control policies of the Justice Department and the US attorney's office for the Western District of Washington. This, he said, amounted to a "tolerance policy" that permitted lawbreaking by the rich, politically powerful pulp mills of the state. This dereliction of duty by the US attorney's office was ameliorated only, he said, "by occasional deceptive acts of bravery by filing criminal actions against a small and weak company" (he was referring to our suit against Farwest Capitol Co.).

The notion of the Seattle US attorney's office operating an environmental tolerance policy could not be left to stand. Not on my watch. It was a gross perversion of the truth, and, given the *Cook* case, about the worst slander that anyone could throw at our office. Durning's allegation demanded a rebuttal, but I was not invited by the committee to rebut his hatchet job. What could I do? For inspiration, I channeled

Chinese General Sun Tzu, who wrote twenty-five hundred years ago in *The Art of War*: "Attack him where he is unprepared, appear where you are not expected."

As Marvin Durning completed his presentation castigating the federal government for not enforcing the Refuse Act for the last fifty years, I, in a coup de théâtre, marched confidently down the aisle to the stage at the front of the auditorium and passed a note to Congressman Floyd Hicks. Hicks, a Democrat from Pierce County in Washington State, a lawyer and former Pierce County Superior Court judge, was temporarily chairing the subcommittee. I identified myself and asked for an opportunity to speak.

Congressman Hicks immediately invited me up on the stage to address the subcommittee. I told them that the remarks of Mr. Durning were factually incorrect and could not be allowed to stand in light of the environmental enforcement record of our office. I said, "I think the facts will show that the US attorney's office in this district, out of the ninety-three US attorney's offices in the nation, has more activity under the Refuse Act than any other district attorney's office in the country."

Then I explained KING-TV's role in promoting false allegations in an attempt to hype their ratings and promote Durning's testimony. I told the committee that two days earlier, after KING-TV first made the allegation of a federal tolerance policy, I had telephoned them and said: "Your sources, I am sure, are not the Environmental Protection Agency, the coast guard, the state Department of Ecology, or the Army Corps of Engineers, because our reputation among those agencies is the most aggressive of the bunch." I said to the subcommittee that I had asked KING-TV what was the source so that we could respond to the particular charge. Their response to me had been "to watch the program."

Next, remembering General Tzu's advice that the possibility for victory "lies in the attack," I would prick Marvin Durning's verbal balloon and deflate his argument. I explained to the subcommittee that it was impractical to file Refuse Act criminal cases against all the pulp mills in the Puget Sound because it wouldn't produce the desired result. The issue really was which companies were complying with remedial cleanup programs and which companies weren't. Only the companies in noncompliance should be sued.

In extensive detail, I went through all our office's environmental enforcement actions under the Refuse Act in the last twelve months. Then, in an argumentative coup de grâce, I scolded Marvin Durning: "I regret it very much, when somebody comes up and attempts to tear down the whole damn system on the grounds that it didn't happen fifty years ago. We weren't that intelligent . . . now we have learned a little bit of our lesson, and my view is that we should take the forward view from the time people became aware." I noticed the committee listening with rapt attention and continued with my admonition: "Let's not go back into the 1950s and early 1960s and cry over spilled milk. Quite frankly, nobody, or very few people, was aware of the problem. There are a lot of dedicated public servants who have worked very, very hard, and I think it is an injustice to lump them all in a bag and say they are part of a tolerance policy or they attempted to sell out the state, because it just isn't true."

After extensive and vigorous sparring among the congressmen, their staff, Durning, and myself, the hearing gradually morphed into a lovefest. For a moment I felt like we were all sitting around a campfire singing "Kumbaya." Marvin Durning summed up our newfound rapport: "I think Bill Erxleben and I agree on this, because I was very proud of the way he handled himself as a representative of the government, before this committee, and I am proud of this committee."

Then Congressman Hicks chimed in as the bonhomie continued. He said, referencing me: "As one member of the committee, I was inspired by the practicality, by the way you are looking at the matter, and the vigorousness with which you are doing the possible rather than tilting at windmills—or, as Mr. Finnegan [the assistant chief committee counsel] would have you, going back and whacking people on the head with this, possibly for criminal actions that we have accepted and tolerated as a public for many, many years. I think it is practical to look to the future and do what we can from now on, but we better be darn sure we do it."

I was amazed and gladdened by this sudden turn in events. At best, I had thought I might manage a draw, but now I smelled victory.

Then, in front of the committee and in the spirit of furthering the camaraderie, I invited Marvin Durning to lunch. He accepted.

That evening there was no mention on KING-TV of any environmental tolerance policy or any other criticism of the federal government or of our office. It was the first, only, and last time the words *tolerance policy* were negatively associated with the Seattle US attorney's office.

***

Orcas of the Pacific Northwest Are Starving and Disappearing
—New York Times, July 9, 2018

The Puget Sound faces an onslaught of new threats today. Studies show that traces of pharmaceutical prescription drugs, which are increasingly found in wastewater discharge, are showing up in salmon and other fish species in the sound, stunting their growth and affecting their metabolism. The effects of water pollution are especially detrimental to the black-and-white killer whales, the magnificent orcas. Since 2005, orcas have been listed as endangered because their primary source of food, the Chinook, or king, salmon, are essentially starving to death due to a complex mix of factors including pollution, loss of habitat, hydroelectric dams, and climate change. The seventy-six remaining southern resident orcas in Puget Sound as of 2018 have not managed a successful pregnancy in three years. Researchers say they will disappear unless the salmon population can be increased. If the salmon population cannot be increased, it will be a travesty for the Puget Sound ecosystem.

Washington State was sued in 2001 by twenty-one western Washington treaty tribes, who claimed that salmon populations were disappearing in the Puget Sound and Olympic Peninsula areas because barriers under highways blocked fish passages and were a violation of the tribes' fishing treaty rights. In June 2018 the US Supreme Court decided to let stand a lower court's decision that required the state to replace fish culverts that block salmon habitat. Fixing 425 culverts will cost the State of Washington an estimated $3.7 billion by 2030, the required completion date.

If warm waters persist and increase due to global warming, despite all the efforts to increase the salmon runs, in the lower forty-eight states at least, the king salmon and the orcas may both disappear. In the minds of many people around the world, orcas are to the Salish Sea as the giant pandas are to the bamboo forests in China. Both species are highly relatable to humans, and their long-term survival is in limbo. To lose the orcas in the Salish Sea may be inevitable. And it will be an uncomfortable commentary on the stewardship of the Salish Sea by the United States and Canada.

Even more disturbing for orcas worldwide are new studies that show PCB contamination in the blubber of orcas. Most at risk are the orcas that eat seals and other animals heavily contaminated with PCBs and those that live near industrialized areas. Researchers predict this contamination may result in wiping out one-half of the world's remaining population of orcas in coming decades.

CHAPTER ELEVEN

THE FIXER

(ONE MONTH EARLIER)

The investigative television show *60 Minutes* first aired in 1968. A bold, gutsy, "gotcha" style of television was its trademark. The investigative reporters at Seattle's KING-TV evening news were *60 Minutes* wannabes, and the US attorney's office was for the first time on the receiving end of KING-TV's zealous pursuit of governmental inaction.

"KING-TV called me today, Bill, and they weren't happy," Stan said, with a frown etched on his face early one morning in November 1971.

"What did they want?"

"They said they have reports that obscene movies are flooding into Seattle from Denmark through the Port of Seattle. They are demanding to know what enforcement program we have in place to deal with this 'dire situation.' Next week they're planning a three-day exposé on the nightly news claiming weak law enforcement by the federal government in failing to seize and destroy these films. We are clearly in their crosshairs."

"What did you tell them?"

"I stalled, and said that we were very busy, but I agreed to an interview at the end of the week."

"What's the plan?" I said, hoping there was one.

"This problem hasn't even been on our radar: there is no program. Never was one. We don't have resources for this, and it's not a priority." Then, throwing the shovel directly at me, he said, "I want you to come up with something to bury this story. Make it go away. This could go badly for the office."

"OK," I dutifully answered, realizing that I had just been handed a Pitkin graveyard burial assignment. "How much time do I have?"

"A camera crew and reporter are coming over on Friday. One more thing—I plan to be called 'unexpectedly' out of the office all day Friday. Will you do the interview for me?"

"I guess so," I said, unable to quickly demur.

Again, I became the designated office fireman, but this fire would be a real challenge. With China's ancient history of enjoying pornographic art, channeling General Tzu would be useless in extinguishing this fire. For the next week, I was now on temporary duty as chief of the office porno squad. It was now late Monday. I had only three days to pull this all together before the KING-TV interview.

I had several serious problems in coming up with an action plan. One, I knew nothing about obscenity enforcement. I had never seen a pornographic movie and had no idea what the difference was between pornography, which was protected by the First Amendment, and obscenity, which was unprotected. And, two, I had never done a television interview before. In four days it would be my TV debut. This would be a challenge. I was a nervous Nellie.

I quickly started to work. Some historical research of worldwide expressions of pornography showed me that explicit representations of human sexuality are nothing new. Ever since the Paleolithic period, in the Stone Age, when humans figured out how to paint and carve, there have been explicit representations of sex, some even derived from religious beliefs.

In contrast with many European countries, the United States, still a young country, had no real history of pornography. It was not until 1953, when Hugh Hefner launched *Playboy* magazine—with a nude centerfold photograph of Marilyn Monroe—that the door opened for pornography to go mass-market in the United States.[1]

Public opinion regarding adult pornography in the United States was mixed. Some saw its repression as a limitation on free speech and sexual expression by a prudish religious majority unable to remove the shackles of the country's Puritan past. But the overwhelming majority view was different: most believed pornography demeaned women—as misogynistic exploitation—caused sexual violence, and resulted in lasting damage to adolescents.

With this brief history lesson in mind, I explored the legal standard for action by our office. Pornography was defined as "movies or pictures that show or describe naked people or sex in a very open or direct way in order to cause sexual excitement." Pornography, per se, was not illegal, but obscene pornography was illegal.

An attempt by the US Supreme Court to define "obscene" pornography occurred in 1957 in the *Roth* case. Here, Justice William Brennan Jr. announced a new test: "whether to the average person, applying contemporary community standards, the dominant theme of the material as a whole appeals to the prurient [lewd or lustful] interest."

The "prurient interest test" was almost impossible to apply because it eluded a conclusive definition. Expressing his difficulty in defining obscenity, US Supreme Court Justice Potter Stewart famously remarked in 1964 in the *Jacobellis v. Ohio* case, "I shall not today attempt further to define the kinds of material I understand to be embraced within that shorthand description [hard-core pornography], and perhaps I could never succeed in intelligibly doing so. But I know it when I see it." This expression, "I know it when I see it," became one of the most famous phrases in the entire history of the Supreme Court.

The US Supreme Court broadened the definition of obscene pornography in a 1966 case, *Memoirs v. Massachusetts*—involving the bawdy English novel *Fanny Hill*—when it said that the material, aside from appealing to the prurient interest, must be "utterly without redeeming social value." This standard made federal prosecutions in 1971 extremely difficult because defendants easily found expert witnesses who attested to the literary and artistic value of sexually explicit films and books.

I decided to follow Justice Stewart's test as my starting point in defining obscenity. I would worry later about whether the material had any redeeming social value. But if "I know it when I see it" was the test—I somewhat implausibly rationalized—then clearly I would need to see pornographic films first to decide if the test worked.

In 1971 there was only one theater in Seattle showing feature-length pornography films, where I could do my "field research." It was the Ridgemont Theater on Greenwood Avenue. I dressed appropriately for my research. Following the stereotypical 1970s attire for porno theaters, I wore a tan trench coat with a belt tied loosely around my waist.

On a rainy Wednesday afternoon in November, I caught the matinee at the Ridgemont Theater, which had a very small boxed-in screen. The theater was only about one-third full, which was good, because the customary spacing among the all-male audience was not to have anyone sit on the immediate left or right of you. Privacy concerns, I suspected. I stood in the aisle for a full minute, until my eyes adjusted to the darkness in the theater, before I sat down. I didn't want to sit in anyone's lap—that was for sure.

The first short film starred Marilyn Monroe and a Coke bottle in fifteen minutes of autoerotic activity. I was really surprised to see her in a pornographic film, and while it was rather disrespectful of Coca-Cola, I couldn't really say it appealed to a prurient interest—whatever that was—or was utterly without redeeming social value.

The feature film, whose name was eminently forgettable, wasn't any better—a lot of dispassionate sex without a story line; pornographic yes, but not obscene. My field research was now complete, except that I hadn't seen any material that I thought was actionable.[2]

***

Something is rotten in the state of Denmark.
                    —William Shakespeare, *Hamlet*

After returning from the Ridgemont to my office, as I was filling out my governmental expense report reimbursing me for attending pornographic films, the phone rang. It was the director of customs in

Seattle. He said his agents seized an "obscene" film from Denmark, and he wanted permission to destroy it. With my newfound legal wisdom, I explained to him that obscenity is a legal judgment, and I needed to review the film first. The customs director said that was no problem at all. He would set up a showing at the customs headquarters office near the Elliott Bay waterfront on Thursday morning, at eleven.

Arriving at the customs office right on time, I expected to be ushered into a small room where I would be left alone to review the film. That was not to be the case. I was shown into a large meeting room with a projector and screen where some fifteen male customs agents, surrounding the director, were seated. "It's a training exercise," the director said with a straight face. A machine in the corner of the room was spewing out copious amounts of popcorn.

I sat down, and—after some pleasantries with a delay for everyone to get a bag of popcorn—the film began. The first minute or so was a travelogue showing the beautiful Danish coastline. Merely a subterfuge, the director quickly explained to me, designed to fool customs agents, who, as part of their inspection, would pull out the first few feet of film to see if it was sexually explicit. And suddenly, the film changed from a travelogue to images of a tall brunette woman and her big German shepherd. This was no Rin Tin Tin movie: it depicted bestiality. *You'll know it when you see it, you'll know it when you see it* was the refrain running through my mind. A bell went off. *I see it! I know it!* No need to focus at all on redeeming social value: there clearly was none. Of course, everyone in the room, including me, stayed to finish off the popcorn and watch the movie to the end. Afterward, I telephoned the director and told him to destroy the film.

I felt I was now ready for tomorrow's TV interview. I understood the law and the history, and, not incidentally, I planned to mention that our office had recently engaged in an aggressive enforcement action by destroying an obscene film from Denmark.

On Friday morning, the KING-TV interview was scheduled: it would occur at two in the afternoon in my office. I was increasingly worried that I would be hit with "gotcha" questions. Would I embarrass the office and myself? Pornography was a subject that I was far from comfortable discussing publicly. I decided to follow the most important rule for answering tough interview questions, a rule followed by most politicians, even though the technique had failed me miserably in law school: "If you don't like the question you are asked, answer a different question." I wrote down on a piece of paper a two-minute explanation of our "vigorous" obscenity enforcement program that I could apply to any question, and hoped for the best.

At the appointed hour, a female reporter and camera crew arrived from KING-TV. I was seated behind my desk as a member of the camera crew applied some fake tan makeup to my face. Then the bright camera lights went on and temporarily blinded me. The reporter asked me a question. I froze like a deer caught in the headlights, and, not even hearing the question, I blurted out my prepared answer.

Forty-five seconds into my memorized spiel, I realized I had not taken a breath. I stopped momentarily, inhaled deeply and audibly with a sort of wheeze, and continued talking. When I completed my prepared answer, I looked at the reporter, awaiting another question. I thought: *Now what do I say?* But the reporter told the cameraman to quit filming. "We're leaving," she said, rather curtly.

Well, that wasn't too bad, I concluded.

When I arrived home at the end of the day, I told Gayle that my interview would run the next week as part of KING-TV's investigative report on obscenity and law enforcement in Seattle. Anticipating my TV debut, each night we anxiously watched the news for the expected thirty-second sound bite from my monologue. But no mention was made at all of the US attorney's office in the entire three-day television exposé. Apparently, my interview was so bad that no part of it was salvageable, and the whole thing ended up on the station's cutting room floor.

On the day after the exposé was over, Stan came down to my office in obvious high spirits and said, "How did you do it? How did you get KING-TV to kill the story about us? Fantastic job!"

"Piece of cake," I replied, without further confession.

AND THEN THE PHONE RANG

One week before Christmas, 1971, my office phone rang. The caller identified himself as Miles Kirkpatrick, newly appointed by President Nixon as the chairman of the Federal Trade Commission (FTC). Chairman Kirkpatrick got right to the point: "I am trying to revitalize the Federal Trade Commission. We're looking for a talented person to head up the regional office in Seattle. A change agent that can shake things up and turn that office around."

This came out of the blue. I was flabbergasted to receive a call from the chairman of the FTC, possibly offering me a job. *How did he get my name?* I wondered.

Kirkpatrick, a prominent Philadelphia antitrust attorney, said he had recently attended the American Bar Association convention in New York, where he spoke with his friend Bob Graham, whom practicing attorneys in Seattle considered the dean of the local antitrust bar. "Bob said you were the right man for the job. If you're interested, jump on an airplane and come to Washington, DC, and we can discuss it."

Bob Graham was a homegrown talent who was formerly the student body president, valedictorian of his graduating class, and a talented athlete at Whitman College in Walla Walla, Washington, before he went on to attend Columbia Law School. With a growing reputation on the national scene, he was very well connected indeed. In 1968, President Johnson had appointed him to a national conference charged with reviewing the state of federal bureaucracies. In 1970, President Nixon appointed him to a US Department of State task force to review embassy operations in the Far East. Most importantly, he was also a good friend of Caspar "Cap" Weinberger, the man President Nixon first appointed chairman of the FTC, who served for a brief period before Miles Kirkpatrick's appointment. Graham remembered me as an assistant state attorney general in the *Flo Villa* case, where he was extremely complimentary of my oral argument on the history of harbor lines in Lake Union. (I said that case had legs.) He had followed my subsequent career in the US attorney's office, and his recommendation would carry a lot of weight. I couldn't have a better advocate.

Like environmentalism, consumer protection was a new wave of populist demand to sweep the nation in the late 1960s, in this case demanding more governmental action to protect consumers. Ralph Nader's book *Unsafe at Any Speed* was a major catalyst that kicked off the 1960s consumer movement. His book decried the auto industry's lack of safety features, like seat belts and padded dashboards, and its reluctance to invest money in improving car safety.

You should always be ready to catch the next wave, I reminded myself. If I wanted to switch my public interest surfboard from the environmental movement and hang ten on the next populist-driven movement—consumer protection—the FTC was absolutely the best place to be. I told Chairman Kirkpatrick that I would be happy to meet with him, and I would arrange a flight as soon as I could.

Stan was initially crestfallen when I told him of my plans to interview with the FTC. But we both knew the US attorney's office was only a way station for both of us. If the Republicans lost the next election, he would be out of a job. Since assistant US attorneys are not civil service employees—instead they are at-will employees subject to the whim of the US attorney and the Department of Justice—I, being so close to Stan, and in a specially created position as executive assistant US attorney, would likely be out of a job as well.

As always, Stan was extremely supportive and wished me success in the interview. I felt bad about leaving, but the allure of another adventure in a new legal arena, where I would call the shots, was simply too strong. In the US attorney's office for the Western District of Washington, I had played the role of first violinist to Stan the maestro. Was I seasoned enough to be a regional maestro in charge of five Pacific Northwest states at the FTC? Would the music be as good? After less than two action-packed years in the US attorney's office, I had accomplished more than I'd ever dreamed of. I had done my duty. *If I stay at the US attorney's office, it probably will be downhill from now on,* I surmised. I ignored the comfort of my current situation. I would spur the white horse of my destiny into a new battle for the common good, this time with the FTC.

***

In 1972 we bought a brand-new house in Bellevue in the Somerset neighborhood on the east side of Lake Washington. For several years, the widow of actor and world-renowned martial artist Bruce Lee lived directly across the street from us with their two young children, Brandon and Shannon. Linda Lee was a lovely lady and her life was thrown a cruel curve ball when Bruce, who had attended the University of Washington, died suddenly in 1973 at age thirty-two in Hong Kong in what was officially ruled as "a death by misadventure." He is buried at Lake View Cemetery in the Capitol Hill section of Seattle.

I remember the monotonous thump-thump-thump of a tennis ball being thrown against the Lees' garage door as Brandon tried to entertain himself in the summer evenings in our otherwise very quiet neighborhood bedroom community. Brandon seemed lonely and withdrawn. I wondered how different his life would have been if his father were still alive.

Later, Brandon, who followed in his father's footsteps, became an actor and martial artist. In 1993 he died at age twenty-eight, in a bizarre accidental shooting on the set while starring in the movie *The Crow*. Brandon is buried next to his father; their gravesites are Seattle landmarks and a national and global pilgrimage. To this day, Bruce Lee's fans come from far and wide to visit the gravesite of the most famous martial artist movie actor ever.

***

Stan Pitkin left the US attorney's office in 1977, after Jimmy Carter, a Democrat, defeated the incumbent Republican president, Gerald Ford. Stan, who saw no local political offices he was interested in running for and who had no desire to enter what he felt was the boring grind of a private legal practice, landed an appointment as the chief counsel of the Western Regional Center of the National Oceanic and Atmospheric Administration (NOAA) in Seattle. Stan was someone who never stood still. He said he loved the land. Irrepressible Stan soon formed a river rafting company and a bus company to ferry rafters and skiers, and he started to develop more than a hundred acres that he had purchased near the city of Gold Bar on the Skykomish River as a dude ranch.

Gayle and I remained close to the Pitkins. Stan and his wife, Anne, had three young children. Our families saw each other often and took a few vacations together. After leaving the US attorney's office, Stan moved from Seattle to Bellevue, and he bought a house only a few blocks away from us in the Somerset area.

One Saturday afternoon in the summer of 1981, Stan and I were sitting on the front deck of my house in the dappled shade of an old native dogwood tree, whose canopy shielded us from the bright midday sun, the tree gently swaying as a soft, warm breeze rippled its leaves. We were enjoying the camaraderie of each other's company as only good friends can. It was a good day to be alive. We were calmly talking, reminiscing, drinking lemonade, and nothing seemed amiss. "Remember that toothache and sinus infection that was bothering me?" Stan said. Then his eyes misted over and his hands started to tremble; he looked at me, and his voice broke as he said softly, "I'm a goner . . . I have cancer."

"I'm sorry. I am so sorry," was all I could say. Later, I realized that I was sorry not just for him and his family; I was grieving equally for myself. Not long thereafter, at age forty-four, Stan Pitkin was dead. I lost a trusted and dear friend, a comrade in arms in the quest for justice. I miss his company.

CHAPTER TWELVE

GRANNY ON STEROIDS

Late in December 1971, I arrived in Washington, DC, via Dulles airport, and checked into the historic Mayflower Hotel, not far from the White House. The following morning, on a sunny, crisp winter day, I took a taxi to the FTC headquarters to meet Miles Kirkpatrick, the chairman.

The FTC building was small by Washington standards, shaped like a flatiron, and located on a prime piece of real estate at the apex of the Federal Triangle between the Capitol and the White House on Pennsylvania Avenue. I was surprised that a small agency like the FTC should inhabit such a coveted location in a town where physical proximity to power is greatly desired. As I walked up to the entrance of the building, I passed famous symbols visually depicting the dichotomy of government regulation of business: two seventeen-foot-tall art deco sculptures showing muscular men restraining powerful horses, titled *Man Controlling Trade*, represented the struggle between regulators and unbridled markets.

I had read earlier that President Franklin D. Roosevelt laid the cornerstone of the building himself in 1937. Referring to the "splendid" architectural setting of the new building, Roosevelt said, "May this permanent home of the Federal Trade Commission stand for all time as a symbol of the purpose of the government to insist on a greater application of the golden rule to conduct the corporation and business enterprises in their relationship to the body politic." *The golden rule is the embodiment of the FTC! I'm going to really like this place,* I thought, absolutely delighted.

One of the smallest of the federal regulatory agencies, the FTC in 1972 had around five hundred attorneys and fifty economists, with a total staff, including the eleven regional offices, numbering under two thousand. Like many independent federal regulatory agencies, it consists of five commissioners appointed for a fixed term of seven years. No more than three of the five commissioners can be from the same political party.

By naming a reformist chairman to head the commission, President Nixon sought to revitalize the FTC. Nixon saw the agency as best suited to capture the populist wave of consumer protectionism, a movement that was driven by a belief that many corporations were exploiting and deceiving consumers.

Miles Kirkpatrick, a graduate of Princeton University and the University of Pennsylvania Law School, had been a partner in the preeminent Philadelphia law firm Morgan, Lewis, & Bockius and had just taken over from Cap Weinberger as FTC chairman. My first impression of Kirkpatrick was extremely favorable. Tall, bespectacled, and scholarly looking, a soft-spoken man with a medium build and thinning white hair, a patrician with a friendly and kindly demeanor, he was refreshingly apolitical and highly principled, exuding intelligence and integrity. He seemed like an uncommonly decent public servant. In the next few years, as I got to know him better, he confirmed my earlier estimation: he simply was the best federal administrator that I would ever have the pleasure to work with. Under Kirkpatrick, the FTC was a haven for young idealists; I would have followed him anywhere.

Our interview took place in his spacious office and lasted less than twenty minutes. I thought of impressing Chairman Kirkpatrick with my understanding of deceptive practices, gleaned from my earlier summer experiences as a door-to-door salesman for Kirby vacuums in Cincinnati and Home Frozen Foods in Seattle, but my better judgment kicked in. I remembered the old sales rule: When you have the customer at yes, shut up and take the order. No glaring faux pas for me. I quickly decided it might be counterproductive to detail my firsthand knowledge of real-world deceptive practices.

The chairman summarized the challenge he was facing: numerous studies had concluded that the FTC had too many high-level employees who were incompetent or do-nothings, and the staff was wasting

FTC chairman Miles Kirkpatrick and Bill.

their time pursuing trivial matters. The president wanted him to fix it, he told me with unmistakable conviction.

Although I was already sold on the position, I waited for the punch line. "I need to hire energetic senior staff committed to changing this organization," he said. Then he broke into a mischievous grin and said, "Bill, do you want to join the fun?"

"I'd love to," I said, and I knew my eyes lit up like a pair of head-lights on high beam. I was not about to play hard to get. I really wanted the job.

In a ritual of welcome and acceptance, Kirkpatrick said, "Let me call the photographer; we'll have our picture taken here by the grand-father clock. It's my favorite piece of furniture in this office."

He is a better closer than I am, I realized. I could learn from him.

And that is how on January 15, 1972, I came to be appointed as the Seattle regional director of the FTC, with jurisdiction over the entire US Pacific Northwest: Washington, Oregon, Alaska, Idaho, and Montana (a five-state territory that is an outdoorsman's dream). If you love nature, if you love the land, if you love salt water, if you love the mountains and rain forests, and the vast open plains, the Pacific Northwest has it all in spades. I was extremely fortunate to find a pub-lic interest legal position so well complemented by my business school background and interest in economics. So, just after my twenty-ninth birthday, I became the youngest regional director in the history of the FTC. A record, I believe, that for better or worse still stands today.

***

Capitalism is the bedrock philosophy for the organization of markets in the United States. As the early-twentieth-century economist Joseph Schumpeter wrote, through the process of "creative destruction," in Darwinian fashion, competition and innovation destroy business models and separate weak competitors from the strong, creating mar-ket efficiency.

Adam Smith, often touted as the world's first free-market capitalist and as the father of economics, postulated in *The Wealth of Nations* the "invisible hand" theory. Minimizing the role of government intervention in markets and letting markets reach their own equilibrium, he said, was the best way to produce maximum economic welfare. The idea was that each person by looking out for him- or herself inadvertently creates the best outcome for all. But there are real-world problems with Adam Smith's theory. To put it succinctly: free markets work, except when they don't; and greed is good, except when it isn't. Economists characterize business behaviors that distort the efficiency of markets as market failures. Price-fixing, monopolization, mergers that create market power, and false and deceptive advertising are all examples of market failures that can distort free markets and produce unwelcome costs to society.

In 1911 the US Supreme Court broke up Standard Oil, triggering a populist wave in the country against industrial behemoths. The power and anticompetitive practices of business trusts were the focus of the 1912 presidential elections, which led to the creation of the FTC by Congress in 1914. The FTC was designed to prevent and correct market failures and enhance business efficiency through the vigorous enforcement of antitrust and consumer protection laws.

Unfortunately, for most of its first fifty years of existence, the FTC was not up to the task of policing the markets. In time it earned the appellation the "Little Old Lady of Pennsylvania Avenue." Through its general ineffectiveness and lackluster enforcement, the agency failed to live up to its responsibilities to the American public and appeared to be in bed with the industries it was supposed to regulate. The agency was preoccupied with trivial cases, hired experienced lawyers that often weren't very talented, and didn't take advantage of its broad jurisdictional mandate.

Beginning in 1969, the Little Old Lady was taken regularly to task for falling far short of her statutory authority. A series of reports, starting with FTC commissioner Philip Elman's scathing critiques in the late 1960s, roundly scolded the FTC for a dismal performance. Elman's critiques were followed by additional criticism of the FTC, most notably in Miles Kirkpatrick's 1969 American Bar Association study and in the Nader's Raiders 1969 study. There were calls to shut the FTC down.

The Nader Report on the Federal Trade Commission was personal and damning. It harshly attacked the leadership and organization of

the FTC, claiming, "the real problem of the FTC . . . can . . . be traced
to people. The FTC should not be a 'friend' to business; it needs to
be feared, and it needs to provide strong disincentives to businesses
for committing violations." In 1971 the President's Advisory Council
on Executive Organization, the Ash Council, joined the chorus, char-
acterizing the FTC unmercifully as overly political and toothless, the
weakest federal agency in Washington. In a remarkable turnaround
beginning in 1969, Cap Weinberger and Miles Kirkpatrick led a vigorous revitalization of the FTC at the national level that changed the
agency's reputation from the Little Old Lady to the nation's champion
of consumer protection. But the FTC's eleven regional offices were still
a work in progress. Headquarters didn't trust them; they had yet to
reform and perform.

The regional FTC offices were traditionally treated as poor country
cousins by the staff in Washington, DC. Viewed as a political necessity
to show concern to Congress for regional issues, these offices provided
some fact-finding investigative efficiency to enforce economically
questionable statutes that were politically popular in many states, like
the Robinson-Patman Act, which was designed to protect small retailers from price competition from chain stores. The regional offices were
tightly monitored by DC and given little authority for the attorneys to
act as full-fledged lawyers. Risk-taking, seen as threatening and potentially embarrassing to the Washington bureaucracy, was highly discouraged. Doing nothing to gain public notice was a virtue, not a vice.
The agency seemed to prize process and a well-written memo discussing a problem over actually accomplishing anything.

The Chinese Taoist symbol of yin and yang represents a perfect
balance of opposites moving toward harmony. It has been said that
behind every crisis, there is opportunity. Crisis begets reform. I viewed
the Seattle office of the FTC the same way: the office was in crisis,
seeking a new direction, and it was my opportunity.

Shortly before my appointment was official, I visited the Seattle
FTC regional office located on Third Avenue, near Pike Street, three
blocks from the bustling Pike Place Market, a tourist mecca in downtown Seattle. Pike Street was the underbelly of the city, filled with topless joints, bars, homeless people, and streetwalkers. The surrounding

area was a seedy part of town inhabited by the dispossessed of the city, with pockets of Hare Krishna devotees sitting on the sidewalks continuously chanting the mesmerizing sixteen-word Vaishnava mantra while clinking their hypnotic finger cymbals. Drug addicts looking to score drugs and peep show and strip club patrons rounded out the ambiance of the neighborhood. The narrow FTC office entrance was in a building next door to the Garden movie theater, which showed feature-length pornography films. The movie *Deep Throat* had just begun what was to be a three-year run.[1] The problem for visitors to the Seattle FTC office was that if you weren't paying attention to where you were going, you just might end up in a sea of trench coats.

I entered the old office building on Third Avenue and took the small elevator to the FTC office. Immediately the soon-to-be-replaced regional director—a bit of an awkward situation—greeted me. He wanted to stay on as a staff attorney, but I successfully urged him to retire.

The office was rather dark and dingy, with a musty smell. It was distressingly unimpressive. No sign of the majesty and might of the federal government here. The regional director introduced me to the staff of eight attorneys, five consumer protection specialists, and the office's administrative support group. After interviewing everyone, I concluded that two-thirds of the staff were definitely keepers—many of whom would really blossom in the coming years and make significant contributions to the success of the office—but one-third would have to be replaced. If this office was to be a real success, it needed to be pruned, motivated, and infused with some top-class talent. I spotted one obvious spot for pruning: the Portland field office that was currently run by one ineffective investigator.

I viewed the turnaround of the Seattle FTC office as a classic business school exercise: define the problems, develop a strategy to overcome the problems, execute the strategy with creative tactics, and measure the results.

I read all the critiques of the FTC to get a grip on its institutional problems. One problem, a lack of tough remedies for consumer protection, was particularly vexing. In 1972, when I began, the FTC was limited to cease-and-desist orders, a directive to "go and sin no more."

A company charged by the FTC did not have to admit wrongdoing; it simply had to say it wasn't going to do it again. If a company violated a cease-and-desist order, it could be fined, but essentially it got one free bite of the apple. It reminded me of the old environmental enforcement policies of the Army Corps of Engineers. Additionally, because Congress allowed American corporations to deduct fines as tax-deductible business expenses, in 1972 a corporation could get a "rebate" of up to 48 percent of any fine paid. If the FTC's statutory remedies were this weak, how could we increase our remedial options to become more effective?

THE PLAN

Our situation was complicated; there was no guarantee of success, and others had failed. We had to identify the obstacles we needed to overcome if we were to be successful. After a great deal of discussion with my staff, we developed a multifaceted strategy.

First, I was used to a great deal of independence in filing and investigating cases, sometimes at breakneck speed. How would we get out from under the heavy thumb of the Washington, DC, bureaucracy that slowed enforcement to a snail's pace? Would DC be willing to decentralize power to the regions to increase the agency's effectiveness? To survive the stifling case review process by DC staff, we would challenge the bureaucracy to improve.[2]

Second, I had to acclimate to the differences between the Seattle US attorney's office and the Seattle FTC office. At the FTC, we had much more freedom to choose the types of cases we wanted to investigate, with far less urgency, but unlike the US attorney's office, only a few cases were presented to us by other governmental agencies. We had to self-generate the case flow.

Third, I needed to navigate the politics of the FTC and run interference for my staff with FTC headquarters in DC. Of course it would help our bargaining position with the bureaucracy immeasurably if I cultivated a relationship with Washington State's powerful Democratic US senators, Warren Magnuson[3] and Henry Jackson,[4] both men widely regarded as lions of the Senate for their seniority and effectiveness in passing legislation. The legislative efforts of these senators would later prove critical to our success.

Fourth, the FTC was criticized for being reactive rather than proactive. What could we do to get ahead of the curve and stop the harm to consumers before it occurred? To strengthen cease-and-desist orders, we needed to develop creative orders that required offenders to do more—like corrective advertising. To increase deterrence, we would borrow from the playbook of the Internal Revenue Service by highly publicizing a few big cases. Cultivating the media and getting wide publicity for our enforcement actions would be a key element of this strategy. Additionally, to expand our reach, we would educate consumers and lobby state legislatures and city councils, using the bully pulpit to promote consumer protection and fight anticompetitive rules and regulations.

Fifth, depending on the groups affected and their ability to protect themselves, consumer fraud has an unequal societal impact. The most vulnerable in the society suffer disproportionately more: the poor, the elderly, minorities, and children are the most at risk for consumer abuses. To address these issues, we needed to triage consumer complaints and focus on the most vulnerable groups.

Sixth, although the FTC had a substantial number of economists in its Bureau of Economics, the agency nevertheless had long been condemned for concentrating its resources on trivial matters of little economic consequence. What could be done to improve planning and economic analysis, and better allocate the regional office's resources? To infuse our case selection with economic discipline, careful planning would be key. To that end, every year we would hold an off-site retreat to develop our enforcement strategy for the coming year. Cost-benefit analysis and a plan to hire an economist would keep our focus on the most important matters.

Seventh, without a significant infusion of new talent, we simply wouldn't have the resources to effectively challenge large corporations, who could hire the best lawyers and investigators around. The FTC was hesitant to pursue cases in federal court outside its own regulatory bailiwick of administrative law, where it was both prosecutor and judge.

I needed to hire aggressive attorneys and investigators as good as or better than those recruited by the major law firms in Seattle, Portland, and Washington, DC—passionate people who could be audacious and groundbreaking, taking us to the cutting edge of the law; people who weren't afraid to take cases to federal court. We decided on a three-part recruitment strategy: aggressively poach some experienced people from the FTC legal staff in Washington, DC; hire from the top law schools; and encourage résumés from highly qualified people in private practice.

And eighth, and last, to develop the optimal strategy for selecting senior staff, I needed to assess my own strengths and weaknesses and determine the need for different skills to round out the team. My mantra was this: *Surround yourself with talent. Don't try to be the smartest guy in the room. (Usually, you are not.) If you are the smartest guy in the room, you haven't recruited very well.*

Although trying and investigating individual cases was exciting, I did not follow the Stan Pitkin model: I would only review cases. With first-class lawyers and consumer protection specialists, there would be no need for micromanagement of cases. The office was big enough and the five-state outreach large enough that it needed a full-time director. I would concentrate on where I thought I could best contribute: hiring the best lawyers and consumer protection specialists, team building, innovation, judgment, and strategy. The big picture. The job would also require a measure of audacity. No problem for me. On the other hand, legal research and legal writing—with all their stylistic constraints and copious footnotes—were among my biggest dislikes. I found these tasks dull and boring. Being the regional director had the potential to be a godsend, freeing me from the drudgery of regular law practice and permitting me to hone my management and leadership skills.

Soon top-notch young attorneys hired from Ivy League and regional law schools joined the team. There were were law graduates from Stanford, Yale, Columbia, the University of California (Los Angeles), and the University of Washington—who had been associates in law firms or working at FTC headquarters in Washington. We had a diverse mix that included minority and women attorneys and consumer protection specialists. Eventually the office would be expanded and consist of thirteen attorneys and eight consumer protection specialists, plus a skilled administrative support group. The entire staff, as a team, represented a cornucopia of talent committed to making the office the best that it could be.

My best hire, and the glue that would keep the team together, was Lola McClintock, the office administrator. She provided the adult supervision for a high-spirited, diverse, and sometimes unruly group of passionate people champing at the bit to change the world. Lola was also the social secretary for the office and supervised a legion of potluck office parties that built esprit de corps.

**

In 1973 the new Henry M. Jackson Federal Building was under construction. Located in central downtown Seattle on a block bounded by Marion and Madison Streets and First and Western Avenues, it is located on a site where the city founders docked their survey boat in 1851. It was not far from my old stomping grounds at the federal courthouse and only three blocks from the waterfront, and ideally sited in the commercial business district. The building enjoyed unobstructed views of Mount Rainier, the Olympic Mountains, the Port of Seattle, and Elliott Bay. It overlooked the ever-changing landscape of a working waterfront dotted with container ships at anchor and ferries navigating varied destinations around the Puget Sound. A striking steel-framed building, clad in precast concrete and completed in 1974, it won the Honor Award from the American Institute of Architects in 1976.

With a bit of adroit lobbying on my part, our office was awarded space in the new building. We would take up most of the twenty-eighth floor of the thirty-four-floor office tower, with prime views of the mountains, the port, and water. From a dingy old office building next to *Deep Throat* in a decrepit part of town to the Taj Mahal of new Seattle office buildings (at least it seemed like that to us)—we had finally arrived. The views from our office rivaled even the views from the high-rise perches of the most prominent Seattle law firms.

My office was well lighted with an expansive view that made Mount Rainier, fifty-five miles away, appear like an apparition as it poked its head up in the sky above the clouds. The cobalt blue waters of Elliot Bay tucked around the container ships anchored below, waiting their turn to unload their container cargoes on Harbor Island. The office was furnished—as befitting my new stature—with the requisite high-backed leather chair, conference table, and massive hardwood desk flanked on either side by the US and Washington State flags. We called it the Flag Room. When we wanted to impress visitors or intimidate miscreants with the power of the federal government, it was the office venue of choice.

***

With the turnaround plan now in place, the successful recruitment of additional attorneys and consumer protection specialists, and a substantial upgrade in our physical location, we were poised to make things happen. But how did we perform?

Like kernels of corn jumping in a skillet of oil on a hot stove, the office was soon popping with creative enforcement ideas. In a parade of firsts, from 1972 to 1979, my team of attorneys and investigators obtained more corrective advertising orders and federal court injunctions against deceptive advertising than all the other regional offices combined. We obtained consent orders against General Motors, Chrysler, and Ford, requiring them to refund millions of dollars to auto buyers who had their cars repossessed and sold for more than the debt owed, without refunding the difference to the buyers.

In a flurry of cases against prominent regional and national firms—including Georgia-Pacific and Pay 'n Save—covering false advertising, retailer liability, and debt collection practices, we pioneered new law.

Of special note, we obtained a groundbreaking order against the Alaska Teamsters, the FTC's first antitrust incursion into collective bargaining and against a labor union. This order prohibited the Teamsters from requiring contractors in master agreements to bind their subcontractors to wage and working conditions, or to sign a master collective bargaining agreement.

Cases were filed against two major national catalog retailers, Montgomery Ward, Inc. and Spiegel, Inc., both based in Chicago, for their collection practices. The case against Montgomery Ward charged that the company unlawfully sued low-income Alaska natives—who lived in remote villages—requiring them to travel in midwinter to courts more than five hundred miles away in Anchorage to defend themselves against alleged defaults on mail order purchases. Likewise, Spiegel brought suit in Chicago against mail order customers in other states who sometimes lived more than one thousand miles away from Chicago. These cases and two other companion cases brought by our office involving "long arm" collection practices were among the first cases filed based upon the FTC's power to define "fairness" in business-to-consumer transactions.

We developed the FTC's first advertising enforcement program that focused on misleading and deceptive advertising directed specifically at black consumers, an area of advertising rife with deceptive and unsafe ads for products like hair-care straighteners, hypertension products, skin lighteners, and facial depilatories. We obtained consent orders against five companies, including Revlon and Johnson Products, for making false claims that their hair-straightening products were safe and effective, when a major product ingredient was lye (caustic soda), which can burn and irritate the scalp or produce temporary blindness.

Our consumer education program was second to none. We helped secure $250,000 in donated advertising to run a multistate truth-in-lending campaign educating consumers about the importance of understanding the annual percentage rate (APR) before consummating a consumer loan. We published consumer handbooks to help people navigate purchases of prescription drugs, advertised specials, and funeral services. We also developed a program of consumer arbitration with the Seattle Better Business Bureau and a program for federal-state relations designed to review anticompetitive actions of local governments. These programs were highly praised by the commission as models of what all regional offices should be doing.

The results were dramatic. In seven years, under four different FTC chairmen—three Republicans and one Democrat—the Seattle regional office of the FTC rose from the ashes like a phoenix to national prominence and became the most controversial, the most creative, the most productive, and widely acknowledged as the best regional FTC office in the country.

What were the behind-the-scenes stories and perils of this journey? How did it all end?

CHAPTER THIRTEEN

CREATIVE JUSTICE

One does not sell the land people walk on.
—Crazy Horse, Oglala Sioux (ca. 1840–77)

Most civil cases brought by the FTC follow a predictable path: investigate, sign a consent order or file charges, and hold a hearing. In our consumer protection matters, some cases required my office to deviate from the usual process and engage in more innovative action to obtain justice.

Several cases involving the FTC's Seattle regional office rank as very unusual and particularly innovative. The plight of the Klamath Indians, in a form of cultural genocide, is one of the most poignant of these.

The Klamath Indian Reservation, located in southern Oregon, was established in 1864 pursuant to a treaty between the United States and the Klamath Tribes—the Klamath tribe, the Modoc tribe, and the Yahooskin band of Snake Indians. The Klamath Tribes ceded to the federal government thirteen million acres of land for one million acres of forestlands. These actions were consistent with the views of most Americans that indigenous peoples must make way, to be replaced by white settlers, under the notions of manifest destiny and rights of discovery, never mind that it had been the Indians' homeland for over ten thousand years.

The history of expansion by European settlers into the New World is the history of victors and the vanquished, with Native Americans being the vanquished. First it was the Spaniards seeking gold and converts to the Catholic Church. Then it was Puritans seeking religious freedom from the Catholic Church. Then came dispossessed and adventuresome Europeans seeking land, fortune, and a new life. Indians were tricked into signing treaties, and the white settlers then ignored the treaties. The forced expropriation of Indian land left a bloody trail of atrocities behind on both sides. But even before the advent of the white man, the frontier was never a particularly peaceful place, with land boundaries shifting from migration and wars between tribes.

The doctrine of discovery became the American doctrine of manifest destiny. It gave Christian explorers the right to claim lands that they "discovered." If the "pagans" inhabiting these lands could be converted, they might be spared. Manifest destiny was based upon a religious belief that the United States should expand from the Atlantic Ocean to the Pacific Ocean in the name of God. Many conquered Indian tribes were relegated to reservations through peace treaties, and in 1860, under a federal policy of assimilation, with the hope of changing Indian children into members of white society, Indian children were separated from their parents and sent to boarding schools, breaking the parent-child bond. The policy goal of assimilation was to eradicate all vestiges of Indian culture and indoctrinate them in the ways of the dominant white culture. Under today's norms, this policy might be best described as a program of legalized kidnapping.

Until the 1978 Indian Child Welfare Act, Native American parents lacked the legal right to deny their children's placement in off-reservation schools. (Today's norms for the treatment of children were ignored in 2018 when the Trump administration separated children from their parents for an indeterminate period when migrant families sought political asylum on our southern border.)

The first boarding school for Indian children was established in 1860 by the Bureau of Indian Affairs on the Yakama Indian Reservation in Washington State. The school was well intentioned and focused on improving the quality of education for Indian children. Christianity would be taught with emphasis on the Ten Commandments, the Beatitudes, and the Psalms, as well as academic subjects. Implanting ideas of sin and a sense of guilt, foreign to the Indian culture, were part of the religious teachings. Possessive individualism would be emphasized over the idea of communal ownership. This was contrary to the basic Indian belief that the land was for all people.

Ninety years later, dissatisfied with the progress in assimilating Indians into the mainstream white culture through the boarding schools, the Eisenhower administration implemented its own "progressive termination policy." One hundred tribal reservations were terminated, with disastrous results. The Indians got poorer, their cultural symbols were destroyed, and, as a result, high rates of suicide and drug and alcohol addiction were exacerbated. The Klamath Indians were among the victims of this policy.

Congress authorized the sale of the Klamath Reservation in 1954. The reservation contained valuable forests of ponderosa pine covering thousands of acres, making the Klamath Tribes one of the wealthiest native groups in the United States. With the sale, the federal government no longer recognized the Klamath Tribes, and all health, educational, and other programs administered by the Bureau of Indian Affairs ceased.

Klamath tribal members were offered a choice of retaining their shares in the former reservation property or receiving a cash payment for their land. By 1961, the withdrawing Klamaths had received $91 million for the sale of their shares in the reservation lands. The six hundred remaining members then voted in 1969 to terminate their trust also. As a result of the second sale, those remaining members were scheduled to receive a 1974 distribution of $71 million, or approximately $120,000 for each person. The Klamath tribal members were ill prepared to handle large sums of money, however. They were largely undereducated and lived primarily on subsistence incomes resulting from the sale and lease of reservation lands. Few were employed.

Most of the tribal members resided in or near Klamath Falls, Oregon, an isolated regional economic center whose economy was based upon timber, farming, ranching, and recreation. The city, located in southeast Oregon, had a population of sixteen thousand. Geographical isolation left residents of Klamath Falls captive consumers to local businesses, making comparative pricing (in the pre-internet era) for consumers very difficult. Racial discrimination against Native Americans, coupled with an attitude by many whites that the termination payments represented a gift from the federal government, acted, in many Klamath residents' minds, to excuse consumer abuse of Klamath tribal members.

Before the first tranche of termination payments was received in 1961, the director of the Oregon Office of Indian Education summarized the upcoming distribution crisis in a letter: "It is a foregone conclusion that a high percentage of people will not have the necessary acumen to handle their proceeds judiciously. Frankly, Congress, the Indian Bureau and the State of Oregon will face a fiasco unless the combined resources of all agencies are thrown into the programs to help solve the problems."

Unfortunately, this warning was not taken seriously, and the process of separating the Klamath tribal members from their first distribution of cash began in earnest. From near and far, like a flock of turkey vultures circling overhead for carrion below, dishonest merchants and hucksters circled the town of Klamath Falls, looking to spot unsuspecting Native Americans and separate them from the sale proceeds of their lands. It wasn't long before a combination of unscrupulous business behavior and bad business decisions severely eroded the Klamaths' assets.

In November 1972 a Stanford Law School classmate of mine, Charles Wilkinson—a staff attorney at the Native American Rights Fund, headquartered in Boulder, Colorado, and later a distinguished professor of Native American law at the University of Colorado—contacted our office. He explained that the initial termination payments paid to the Klamaths in 1961 had been exploited by a wide variety of unfair and deceptive practices.

With the impending payment of another $71 million, it looked like history was about to repeat itself. Wilkinson asked our office to help. But FTC enforcement actions after the fact aren't always the best way to address unfair and deceptive business practices. That was certainly the case with the Klamath Indians: they needed a coordinated federal-state program to focus on the forthcoming cash distributions and alter the otherwise to-be-expected tragic outcome. But perhaps we could help. Over the past ten months, we had been holding well-publicized consumer problem fact-finding hearings in our five-state territory. We already knew how to bring the spotlight of publicity to bear on important issues. A highly publicized hearing in Klamath Falls, Oregon, to focus on consumer abuses and the necessary solutions might be exactly what the medicine man called for. Former US Supreme Court justice Louis D. Brandeis explained this strategy best: "Publicity is justly commended as a remedy for social and industrial diseases. Sunlight is said to be the best of disinfectants; electric light the most efficient policeman."

Following Justice Brandeis's advice, we decided to sponsor a high-profile public FTC hearing in Klamath Falls before the 1974 distribution of $71 million to the Klamath tribal members occurred.

The hearing panel consisted of the chief counsel of the consumer protection division of the Oregon attorney general's office, the Klamath County district attorney, a representative of the Klamath Tribes, and me as chair of the panel. The hearing, on December 13, 1972, was packed with spectators and the media. I had been concerned that a hearing in remote Klamath Falls would go unnoticed. That didn't happen. Reporters from Oregon newspapers and television stations were present, anxious to cover the event. People were on the edge of their seats as sixteen witnesses, mostly Indians, described consumer abuses in Klamath Falls, abuses that would have been tolerated nowhere else.

The testimony at the hearing was dramatic and heartrending. The tenor of the testimony can be best summarized from the transcript of the testimony of two Klamath Indians. One witness told the panel, "I think that we have sat back and rather expected the business people or lawyers, the bankers, the real estate agents to deal with us honestly because we feel they are in a reputable business in a reputable community, supposedly, that they would deal fairly with us, and now we know better and we know that actually they do not deal with us honestly and fairly, and actually our money is more valuable to them than to us . . ."

Another witness angrily outlined the historical plight of Indian nations in the United States. "Three times we have been taken, first by beads, then by bullets, and now by politics. I guess we are safe. We have nothing they want but our pride, and they sure as hell can't cash in on that."

With a splash of sensationalism—which we were delighted with—the hearing made the Oregon evening news and was broadcast state-wide on television. The next day, the state's only afternoon newspaper, the Portland-based *Oregon Journal*, carried the story with the front-page banner headline "Klamath Indians 'Cheating Routine.'" As an example of the rip-offs, the paper told of a two-tier pricing system by some Klamath Falls auto dealers: one price for whites, and a sub-stantially higher price for Indians. Also, there was testimony that the Klamath County Bar Association had set guardianship fees several times higher for Indians than for Caucasians.

Once we had mobilized Oregon public opinion, the question was what to do next. I knew that when the publicity died down about the consumer abuse of Klamath tribal members, the problem was likely to reemerge and affect the upcoming distributions from the sale of the reservation lands. So we continued our investigation to fully doc-ument the consumer abuse and economic exploitation of the Klamath Indians. While we knew we could not remedy the underlying social and economic problems, we could be a catalyst and take a leadership position to galvanize protective measures before the second distribu-tion was paid out.

In January 1974 our office published a report—formally adopted by the FTC—titled *Consumer Problems of the Klamath Indians: A Call for Action*. We made four recommendations urging Congress and federal, state, and local governments and agencies to address both consumer abuses and the longer-term social and economic needs of the Klamath Indians. Our most immediate recommendation was for a congressio-nal appropriation and private grants to fund a consumer counseling staff with experience in investments to assist the tribal members before the second distribution payments were received. We eventually helped secure $500,000 for financial counseling to tribal members, thereby mitigating another tragedy in the treatment of Native Americans.

***

Despite some improvements in the economic and social conditions of America's roughly five million Native Americans—including a few small tribes benefiting disproportionately from their tribe's ownership of gambling casinos because of their proximity to highly populated areas—Native Americans are among the poorest and unhealthiest of all communities. Their plight today remains an unsolved political-cultural quagmire.

The *Seattle Times* reported on December 18, 2018, in a story headlined "Jesuits sent abusive priests to return to Gonzaga campus," that the plight of Northwest Native Americans is still unfolding. From the early 1980s until 2010, the *Times* reported that that Native American villages and Indian reservations in the Jesuit Oregon province—an area encompassing Oregon, Washington, Alaska, Idaho, and Montana—were subjected to outrages of sexual abuse by Jesuit priests. The province had ninety-two Jesuits accused of criminal activity during this period, a figure far exceeding any other Jesuit province in the country.

PSYCHIC SURGEONS

A bizarre and heartrending type of consumer abuse—covered extensively in national media—occurred in January 1974: the case of the Philippine psychic surgeons. It was the first case in the nation brought under the FTC's newly acquired federal court injunctive powers, authorized under Senator Jackson's amendment to the 1973 Alaska pipeline bill. This case also required a very creative and unusual enforcement approach by our office.

It all started in the 1960s with airline pilots from Trans World Airlines (TWA) and Pan American Airways (Pan Am) who flew between the Pacific Northwest and the Philippines. The Philippines, formerly a US colony and a mostly devout Catholic nation—where divorce is, even as I write this in 2018, illegal—had become a center for "psychic surgery," a procedure that promised miraculous cures for almost any ailment. The pilots—mesmerized by what they had witnessed, with breathless amazement—brought tales of these "miracles" back to the United States, and seriously ill people started to consider flights to the Philippines to visit a psychic surgeon.

The practice first appeared in the Spiritualist communities of the Philippines around 1950. Psychic surgery came to the attention of the American public with the 1959 publication of *Into the Strange Unknown*. The authors, Ron Ormond and Ormond McGill called the practice "fourth dimensional surgery," and concluded that "[we] still don't know what to think; but we have motion pictures to show it wasn't the work of any normal magician, and could very well be just what the Filipinos said it was—a miracle of God performed by a fourth dimensional surgeon."

Although psychic surgery procedures varied somewhat between practitioners, there were common practices. The surgeries were often performed in a "clinic" staffed with multiple psychic surgeons, who took the patient into a small room with a single bed and, often, a Bible noticeably placed on a nearby nightstand.

With the patient lying on his or her back on the bed, the practitioner, after first swabbing the area clean with cotton and alcohol, pressed the tips of his fingers into the patient's abdomen, kneading the area, creating a depression that, to the onlooker's amazement, suddenly filled with blood. The practitioner's hands appeared to penetrate the patient's body and extract organic matter said to be the diseased tissue. The area was then wiped clean of blood, with the patient's skin amazingly showing no wounds or scars.

To cash in on the medical tourism opportunity presented by this phenomenon, TWA and Pan Am, along with several West Coast travel agencies, started to promote trips to the Philippines for psychic surgery. Beginning in the 1970s, travel agencies in Oregon and Washington widely advertised these trips through newspaper advertisements and brochures. The brochures were printed and paid for with the cooperation of Northwest Airlines and Pan Am. The travel agencies also rented hotel conference rooms to show films of the procedure to packed audiences and provided testimonials of people who claimed to have been cured of a variety of diseases. Soon the rush was on: over one thousand people, many incurably ill, booked $1,000 travel packages to the capital of the Philippines, Manila, the location of the largest congregation of psychic surgeons.

Complaints about the fraudulent nature of psychic surgery first came to our attention with pleas for help coming from Seattle Children's Hospital. The hospital lamented that, desperate for a cure, a number of parents had discontinued their child's cancer therapies and had taken their child to the Philippines for psychic surgery. The surgery was unquestionably a fraud and life-threatening to the health of the children, the hospital officials said. We were urged to take immediate action to help avoid certain tragic consequences.

I was stumped. Without any idea of how to address a consumer problem in a foreign country, where we had no jurisdiction, we opened a preliminary investigation anyway. We believed the practice to be clearly fraudulent. The results of our investigation were alarming. We learned that not only children but also many adults suffering from terminal illnesses, or with chronic or permanent conditions like multiple sclerosis, blindness, and paralysis, in a last-ditch search for a cure, had taken tours to the Philippines for psychic surgery. At times psychic surgeons manipulated cancerous tumors with adverse results. We needed to act promptly. But what action was possible? The FTC had no jurisdiction over consumer fraud in the Philippines.

We couldn't prove psychic surgery actually fraudulent until we discovered how it was done. And because there were religious overtones associated with the procedure, any US enforcement was potentially tricky, both constitutionally and politically. Did the First Amendment protect this arguably "religious" faith healing? Pentecostal churches sometimes involve spontaneous healings, where parishioners throw away their crutches and walk away unassisted. Was this a scientifically inexplicable cure based on religious faith that qualified under Catholic Church doctrine as a miracle? How were claims from this procedure different from the claims of other miraculous church healings that occur at the center of some of the main Catholic pilgrimages, like Lourdes in France and Fatima in Portugal? (At Lourdes, as of 2018, Catholic bishops have recognized seventy miraculous cures.) Was this "surgery," because of a placebo effect, nevertheless an effective cure regardless of its deceptive nature?

Our first thought was to contact the US State Department and ask them to request an investigation by the Philippine government, long an ally of the US government. The Philippine president, Ferdinand Marcos, was both a fervent anti-communist and a corrupt right-wing dictator. No matter: the US government at the time was an equal-opportunity supporter of anti-communist regimes run by corrupt right-wing dictators.

The State Department informed us that the Philippine government had no interest in pursuing the matter. Psychic surgery was considered a native religious practice that people had the option to participate in or not. Part of the problem, the State Department surmised—off the record—was that psychic surgeons paid kickbacks to President Marcos.

We were back to square one. If we couldn't shut the practice down in the Philippines, the only remaining option was to stop the US advertising that promoted psychic surgery in the Philippines. For fast action—using the FTC's newly acquired federal court injunctive powers—an injunction against the travel agencies promoting the trips seemed the best option, but we needed witnesses to help us meet the legal test for an injunction: the possibility of irreparable harm and likelihood of success on the merits.

Since over a thousand people had already participated in these tours, we were able to interview a number of people in the Seattle area who had been to the Philippines, witnessed psychic surgery, and felt they were defrauded. Many were willing to provide affidavits or live testimony in support of an injunction. *At last this case is starting to come together,* I believed.

Then our search for witnesses came up with a tantalizing opportunity to have an actual psychic surgeon testify at the court hearing. By chance, a Philippine psychic surgeon was temporarily practicing in Portland, Oregon—and, therefore, subject to the federal court's subpoena power. We felt certain that the man could be easily impeached on the witness stand, which would greatly bolster our case. We immediately dispatched a federal marshal to serve him. Unfortunately for us, the psychic surgeon got wind of the subpoena and fled to the Yakama Indian Reservation near Yakima, Washington. In an unexpected turn of events that astonished us, the Yakama Indians—sensitive and protective of their own shamanistic healing practices—granted the psychic surgeon sanctuary on the reservation and refused to give him up. We then had to scratch a potential star witness and continue our search.

Time was running out. Because a number of tours were scheduled for imminent departure, including a flight of several hundred people headed for the Philippines from San Francisco within a week, we had to move fast. We wanted to warn these passengers that psychic surgery was fraudulent and encourage them to cancel their trips.

We immediately petitioned the federal court in Seattle for a temporary restraining order (TRO), seeking to warn those signed up for Philippine tours that psychic surgery was fraudulent. The TRO sought to require three West Coast travel agencies based in Seattle and San Francisco to warn passengers leaving on flights to the Philippines that "psychic surgery . . . is not an actual surgical operation, no incision is made, and diseased tissue is not removed from the human body." The *Washington Post* proclaimed in a headline, "FTC Hits Psychic Surgery, 'Spiritual Pilgrimages' to Philippines Under Attack."

After reviewing our affidavits and a court hearing, the judge granted the TRO and authorized the sending of warning telegrams to all members of a San Francisco–based tour scheduled to fly to the Philippines the next day. This became the first TRO awarded to the FTC by a US district court under the FTC's newly acquired authority. FTC chairman Calvin Collier was delighted with the result and congratulated our lead office trial attorney, Greg Colvin, and our office on a "glowing" performance.

We had high hopes that the passengers would heed the warning in our telegram. But to our dismay, we learned that of over two hundred persons on the flight, not one had canceled. Feedback from the tour members highlighted the nature of the problem: Most of the travelers had long given up on conventional medicine, and many of them felt they had no hope. Many were willing to pursue the proverbial needle in a haystack on the slimmest chance that a cure existed outside of mainstream medicine; others were suspicious that the court order was a conspiracy by the American Medical Association and the US government to stifle alternative medicine.

After the TRO, the federal court later granted a preliminary injunction. We then filed an FTC administrative complaint, transferring jurisdiction from the federal court to the FTC. The FTC administrative law judge flew to Seattle and held a hearing at the federal courthouse to decide the case on the merits. For the case to be really effective and discourage people from going to the Philippines, we needed to come up with additional evidence proving that the procedure was fakery; otherwise, many US residents would continue to seek psychic surgery. How could we prove something was fraudulent without actual proof of the fraud? We needed expert witnesses. Luckily, we found them.

In a dramatic surgery-focused Scopes Monkey Trial–type hearing, pitting faith, science, and common sense against each other, a procession of forty-eight witnesses were called to testify over a two-week period. The testimony was riveting and often dramatic. Thirty-three witnesses testified for the FTC and fifteen for the travel companies.

During the hearing, there was a particularly bizarre federal courtroom moment when one of the Seattle attorneys representing the travel agencies suddenly held up a mason jar filled with a clear liquid preservative and what appeared to be blackened tissue. He said that the jar contained his diseased heart valve. I was stunned as the attorney claimed in open court that this tissue had been removed by a psychic surgeon in the Philippines and that he had been free of heart disease ever since.

Unbelievable, bizarre behavior, yes, but it wasn't evidence, and the judge was not impressed.

One of the FTC's first witnesses was Richard Douglas of Seattle. He said he and his wife spent their life savings of more than $2,000 to go to the Philippines with the hope that the psychic surgery would cure his wife of cancer—including a neck tumor that doctors said could not be removed. A psychic surgeon performed the procedure and removed the "cancerous tissue." Mr. Douglas took the tissue from the psychic surgeon and put it in a bottle of preservative. Later, he asked a Seattle pathologist to analyze it. The "tumor" was found to be a segment of "what appears to be a small bowel . . . of a small animal." Because of the expense of the trip to the Philippines, he and his wife were now having a hard time paying for regular medical treatment. "If

I knew what I know now before I went on the trip, I never would have gone to the Philippines," he said.

This was great evidence, but how had the sleight of hand been performed?

Our next witnesses, an extrasensory perception instructor from Iowa and a professional magician from Arizona, answered that question. What better way to expose fake magic than with fellow magicians who could explain the deception?

Our first magician witness was Donald Wright. After his father-in-law appeared to have been cured by psychic surgery, Wright, an instructor in extrasensory perception, went to Manila to learn how to perform psychic surgery himself. Wright estimated that he subsequently performed twenty-five to thirty surgeries, but he became convinced that the patients weren't being helped. He then made numerous attempts to alert others of the fakery involved.

To demonstrate the sleight of hand involved, we asked the judge to allow Mrs. Wright, Donald's wife, to lie down on the counsel table and expose her abdomen to provide a courtroom demonstration of how the surgery was performed. The administrative law judge, Daniel Hanscom, responded sternly, "Not in my courtroom." He thought that such a demonstration in the imposing, high-ceilinged Seattle federal courtroom would be unseemly.

Improvising on the spot, Mr. Wright placed on the counsel table—instead of his wife—a towel covered with a nonpermeable surface as a substitute for a human abdomen. He then created a depression in the material with his left fist. With his right hand, he dipped a wad of cotton into a pan of water and ran it over the depressed area as if to clean it. Next, unseen to the human eye, he palmed a cotton wad "bullet" containing blood and animal tissue covered by a membrane. With both hands now in the depressed area, he pierced the bullet with his fingernail to release the blood, creating the appearance of an open, bleeding wound. From the bloody "wound," he then withdrew animal tissue from the bullet in such a way that the tissue appeared to have come from inside the simulated abdomen. Lastly, he wiped the area clean with fresh cotton, leaving no trace of any "incision."

Donald and Carol Wright demonstrated the sleight-of-hand they learned in the Philippines before Daniel Hanscom, an administrative-law judge.—Staff illustration by Steve McKinstry.

Courtesy of Seattle Times.

Our second magician witness, Robert Gurtler, performed magic acts in Las Vegas under the stage name Andre Kole. He had witnessed psychic surgery the previous year while in the Philippines. "The Filipino faith healers," he said, were "the most fantastic artists I've ever seen." He went on to say: "Their sleight-of-hand ability is better than 95 percent of the magicians I've seen operate anywhere in the world. I was shaken. I thought I was witnessing the supernatural." But after observing several surgeries, he detected the fakery. "Some of the cleverest trickery I had ever seen. . . . I could do any of it [the psychic surgery] without any clothes on at all [to hide the bullet]."

Following the hearing, Judge Hanscom wrote a seventy-five-page decision in which he described psychic surgery as "pure and unmitigated fakery." He concluded in the vernacular: "More bluntly, the 'surgical operations' . . . [performed] with the bare hands are simply phony."

The *Seattle P-I* trumpeted our success in obtaining federal court injunctions, including in the Philippine psychic surgeon case, by running a long story under a banner headline: "New Life for U.S. Agency: FTC Finally Armed to Defend Consumer." I explained to the *P-I*: "Congress has given the FTC a brand-new box of dynamite, and we're beginning to light some fuses."

***

Psychic surgery still thrives in the Philippines, but it is no longer overtly promoted in the United States. From time to time, psychic surgeons still make their way to remote areas of this country to ply their trade. One Filipino man, Placido Palitayan, was arrested in 1989 in the small town of Colville, Washington, not far from the Colville Indian Reservation. On the day of his arrest, he was scheduled to see about 130 patients over two days at seventy-five dollars each. A bucket near the house containing blood and tissue that purportedly had been removed from patients was found to contain tissue from a bovine animal. He was charged with theft and the unlicensed practice of medicine. Palitayan was known to have treated at least twelve hundred people in the Colville area during the six or seven visits he made from the Philippines between 1984 and 1989.

In 1984 a sensational celebrity case of psychic surgery made US tabloid headlines: comedian Andy Kaufman, who hit the mainstream playing Latka Gravas—a mechanic of indeterminate national origin—in the sitcom *Taxi*, was diagnosed with a rare lung cancer. He traveled to the Philippines for six weeks for psychic surgery treatments. The psychic surgeon treating him claimed to have removed several large cancerous tumors, and Kaufman declared that he was cancer-free. He died from renal failure as a result of metastatic lung cancer two months after returning to the United States. In the 1999 movie *Man on the Moon*, based on Kaufman's life and starring Jim Carrey, during the psychic surgery operation, Kaufman notices the sleight of hand and starts laughing in seeming despair. In the next scene, he is seen dead at his funeral.

WASEM'S DRUGSTORE

The FTC developed corrective advertising in the 1970s as a method of putting the market back in balance. Here's the theory: When a company engages in false advertising and is ordered to stop, unless something more is done, the false message lingers in the marketplace, and consumers may continue to be deceived by the lingering deception— unless the company runs corrective ads. Cliff Wasem's drugstore became the unlikely recipient of the FTC's "toughest yet" corrective advertising order of the Seattle Regional Office, according to a headline in *Advertising Age* on February 22, 1974.

Wasem's Rexall drug and general merchandise store in Clarkston, Washington—1970 population, about six thousand—is located in a lightly populated, remote southeast corner of Washington State, across the Snake River from Idaho. The drugstore has a classic old-style breakfast and lunch counter that has been open continuously since the store was founded in the 1920s. The early-bird breakfast special is still reportedly available today for $2.99: "One egg, as you like it, one pancake, and a choice of sausage or bacon."

Thiamine, or vitamin B, was subject to a craze for nutritional perfection in the 1930s and 1940s. The *New York Times* said thiamine was "vitalizing" and provided "charm, composure, and good digestion." In ensuing years, a raft of B-vitamin products came out with various sets of claims to improve the nation's well-being. *Vitamania*—a term coined in 1942—continued unabated, creating an empire of poorly regulated and often pointless nutritional supplements worth billions of dollars. (Nearly $133 billion in supplements were sold in the US in 2016.) By 1970, the stage was set for Wasem's to join the gold rush. It developed its own store brand of nutritional supplements: Wasem's Super B Vitamins.

Cliff Wasem, the proprietor of the drugstore started by his father, advertised Wasem's Super B Vitamins in local newspapers and on regional television with the enthusiasm of an old-time snake-oil sales-man. The advertising, often starring Cliff Wasem himself, made a wide variety of health claims, including "Super B works, builds up your blood and nerves." Contrary to the requirements of FTC advertising law, none of the health claims were substantiated.

The conventional wisdom of the scientific community was that most people had no need to supplement their diet with nutritional supple-ments and that no evidence existed for the claims of cures often made. The Northwest regional office of the Food and Drug Administration (FDA)—lacking enforcement power over nonprescription drug advertising—wanted us to investigate Wasem's vitamin B advertising claims. We told the FDA that the matter was local, with far too small an economic impact to justify the use of our limited resources.

But that was not the end of it. A few weeks passed, and I received a phone call from the exasperated regional director of the FDA. "You won't believe this," she said. "Now Cliff Wasem is claiming in his advertising that his ads are true because the FDA has approved them."

Wasem was a member of the national council of the John Birch Society and held leadership positions with the Asotin County Republicans. Like many eastern Washington conservatives, he didn't like government interference in business, particularly the federal gov-ernment interfering in his business. But for us it was too late for him to retreat and call it a day. He had crossed the Rubicon. One simply does not willfully represent, untruthfully, that the federal government has approved a health-related product when it hasn't. He would have to pay for his transgressions. This situation was ripe for a corrective advertising order.

Following a protracted negotiation with our office, Wasem agreed to sign an FTC consent order. It required that 25 percent of all adver-tising for Wasem's Super B Vitamins during a one-year period be for corrective ads. In the first FTC case to require corrective advertising on television, the order also required Wasem to drop the word *super* from its brand name and place seven sixty-second corrective spots on consecutive days on the same TV stations at the same approximate time of day used for the previous misleading ads. In the audio portion of the TV ads, Wasem was to say the following:

This advertisement is run pursuant of an order of the FTC. I have pre-
viously been advertising Wasem's Super B Vitamins, and have made
various claims, which are erroneous and misleading.

Contrary to what I told you, Super B will not make you feel better
nor make you better to live with nor work better on the job. There is
no need for most people to supplement their diets with vitamins and
minerals. Excess dosages over the recommended daily adult require-
ment of most vitamins will be flushed through the body and be of no
benefit whatsoever.

Contrary to my previous ad, neither the FDA nor the FTC has rec-
ommended Super B or approved our prior claims. Super B Vitamins
are sold on a money-back guarantee, so if you are not fully satisfied,
then return them to me at Wasem's Rexall Drugstore in Clarkston for
a refund.

Before the consent order was final, there was a firestorm of criticism against it. *Advertising Age*, the main national trade publication
for the advertising industry, opposed the order in a lead editorial headlined "FTC 'cure' is worse," claiming that the corrective ad had as much
hyperbole as Wasem's original copy:

We are not so sure this description of the role of vitamins and miner-
als is so noncontroversial that it should be incorporated into an FTC-
approved corrective ad, disseminated to the public as authoritative
truth. Any way you look at it, the settlement which the FTC secured
from Mr. Wasem cuts so much new ground for diet supplement mar-
keters and for advertising generally that it is of considerably more
than local interest.

Other commentators railed that the FTC was picking on a
small-business owner who couldn't afford to defend himself. The enemies of corrective advertising were piling on. Would the FTC stand up
to the criticism and support the Seattle office by accepting our consent
order? I was really concerned that the commissioners would buckle
under the avalanche of advertising-industry criticism.

As I feared, the commissioners, ever sensitive to criticism from the press that the FTC was overreaching in the exercise of its regulatory authority, began to get cold feet and decided to reconsider their preliminary approval of our consent order. But FTC commissioner Mayo Thompson, a Texas lawyer known for his colorful language, saved the day, saying in a memorandum to other members of the commission:

> *The situation is this: We have a tough sheriff out in Seattle. He caught a rustler in the act, gave him a fast but fair hearing, and imposed a sentence that eminently fit the crime. Then the townspeople started getting a lot of criticism from the eastern press about how "harshly" it had dealt with the varmint.* (Advertising Age *shed some editorial tears of crocodile size.) The folks got scared, fired the sheriff, and were all set to let the rustler out of the pokey. Whereupon the good guy sheriff stood his ground, shamed the city fathers for the color of the stripe down their backbones, and won their support once more.*
>
> *I think the Seattle sheriff was entirely right—as does Staff. Therefore, I move that we accept the consent order as originally submitted by Seattle.*

The commissioners then voted unanimously to accept the consent order.

Shortly after their acceptance of the final order, one of my staff told me that Cliff Wasem had started to run the required corrective advertising on television. I was relieved to hear that this highly controversial matter was finally concluded.

"There's one problem," my staff member said, sounding rather alarmed.

"What's that?" I inquired, fearing that this case was never going to go away.

"You won't believe this, but Cliff Wasem is following the corrective TV ad with his own TV ad. He is saying that 'big government FTC' is making him run the corrective ad against his own wishes and beliefs."

"For Christ's sake," I said, "don't tell me that," not believing my ears.

"What do you want to do about it?"

"Absolutely nothing," I said, with a note of irritation. I was tired of playing a game of whack-a-mole with Mr. Wasem.

And that's the saga of one of the toughest corrective ads ever ordered by the FTC.

CHAPTER FOURTEEN

THE MOUNTAIN, THE WOODSHED, THE FARM

Mount Rainier, an active volcano, with a summit elevation of 14,411 feet, is the highest mountain in the Northwest. It is considered to be one of the most dangerous volcanoes in the world and is the most glaciated and topographically prominent mountain in the contiguous United States. The mountain dominates the Seattle skyline with mesmerizing beauty and can be seen from afar in both eastern and western Washington. If you live anywhere in sight of this mountain, you may want to climb it—not to dominate the mountain in some sort of misguided triumph, but to honor it. Considered sacred by Indians and called Mount Tahoma—"the mountain that was God"—Mount Rainier has a life force all its own, both dangerous and beautiful, and fully worthy of worship.

After six months as the regional director of the FTC in Seattle, I wanted to press forward with my plan to bond with the Washington, DC, headquarters. What better way than by inviting the director of regional operations, Al Cortese, on his next visit to Seattle, to join me in an expedition to summit Mount Rainier.

If you are in good hiking shape, the weather is good, and you are not prone to altitude sickness, summiting Mount Rainier is not overly

difficult. Although climbers are roped together at the higher elevations—where crampons and an ice ax are essential safety equipment
in the snow and ice—the climb on the main route is not considered
technical; more often it is described as a long, slow slog, punctuated
by rest steps at altitude. But the mountain is deceptive and can be
unforgiving. More than a hundred people have died trying to climb
it—including one of the world's best mountain climbers. Leading a
climb on Mount Rainier, legendary Northwest mountain climber Willi
Unsoeld, a member of the first American expedition to successfully
summit Mount Everest in 1963, died in an icefall that broke off a glacier, along with one of his climbing students, in 1979.

Al Cortese responded enthusiastically to my invitation. Since
Washington, DC, is a former flatland malarial swamp, mountain and
hill deprived, Cortese saw this as an interesting physical challenge and
an opportunity to get out of the humid and sweltering July weather in
DC. For a climbing companion, I paired him with Harrison Sheppard,
a former FTC attorney in DC, now with the Seattle office. For my
climbing partner, there was only one person I really wanted on this
adventure: Dave Pender, my roommate and parachuting buddy from
law school. Later, Dave left a law firm in Los Angeles to reunite with
me at the FTC in Seattle. Eager for another adventure, Dave didn't have
to be asked twice.

In late July 1972 the four of us made the two-hour drive to Mount
Rainier and spent the night at Paradise Inn, at 5,400 feet of elevation. I
had arranged with RMI Expeditions, a guide service run by the identical-
twin Whittaker brothers, Jim and Lou, to lead us up the mountain.
(Jim Whittaker had joined the pantheon of famous alpinists in 1963,
when he became the first American to summit Mount Everest.) A full
day's safety training on the mountain above Paradise was required by
RMI, during which we focused on the use of the ice ax to self-arrest in
the event of a fall.

The day following our training—with eager anticipation and some
trepidation about our untested alpine abilities—the climbers separated
into five guided groups for the trek to Camp Muir, a high-altitude base
camp at 10,188 feet of elevation. Dave and I were assigned to one team,
and Al and Harrison to another. The temperature was warm and the

sun was shining; it was a splendid day to begin the climb. The RMI guide leading our group, Marty Hoey, an attractive, free-spirited twenty-two-year-old woman, had been the camp cook at Muir, and this was her first opportunity to work as a guide. Both Dave and I found her presence a great motivator, helping us to maintain a brisk pace on the four-hour climb in beautiful, warm, sunny weather to Camp Muir from Paradise.

At Camp Muir we had a campers' dinner and spent the night in the bunkhouse before striking out for the summit. Because rising temperatures increase the risk of snow avalanches, glacier icefalls, and snow bridges over crevasses failing, our rope teams had to depart at 3:00 a.m.—well before sunrise—when the snow conditions were favorable. The objective was to summit and get back down to Camp Muir by noon the same day. Although the night was clear and the moon was shining, we turned on our head lanterns to see the trail and fastened the crampons onto our boots for secure footing on the ice and snow.

We began the climb taking the most direct route to the summit by way of Disappointment Cleaver and Ingraham Glacier. The six o'clock sunrise was beautiful. It looked like it might be a glorious day with fantastic views awaiting us at the summit. I was excited to permanently capture the view. Somewhat incongruously, in my pack, next to my toothbrush that I sawed in half to lighten the weight, I had my four-pound Kodak Super 8 film camera ready to record the view at the summit.

Just after sunrise, Marty Hoey received a warning on her radio that the weather was deteriorating above 12,000 feet, and only the strongest two of the five rope teams would be allowed to try for the summit. Our rope team was selected as one of the two strongest teams based upon the speed that we climbed from Paradise to Muir the day before. (Of course, the only reason we were fast was that we were trying to impress Marty.) Al Cortese's team, which spent more time enjoying the scenic views, was slower to arrive at Camp Muir and wasn't designated a strong team. They returned with two other teams to Camp Muir, denied an opportunity to try for the summit. Statistically our experience was typical: the average summit success rate of summer climbers is only 51 percent.

Maybe Cortese was lucky his team wasn't selected. At different altitudes, the weather on Rainier can vary from sunshine at 10,000 feet to storm conditions at higher elevations. We were soon to experience this phenomenon. As we climbed above 12,000 feet, the weather suddenly changed. Snow began to fall heavily and the wind howled. We had to brace ourselves to remain standing. Soon we were in a blizzard and total whiteout conditions, with no visibility whatsoever. I was rapidly getting concerned.

Eventually we found ourselves stranded in the midst of a snowfield, where orange bamboo wands with flags were supposed to guide us around a series of crevasses—deep fissures in the snowfield, often covered by unstable snow bridges. One mistake in this snowfield could take our whole team down a hole to an icy prison. But with the wind and the heavy snow, the wands marking safe passage were nowhere in sight. Surrounded by crevasses with yawning mouths ready to swallow us, we were lost and now beyond concerned.

The snowdrifts were thigh high, and several times we all had to self-arrest with our ice axes when a team member slipped and fell. This climb was turning out to be far more than we had bargained for. I wondered if Dave—who was behind me at the end of the rope—was as worried as I was. Everyone had their heads down to keep the driving snow off their faces and to survey closely the ground ahead. No one was talking. I remembered that I survived unscathed from a hurricane at sea; I survived unscathed from jumping out of an airplane; I survived unscathed from serving in the military in the Vietnam War; and I survived going over a dam on a river on top of a man on an air mattress. *Hell, I can do this*, I convinced myself.

Our packs contain no shelter or sleeping bags, I thought. There was no feeling of impending doom, but I think we all wondered how it was going to end. On her first trip as a guide, Marty Hoey and her team of novice climbers were in big trouble.

Hoey stopped the rope team to assess the situation.

"Marty, what are our options?" I asked, hoping there were some good ones.

"I'll radio base camp and let them know our position," she answered, surprisingly unfazed. "Our best option is to go forward and climb above this storm."

Calmly and coolly, she led us carefully through the snowfield as she worked her way up the mountain, testing the snow ahead of her

Bill summits Mount Rainer holding his frozen movie camera.

with a long pole to see if a crevasse lurked beneath our feet. Our team followed Hoey in lockstep, still unable to see more than a few feet ahead. Finally, after about an hour, the fierce storm abated as suddenly as it had started, and we were able to locate the wands and continue up the last 1,500 feet to the summit.

Summiting was anticlimactic. Where were the magnificent views of the Puget Sound? It was the end of July, 25 degrees above zero; the winds were 20 miles an hour, and the visibility was less than 40 feet. I tried to take pictures with my movie camera, but it was useless. The camera was frozen.

We climbed the mountain high, but disappointingly, there was nothing to see and record on the other side.

Coming down the mountain, I was exhausted, mentally and physically, but also ecstatic that Dave and I had summited under difficult conditions.[1] By late in the afternoon, we had completed our descent back to Paradise. Al Cortese said he had enjoyed the hike to Camp Muir but was disheartened that he was not allowed to summit the mountain. The fact that Dave and I had summited, and Cortese did not, did nothing to further our relationship with Washington, DC, but my staff enjoyed the story of our adventure. They considered it further evidence of the Seattle office's superiority over Washington, DC. This super-competitive attitude would eventually cause us big trouble.

＊

Marty Hoey went on to climb Mount Rainier over a hundred times and also led expeditions on Alaska's Denali. In an attempt to become the first American woman to summit Mount Everest, the tallest of all mountains at more than 29,000 feet, she accompanied the Whittaker twins and Jim Wickwire, another famous American alpinist and a Seattle lawyer, on a seventeen-person expedition to Nepal. In 1982, at age thirty-one, at an altitude of 26,600 feet, her lifeline buckle suddenly became unhitched, and Hoey plunged over the edge of the Great Couloir on Mount Everest to her death, falling 6,000 feet into a crevasse.

Marty Hoey's body was never recovered. Expedition leader Lou Whittaker said she was probably the world's best female high-altitude mountaineer at the time of her death.

THE WOODSHED

To my consternation, the relationship between our office and the Washington, DC, staff continued to deteriorate. DC had multiple layers of very bright young attorneys reviewing our cases, including Robert Reich, the diminutive director of policy planning, who had been a Rhodes scholar with Bill Clinton and would become President Clinton's secretary of labor and then an academic and political pundit often seen on national television.

Distressingly for our work, however, the DC review system had no standards of timeliness, and our cases often languished. Our goal in the Seattle office was transformational. We wanted to convert the FTC regional offices into an effective fighting force championing the consumer, from the bottom up if necessary. To accomplish this task, we would embrace the ethos that it is better to beg for forgiveness than ask for permission—a dangerous and risky strategy, because bureaucratic power is seldom transferred willingly, and obedience to hierarchy is expected.

We found ourselves in an odd situation. We had top-of-the-class legal and investigative talent, but like the other regional offices, we were treated as second-class citizens. "All good ideas emanate from Washington, DC, the seat of all knowledge; if you were really any good, you would be at the headquarters"—that was the conventional wisdom of the DC bureaucracy.

A bit of chaos and conflict can spur creativity and innovation, but too much can create problems. Friction escalated between our office and the reviewing staff at headquarters. Rather than trying to artfully finesse the bureaucracy to get things done, a few of my staff members were overly aggressive in their contact with headquarters and qualified for a time-out in charm school. But I, too, was guilty of pushing the boundaries of DC tolerance. By using the bully pulpit where the FTC had not yet announced a policy, I stepped on a few toes too. As a result, our relationship with the DC staff could be best described as strained. It was an untrusting marriage: neither side thought the other side had its best interests at heart. East Coast is East Coast and West Coast is West Coast, and the twain shall never meet.

The irony in our situation was that everyone else, except the DC bureaucracy, loved what we were doing—except, of course, for the hapless recipients of our enforcement efforts. The media, consumer groups, Senator Magnuson and the Senate commerce committee staff, Senator Jackson, and the FTC commissioners themselves thought we were doing a wonderful job. But the executive staff in DC saw us as too independent, a maverick office difficult to control. And they were not to be trifled with.

One day, sometime in 1973, I received a curt telephone message to report to the executive director of the FTC, Basil Mezines, in DC, within the next two days to review my performance. Naively, I thought at first I was going to receive a good-performance award. Then it dawned on me that I might get fired for insubordination. In the pit of my stomach, I had a queasy feeling and a dark foreboding that I had miscalculated and been overzealous in our pursuit of the public interest. Had we been consumed by hubris and flown too close to the sun? Were we about to crash and burn? Was I going to be held to account? I asked Lola McClintock, our office administrator, to arrange a flight for me to DC the next day. She said that only first-class seats were available on the one direct flight from Seattle to Washington, DC. *If I'm going to be fired, I'm going out in style,* I thought. "Book me on first class," I said.

Arriving in Washington the next day, I stayed, as usual, at the Mayflower Hotel, a place where J. Edgar Hoover and his assistant director and alter ego, Clyde Tolson, daily had lunch and discussed the most salacious gossip of the day—overheard on the bureau's political wiretaps. To clear my head and steady my nerves for my meeting, the following morning I put on my running clothes and headed out the door for a four-mile jog that would take me past the White House and the reflecting pools on the National Mall. As I ran past the reflecting pool at the Lincoln Memorial, I looked up at Abe's statue for inspiration and realized how my predicament paled next to the challenges he and countless others had faced. *Perhaps this won't be so bad,* I hoped.

In the early afternoon I was ushered into Mezines's office, where Al Cortese, the regional office director, and Mezines, the executive director and top staffer in the agency, were waiting. There were no hellos. Mezines greeted me sternly, saying, "Bill, sit down," and pointed to a chair. I immediately knew I was not going to get an award. It was a trip instead to the woodshed.

While Cortese sat silently in the background, Mezines perched on the edge of his desk, barely three feet in front of me, waved his finger at me, and began to scold. For thirty minutes I was read the riot act. The main offense: the Seattle regional office wasn't paying proper attention to the instructions and formal procedures required by the staff in DC. As the Seattle regional director, I needed to crack down on my errant staff and have them show more respect for the chain of command. And by the way, I should stop poaching students at nationally recognized law schools like Harvard. National law school recruitment is the province of DC, not the regional offices. "Hereafter you are limited to recruiting in your own region," Mezines said with a steely gaze.

I didn't say much during the lecture. I thought of saying, "I'm guilty," and looking as contrite as I could—apologize, like I often did in the air force, when I regularly violated protocol—but I couldn't bring myself to do it. Was it game over?

I felt like I was trapped in a modern-day Greek tragedy, like Prometheus, about to be bound to a rock for overreaching. I was becoming despondent at my prospects. Would an intervention occur to end my punishment? Would someone, like my protector, the centaur Chiron—first among the centaurs, and the astrological symbol of my birth—step forward to save me like Chiron and his buddy Hercules stepped forward to save Prometheus?

After I was excused from Mezines's office, I decided to observe the commissioners' weekly meeting, where they review and discuss enforcement actions, which this week would include one matter my office had on the agenda. The meeting took place in a large conference room at FTC headquarters. In the center of the room was a huge oval conference table where the commissioners and their assistants sat, with the chairman at the table's head. Along the interior walls of the room were armless chairs occupied by twenty to thirty staff members who either had cases on the agenda; were there to observe or divine, by osmosis, the direction of the commission; or had nothing else to do. Among the regular attendees, I immediately noticed my two antagonists from the woodshed, Mezines and Cortese.

Among the FTC commissioners in attendance was Elizabeth "Liddy" Hanford, a pleasant-looking and well-coiffed lady with a southern accent and a Harvard Law degree. In 1975 she would marry Bob Dole, who would become the 1996 Republican presidential nominee and a longtime Senate majority leader.[2] I had recently met with Commissioner Hanford when she visited our office in Seattle, and we later entertained her with a Seattle staff office party. She was decidedly impressed with my staff and the enthusiasm of our office.

My punishment was short-lived as Commissioner Hanford—in my Chiron-Hercules imagined moment—interrupted the meeting as soon as she spotted me in the conference room and rescued me. "Bill, I am so glad to see you again! Welcome," she said, with her sweet drawl and southern charm fully on display. Then she began effusively to praise our office as a model for other regional offices. Amazingly, the compliments flowed around the room as other commissioners, in lockstep, including the chairman, chimed in and heaped even more praise on our office.

I looked over at Basil Mezines, who, with his eyes cast downward at the floor, appeared to be glowering, the color rising in his neck. I imagined billows of smoke coming out of his ears. Acknowledging the commissioners' accolades, I broke into a big smile and raised my hand and waved to them in a mental victory lap.

On my return to Seattle the next day, Lola, showing obvious concern in her voice, said, "How did it go?"

"It went swimmingly, absolutely swimmingly," I answered, fully realizing that I had almost drowned.

***

In February 1973, Miles Kirkpatrick resigned from the FTC to return to his law practice. There was speculation at the time that the Nixon administration had pushed him out because of his unresponsiveness to political influence. Lewis "Lew" Engman, a tall, handsome, youthful-looking man with a broad brow and deep-set, piercing blue eyes, replaced Kirkpatrick. Engman was another Harvard Law graduate, who previously had practiced antitrust law in his hometown of Grand Rapids, Michigan, and in Washington, DC. Before his appointment to the FTC, Engman had been the assistant director of the White House Domestic Council. Highly qualified, yes, but Miles Kirkpatrick was a tough act to follow.

As FTC chairman, Engman rose to the challenge and pushed for greater competition in medical services and prescription drugs. He soon established a reputation as a strong consumer advocate. He liked our office, and he and I got along well. On one of his visits, we entertained him at my house with a great summer party on the patio, featuring one of the Seattle office's delicious potluck dinners, our tried-and-true bonding technique with FTC commissioners. I still vividly remember those potlucks. In my mind's eye, I can see the glorious assortment of delicacies that were our repast: Greek dolmades, taramosalata, and moussaka provided by Lola McClintock; an array of salads, shrimp, and breads, with hot, cold, and spicy dips to tickle your tongue; a sumptuous display of specialty hors d'oeuvres; and for the pièce de résistance, an array of desserts, including a classic cherry cheesecake made by our resident baker, attorney Ivan Orton.

⁎

After two years as chairman, Lew Engman in 1975 exited the commission to become the president of the Pharmaceutical Manufacturers Association. Calvin Collier, the FTC's general counsel, who was widely perceived as being President Ford's White House political point man at the FTC, succeeded him.

BACK TO THE FARM

Because of the interminable delays in processing casework, I became increasingly interested in structural reform at the FTC, particularly in the regional office system. Due to the varied nature of their work, lawyers often harbor the delusion that they can do anything, but good management is seldom their forte. I was convinced that the efficiency of the agency could be greatly improved with the various management skills taught in graduate business schools. One day, a flyer from the Stanford Graduate School of Business for its Sloan Fellows Program caught my eye, and I had an epiphany. I would go back to Stanford and study advanced management at their top-ranked national business school and share my learning with the FTC. I was ready for an intellectual recharge, and the idea of a sabbatical for the entire family in sunny California was particularly enticing.

The Sloan Fellows Program—favored by large corporations like the Boeing Company—was a ten-month residential course of management study designed for midlevel executives who demonstrated a potential for senior management. One-third of the forty-five-member class was composed of American managers; another third was foreign managers coming from Africa, Asia, Europe, and Latin America; and the final third was US public sector managers, like me.

The program required a sponsor to nominate an individual, and then, upon the student's acceptance by Stanford, pay all expenses, including moving expenses to Palo Alto, and continue the student's full salary while they were in the program. It was costly. Tuition alone exceeded $50,000—today, in a revamped degree version, it's more than $100,000—but it came with premier benefits. You were promised the crème de la crème of business school professors, cultural excursions, a campus program for spouses, and class field trips to Washington, DC, and New York City to meet with top political, governmental, and business leaders. There was one catch: the student had to agree to three additional years of employment with his or her sponsor after the end of the program, or pay the costs of the program back. All I had to do was convince the FTC chairman, Lew Engman, to nominate me—a bit of a challenge, because according to anyone's memory, I would be the first lawyer nominated by the FTC for an extended educational leave program like this.

"Ask, and it shall be given you," the Bible says. So I approached the FTC with the idea. And to my surprise, the agency—with Chairman Engman's blessing—offered to sponsor me. I think they recognized that the FTC needed some new thinking regarding its organization and management, or maybe they just wanted to get rid of me for a year. Either way, I had just won the lottery. (It turned out Chairman Engman really did like me. In 1974 he recognized me with the Chairman's Award for Outstanding Supervision.)

I was accepted into the program for the 1975–76 year, as the only lawyer in the class. I left the Seattle regional office in the capable hands of my assistant regional director, Tom Armitage, a former clerk for US Supreme Court Justice William O. Douglas.

Gayle and I rented out our house in the Somerset neighborhood of Bellevue to a nice family and found a modest Eichler home for rent on a small lot in a quiet and leafy Palo Alto neighborhood. (Today this home would sell for about $2.5 million.) Our two children were soon enrolled in the excellent Palo Alto school district's preschool and first grade. I rode my bicycle to class most days in delightful weather, enjoyed intellectually challenging classes, and took up a new sport, racquetball, to stay fit.

On one of my first trips to the business school, on a second-story balcony in the interior quadrangle of the school's classroom complex, I encountered a lovely MBA student wearing a white wedding dress, holding a bouquet of flowers, with a beaded lace wedding veil over her face. She was standing next to a white-collared minister dressed in black, ready to officiate the wedding. In the courtyard below, playing the "Wedding March," was the infamous and rowdy Stanford band.

How very sweet of the band to play for an MBA student's wedding, I thought. *Perhaps they have changed and gone mainstream.* But then, to my astonishment, I watched as the man dressed as a minister picked up a bulging white cloth bag emblazoned on the side with a large black dollar sign.

My God, they are going to marry her to the bag of money! I realized, as my jaw dropped. Yes, the "minister" did marry the woman to the bag of money. The band was in fine fiddle, with an entertaining piece of performance art. A large group of MBA students watching the performance cheered and applauded the ceremonial satire. These business students were decidedly unashamed by this overt unveiling of the mercenary motives in their choice of a graduate education.

My return to Stanford was richly rewarding. It was everything a sabbatical should be and more. The professors were outstanding. The courses were interesting. With my own interest piqued by the trial of the Seattle Seven, I even signed up for a popular elective undergraduate course in Marxist philosophy.

Despite the prominence of the school, the faculty had a remarkable sense of humility about the function they might be serving in the academic community. "We are not sure that students learn any more about business in the MBA program than they would have learned on the job. Perhaps our contribution is more modest. We may primarily act as a high-priced finishing school that identifies the most talented people for business, streamlining the selection process," one professor candidly confessed. While I thought his observation overly judgmental, I do think I gained the most value in the program from my fellow students. I particularly enjoyed my interactions with my classmates who were from cultures and backgrounds different from mine. The friendships and networking connections—both domestic and international—were invaluable.

Our field trips to Seattle, New York, and Washington, DC, were eye-opening and educational as well. In Seattle we were feted by a reception with Boeing's CEO and a special tour of Boeing's Everett airplane assembly plant, the largest manufacturing building in the world. In New York we met with several Fortune 500 CEOs in the twin towers at the World Trade Center. In Washington, DC, after a special tour of the White House, we headed to the World Bank for a six-course lunch hosted by the World Bank's president, Robert McNamara, President Johnson's secretary of defense during the Vietnam War. With McNamara at the head of a long table, we were seated in the cavernous executive dining room for a lunch prepared by the resident French chef, accompanied by a variety of aperitifs and fine French wines. A true banker's lunch, where unless you used the multiple utensils next to your plate correctly, there was little chance of being taken seriously.

McNamara, the chief Vietnam War strategist for President Johnson, had been profoundly conflicted about what the US was doing in Vietnam at the time, and was haunted by his decisions for the rest of his life. At the lunch he did not talk about the war, and I wisely chose not to bring the subject up—although I was sorely tempted to do so. It would have spoiled for everyone the magnificent repast.

We met privately with Chief Justice William Rehnquist at the US Supreme Court, a Stanford Law School graduate who I later learned was the only Lutheran to serve on the court. In 2019, of the nine justices, a majority of five are Catholic justices—six if you count Neil Gorsuch, who was brought up Catholic but now attends an Episcopal church. If you count Gorsuch, it gives the court a majority of five conservative Catholic Republican appointed justices. The other Catholic justice is a liberal Democratic appointment, Elena Kagan. Of the remaining justices, three are Jewish; all are graduates of only three Ivy League law schools, Harvard, Yale, and Columbia; one of the nine justices is African American and one is Latina; and only three are women. Considering the increasing polarization of the court on political, social, and religious value issues, this remarkable imbalance illustrates a seemingly undemocratic lack of diversity.

The most recent Catholic conservative appointed to the US Supreme Court was Brett Kavanaugh, only fifty-three years of age when he was appointed by President Trump in 2018, after a contentious Senate confirmation hearing where Kavanaugh was accused of a sexual assault on a woman, Christine Blasey Ford, a professor affiliated with Palo Alto and Stanford Universities. Kavanaugh was confirmed. Liberal opponents of Justice Kavanaugh fear his presence will increase the political and ideological polarization of the court and could be a key vote in overturning *Roe v. Wade* or, more likely, eroding the decision by allowing incremental restrictions by the states on abortion. Kavanaugh also represents a potential threat to the independence of the FTC. When sitting on the US Court of Appeals for the District of Columbia, in an eighteen-thousand-word dissent in 2008, *Humphrey's Executor v. United States*, he suggested that the high court erred in a

1935 decision upholding the constitutionality of independent agencies like the Federal Trade Commission because these agencies encroached on the president's right to dismiss executive branch employees for any reason.

We had a special tour of the White House and Congress, meeting a variety of colorful and memorable politicians, including Bella Abzug, Democratic congresswoman from New York and cofounder of the National Women's Political Caucus, a liberal firebrand who wore outrageously large hats; and Senator Hubert Humphrey, former vice president and the ever-voluble "Happy Warrior." But the session I enjoyed the most was with the humorist and Pulitzer Prize–winning political columnist for the *Washington Post* Art Buchwald. His political commentary was both witty and insightful.

During the Sloan program, I also enjoyed a triumphal return to the classroom at the Stanford Law School. One of the law professors, Byron Sher, invited me to teach a class in his consumer protection course. I regaled the students with FTC consumer protection war stories. They absolutely loved it. (I did not mention my record low score on a law school practice exam.)

At the end of the program, I was chosen to be a commencement speaker for my class. I can't remember what I said. I hope it was irreverent and funny. Then, with the program behind me, our family returned to Seattle and I resumed my position as regional director for the FTC, wondering if I would be able to use my Sloan experience to help reform the management structure and case review procedures at the agency. It would prove to be an undertaking of great risk fought for all to see in the Congress of the United States.

CHAPTER FIFTEEN

SPEAKING TRUTH TO POWER

There is only one way to avoid criticism: do nothing, say nothing, be nothing.

—Aristotle

I quickly learned that it is one thing to speak truth to power, but what do you do if power has no capacity for truth?

The *Oxford English Dictionary* says that *bully pulpit* means "a public office or position of authority that provides its occupant with an outstanding opportunity to speak out on any issue." Like my trustbuster and national-park-creation hero, President Teddy Roosevelt, I now had a bully pulpit. At the risk of making enemies, I was determined to use my FTC position to speak out when necessary to protect consumers. As US Supreme Court Justice Antonin Scalia once said, "A man who has made no enemies is probably not a very good man." If I am to be judged only by the number of enemies I ended up making by using my bully pulpit as regional director of the Seattle FTC, I was a very good man indeed.

I knew that if we could motivate voluntary reform by use of the bully pulpit, we could greatly increase the enforcement effectiveness of our limited office resources. This strategy, seldom used in the FTC, was not without its risks. But sometimes you must venture forth; you must be willing to lose a job to do a job. Truth-telling to the powerful would be in our arsenal of law enforcement weapons.

But I was not Ralph Nader. As a nonelected government official, I had constraints on the use of the bully pulpit. In the case of the FTC, the subject matter must relate to antitrust and consumer protection issues and be aligned with the agency's mandate to make the market-place fairer and more efficient. Our strategy: We would develop a federal-state relations program and work behind the scenes to identify state and local anticompetitive rules and regulations. Once the harmful regulations were identified, we would nudge (or push) the legislative authorities to repeal or modify them.

But there were times when an even more aggressive public approach was needed. A vested business interest or profession can often effectively control a state or local regulatory authority. Most professional state boards are composed of only the members of the profession, creating a conflict of interest with the consumers of their services. Letting the professions wield the power of government through the licensing authority to control access and affect prices is costly and foolish. State-sanctioned governmental entities were not about to listen to a federal agency that they believed lacked jurisdiction to do anything about their anticompetitive behavior. These were the cases where an aggressive and innovative frontal assault using the bully pulpit was required, where in other cases a simple warning letter might have done the trick. By exposing the deceit that was undermining parts of our capitalist system, we would embark on a calculated but perilous crusade in pursuit of fairness and justice for the American consumer.

As a nonelected official, for me to use the bully pulpit to accomplish change was an unusual strategy in a high-stakes game. Even with the wind of the populist consumer movement at our backs, the bully pulpit strategy was useless without the cooperation and support of the media. Fortunately for us, media and consumer advocacy groups came to our aid by doing consumer surveys documenting consumer abuses and favorably publicizing our attempts to bring wrongdoers to account. The media also provided a bulwark of public opinion protecting us against political retribution for our audacity and unconventionality. But as the following examples show, the powerful do not fall lightly from their privileged perches, regardless of how much public attention is drawn to them.

STEPPING UP TO THE BAR

When I started to work at the FTC in 1972, my knowledge of antitrust law was limited to an excellent course I'd had in law school taught by Donald Turner, a visiting professor from Harvard, who then headed the Justice Department's antitrust division from 1965 to 1968. After only a few months on the job at the FTC, I put his teaching to work when I learned that my own legal profession was not averse to using its own professional associations to gain economic advantage by fixing prices.

The King County Bar Association (KCBA), which includes Seattle, had promulgated an ethics rule prohibiting lawyers in King County from charging less than twenty dollars an hour for their services. Apparently, the dubious rationale for the rule was that the rule actually protected consumers because any attorney that charged less than twenty dollars an hour must be incompetent. This struck me as nothing more than a blatant attempt at price-fixing of professional fees in violation of the state and federal antitrust laws. Being ecumenical in my choice of law enforcement targets, I wrote the leadership at the KCBA and told them they were likely engaging in price-fixing and should eliminate the rule. The KCBA didn't reply to my letter, but several months later I noted with satisfaction that they had quietly removed the rule from their code of ethics. Three years later, the US Supreme Court authoritatively settled the matter in *Goldfarb v. Virginia State Bar*, when it ruled that bar association minimum-fee schedules violated federal antitrust laws.

Several years later, in another attempt to encourage competition in legal services, I also jousted with the Washington State Bar Association (WSBA). In this case, I wrote them saying that their blanket prohibition on lawyer advertising in their professional rules of conduct was without justification and anticompetitive. WSBA's stated rationale for the prohibition was that both the image of lawyers and society's respect for them would diminish if lawyers advertised. Ever since Dick the Butcher—a character in Shakespeare's *Henry VI*—as an antidote to society's ills said, "The first thing we do, let's kill all the lawyers," lawyers have been highly sensitive about their image.

After receiving a reply from the president of the WSBA that they would look into the matter, one the WSBA's governors, Neil Hoff, from Tacoma, a former Republican state senator and legislator, said in a letter to me what the WSBA really thought: "What you describe as a 'magnificent opportunity to recognize the needs of consumers of legal services' is nothing more than the bleating of a beaurocrat [*sic*] who either couldn't hack it in the private practice or wouldn't really try."

It took decades and more pressure from both the Justice Department and the FTC before the WSBA and other state bar associations succumbed to the proposition that the blanket prohibition on advertising was anticompetitive. Now the WSBA expressly allows advertising by lawyers in its professional code of conduct: what the WSBA once considered professionally unethical is now, belatedly, considered ethical.

RX FOR PHARMACISTS

The absence of prices in prescription drug advertising by retail pharmacies in Oregon, which often caused consumers to overpay for their health care, provided a classic case of competitive market restraints by a professional association in cahoots with the state government. The culprit was the Oregon Board of Pharmacy, ostensibly charged with protecting the public interest.

Early in 1974, the FTC opened an industry-wide investigation to determine whether retail druggists engaged in unlawful practices by not disclosing prescription drug prices. Numerous surveys showed a wide variance in commonly prescribed prescription drug prices—of as much as 1,200 percent in the same community. There was one problem, however, with a potential FTC solution to the issue: the FDA, not the FTC, had responsibility for prescription drug advertising, which called in to question the scope of FTC authority. Nevertheless, the

FTC, under chairman Lew Engman, was determined to find out why the market wasn't working and to suggest solutions.

In more than twenty states, pharmacists' boards sanctioned by the state legislature managed to exercise their political power by using rulemaking to ban prescription drug price advertising by pharmacists altogether, as in Oregon. Or they accomplished the same result by declaring prescription price advertising by a pharmacist unprofessional conduct in their association codes of ethics, as was done in Washington State. The Oregon Supreme Court had overturned the Oregon Board of Pharmacy's ban on advertising in 1966. But in brazen disregard of the law, the board continued to publish the overturned regulation as if it were still in force, confusing pharmacists regarding the state of the law.

Despite the legality of prescription price advertising, few pharmacies in Oregon advertised drug prices. Most retail pharmacies did not even post prices on the premises or give price information on the telephone. A customer had to walk into the store with a prescription before they could learn the price. Our office saw an opportunity to challenge restrictions on prescription price advertising by making Portland, Oregon, a laboratory for an innovative experiment to encourage prescription price advertising and comparison shopping by consumers.

In April 1974 we sent a memorandum to the FTC outlining our strategy and pointing to possible savings of millions of consumer dollars if more price comparison of prescription drugs took place in Oregon. Our champion on the commission, Mayo Thompson, helped shepherd the approval of our request through what was supposedly a secret session for the commissioners to review regional office cases. Commissioner Thompson's ringing endorsement at that meeting was later leaked and published by both *Advertising Age* and *The Economics and Antitrust Law Journal*:

> *If I had any doubts about the quality of our regional office personnel, they would have been resolved by a matter that has just reached my desk, the request by the Seattle Regional Office to investigate certain alleged restraints in the advertising of drug prices in the Oregon area. The analysis in that file is, I believe, the best that I have seen since*

*coming to the Commission. . . . The public benefits of that single case
are likely to exceed anything that we can expect from the 38 cases we
are discussing here as a group . . . I want to offer my personal congrat-
ulations to Mr. Erxleben of the Seattle Office and to his staff people
who have worked on this case. It is a model, in my view, of what all of
our regional offices should be doing.*

Following approval of our investigation by the commissioners, we
hit the Portland media with an opening salvo. I sent a letter to every
newspaper, every radio and TV station, and every consumer group in
the area, inviting interested parties to attend a press conference, where
we would kick off a campaign to promote price advertising of the most
commonly sold prescription drugs.

At the packed press conference, extensively covered by all Portland
media, I laid out the economic case for price advertising. Why, I asked,
had there been almost no advertising of prescription drug prices since
the 1966 decision of the Oregon Supreme Court overthrowing the
Oregon Board of Pharmacy's ban on such advertising? I noted that
the Oregon Board of Pharmacy "has contributed to the suppression of
drug price advertising by continuing to publish regulations that pro-
hibit advertising, as if they were in force." I also praised two Portland
drugstores, Fred Meyer and Central Drugs, for running prescription
price ads right before our press conference. And finally, I called on
the Oregon State Legislature to "enact legislation requiring the posting of prescription drug prices and requiring response to telephone
inquiries."

In a moment of additional drama that heightened the publicity for
the event, several druggists, protesting the press conference as a public relations gimmick, stormed the meeting with criticisms and challenged me to a public debate. As the newspapers reported the following
day, I accepted the challenge. Of course, I would choose the time and
place and forum for that confrontation.

Immediately after my press conference, Fred Meyer and Central
Drugs expanded their newspaper advertising showing their prices for
commonly prescribed prescription drugs. I sent them a congratulatory
letter on official FTC stationery, commending them for their "spirited

recognition of the public interest." I expressed my hope that "you will continue to provide consumers with important price information." The two drugstore companies then published a copy of my letter in Portland newspapers, side by side, in full-page ads next to their prescription drug prices.

Shortly afterward, the Salem, Oregon, *Capital Journal* published an editorial headlined "Post Prescription Drug Prices." They admonished druggists and demanded prescription price advertising, saying: "Druggists should not require such a club over their head to bring their prices out into the light of day. They should respond to this legitimate consumer request without waiting for legislatures to force such action."

The Portland Retail Druggists Association was seething. They flooded the FTC's DC office with letters of protest against me personally and fired off a letter to the FTC chairman, Lew Engman, seeking a retraction of my remarks at the press conference and a public apology from me. Asked to comment on the letter by the *Oregon Journal*, my response was summarized under the headline "Druggists Won't Get Apology." Decidedly unrepentant, I said, "Are we going to apologize for those statements? Are you kidding? We are right."

The next step was to schedule a hearing and "debate" in the Portland City Hall council chambers to discuss ways of getting pharmacies to advertise prescription drugs, including urging the Oregon State Legislature to make price posting and consumer telephone responses by pharmacies mandatory.

The FTC public hearing in Portland was quite a production. We had a sold-out crowd for the spectacle, with all the media and interested parties in attendance. I chaired the hearing, and much like the director of a stage production—or the chairman of a congressional committee—I orchestrated the testimony to clearly identify the heroes and villains.

An impressive list of witnesses testified. Bernard Kaplan, the manager of Central Drugs, said that the results from prescription drug advertising had been "more than gratifying," as his prescription business had greatly increased since he started advertising.

Sid Lezak, the widely respected Oregon US attorney—who would later hold the record, at twenty-five years, as the longest-serving US attorney in American history—called the pharmacy board's failure to remove the ban on prescription drug advertising after it had been outlawed by Oregon courts "about as reprehensible as any act I can remember in recent years by a supposedly responsible state board."

Dean Killion, the president of the Oregon AFL-CIO, said pharmacies should be encouraged to advertise so that competition could eliminate "the gross disparities in drug prices that currently exist."

Lindsey McGrath, of the Oregon Students Public Interest Research Group, testified about her organization's 1973 study that documented wide disparities in drug prices in the Portland area. She said, "For instance, one drugstore charged $12.95 for the same drug—erythromycin stearate—that costs one dollar at another pharmacy." Testimony from other witnesses supported the findings in the organization's study.

Toward the end of the hearing, pharmacy and industry drug representatives had their opportunity to testify. The main thrust of their arguments was that the consumer surveys were not representative and that the FTC lacked jurisdiction to pursue the matter. *Weak rebuttals, and not very persuasive,* I concluded.

At the end of the hearing, I announced, as the pièce de résistance of our effort, that the Oregon Board of Pharmacy had capitulated. It agreed to eliminate further publication of its overturned rule banning prescription drug price advertising.

The Portland Retail Druggists Association, however, was not about to go down without a further fight. They had been embarrassed and wanted a pound of flesh: mine. Their strategy was simple and uncompromising. Apply political pressure to get me fired.

In a second letter to Chairman Engman—now escalated with copies to the Oregon Congressional delegation and General Alexander Haig, who was then President Nixon's chief of staff—Stanley Hartman, on behalf of the executive committee of the Portland Retail Druggists Association, first challenged the FTC's jurisdiction. Then he went after my scalp. He said that my actions, publicly endorsing Oregon drugstores that advertised, were "documentary evidence of gross impropriety and use of authority reminding one of Watergate." *A curious subject to bring up with the Nixon White House,* I thought—the irony was apparent. Then the letter demanded my dismissal: "The Portland Retail Druggists Association . . . demands that the Federal Trade Commission discharge William C. Erxleben, FTC Regional Director, Seattle, Wash., on grounds of actions in excess of authority and gross abuse of authority. As a former White House aide, you [meaning Chairman Engman] are cognizant of the gravity of these charges and the need to conduct a complete investigation of the documented charge."

Oh boy, I reasoned. *I'm glad I work for an independent agency that is less susceptible to White House influence.*

To my relief, Chairman Engman did not respond to either of the Portland Retail Druggists Association's letters. Neither, to my knowledge, did the Nixon White House.

The final step in our strategy was to develop a handbook to increase consumers' awareness of the need to comparison shop for prescription drugs. The Seattle office staff thus completed a thirty-page "Consumers' Survey Handbook on Prescription Drug Prices" in October 1974 and distributed it broadly. The *American Pharmacists,* a national trade journal of pharmacy associations, predictably was less than thrilled by the handbook. They published an article headlined "FTC Price-Survey Guide Tells Public How to Exploit Pharmacists." The article also acknowledged that the FTC's Seattle regional office "has been in the forefront of the FTC's nationwide campaign to abolish 'secrecy' with regard to prescription prices." They noted that the Seattle FTC office "has generally been one step ahead of Washington, DC, in the drive to force or scare pharmacists into advertising Rx prices."

The US Supreme Court soon validated our challenge to boards of pharmacies. In 1976, in a case brought against the Virginia Board of Pharmacy by a consumer group, the court stated that a Virginia statute declaring it unprofessional conduct for a pharmacist to advertise prescription drug prices was unconstitutional.

***

Efforts by the federal government to increase prescription drug price advertising in the United States have been largely unsuccessful. Even though the FTC has brought enforcement actions to encourage generic drugs in the marketplace, in the United States we spend 44 percent more on drugs per person than Canada, the country with the next highest costs. This is largely due to perverse incentives in Medicare inserted by Congress at the behest of the drug lobby. Today, in an ironic turn of events, large pharmaceutical companies advertise prescription drugs—but not their prices—in an attempt to create patient demand for expensive drugs that their doctors might not otherwise prescribe, further exacerbating the problem by driving demand for expensive drugs despite the clinical effectiveness of less costly alternatives. The United States and New Zealand are the only two countries that allow direct-to-consumer advertising of prescription drugs. In 2015 the American Medical Association called for a ban on direct-to-consumer advertising of prescription drugs to no avail.

In 2018 the Trump administration proposed that list prices must be included for most drugs in television ads. The Department of Health and Human Services (HHS) Secretary, Alex Azar, described it as a small step in the right direction in providing real transparency to the "sky-high list prices many patients pay." HHS's proposal rule was criticized by the *Wall Street Journal* "as political advertising" because almost no one pays list price, and HHS lacks the statutory authority to enact the rule.

WHO'S AFRAID OF VIRGINIA GALLE?

Virginia Galle, upon her appointment by Seattle mayor Wes Uhlman as the head of the Department of Licenses and Consumer Affairs, became the first woman department head in Seattle city government history. I worked closely with her on numerous consumer issues where she perceived companies to be swindling the public. In January 1977 she and her top aide, Charles Ehlert, suddenly and unceremoniously "resigned." The timing of their resignations fell in the aftermath of a highly publicized three-day real estate conference cosponsored by the City of Seattle and our Seattle FTC office; possible price-fixing in residential real estate commissions and title insurance was the highlighted topic. There were widespread rumors that Mayor Uhlman had dumped Galle because she was too aggressive in pursuing violations of law against some of the mayor's political supporters, particularly Realtors. Protesting her departure, her assistant, Charles Ehlert, followed her out the door.

Shortly after Galle's "resignation," I was called by the *Seattle P-I* to comment. Since I didn't trust Mayor Uhlman—who had been a political antagonist ever since my encounters with him in the perjury trial of his assistant chief of police, Buzz Cook—I wasn't about to give him the benefit of the doubt. The *P-I* quoted me as saying, "If you get too close to some particular interest or campaign contributors, you can be removed. I think it's entirely appropriate to ask what's going on." Like pack dogs on the scent of a good story, eager to escalate the rhetoric and continue the chase, other Seattle papers published my quote.

The Seattle City Council joined the hunt: they wanted to know what was going on too, especially since a city ordinance required the mayor to explain his actions when removing the head of a city department. In a letter written by council member Randy Revelle and signed by all other city council members except Wayne Larkin—a former Seattle police officer and a member of the notorious vice squad during the Seattle police payoff era—Mayor Uhlman was asked to explain his reasons for removing Virginia Galle.

Uhlman refused, stonewalling with a quibble. He did not "remove" Galle, he said: "She resigned."

The *P-I* summarized the fray with a lead editorial headlined, "What Is Going On?" and concluded, "All of which makes us say again, in Erxleben's phrasing, that it's entirely appropriate for the public to know in the Galle case just what in the devil is going on?"

The editorial also pointedly noted that the mayor was hell-bent on revenge in response to my challenge to him to explain the circumstances of Galle's dismissal. "Uhlman indicated that he is even going to take his case to the president of the United States, Jimmy Carter, to get William Erxleben fired from his job as the zealous director of the regional office of the FTC. Uhlman said he has already asked U.S. Sens. Henry M. Jackson and Warren G. Magnuson to help him collect Erxleben's scalp." In his letter to Senator Jackson, Uhlman said: "His [Erxleben's] entire conduct in this instance was in the finest tradition of the chilling smear and innuendo of the Nixon years . . . Mr. Erxleben's conduct should preclude him from consideration for continuation in this important nonpartisan position." On the editorial page—in a large political cartoon by Bob McCausland—the *P-I* dramatized the mayor's anger: Mayor Uhlman was depicted as a snorting, enraged bull, with pictures of Galle and myself stuck on his horns.

Courtesy of Seattle Post-Intelligencer.

Following the Democratic mayor's diatribe, in which he attempted to brand me a "partisan Republican," Uhlman and I, mano a mano, engaged in daily dueling press conferences that played out like a fencing match and were joyously captured by the media. It seemed that both the mayor and I had a proclivity for the jugular. In a riposte, captured by a *Seattle Times* story carrying the provocative headline "F.T.C. Official Lashes Back at Mayor," I said that Uhlman's branding me as a partisan Republican "won't wash," because I had never been affiliated with a political party and that the mayor's attack on me was "merely a smoke screen . . . to evade public accountability." I added, "The new

post-Watergate politics demands that public officials be held accountable to fully explain their actions."

Mayor Uhlman never received replies to his widespread call for my
resignation. FTC headquarters never contacted me to ask me to tone
down my rhetoric either. One of Senator Magnuson's staff members
quoted the senator as saying, after reading the letter from Uhlman
asking that I be removed from office: "Sure, over my dead body."

***

Although none of the parties involved ever publicly acknowledged the
truth of Virginia Galle's firing, in a delicious twist of fate, justice prevailed. I felt a moment of schadenfreude, when one year later, Mayor
Uhlman decided not to run for reelection as mayor. His political career
was over. After her dismissal by Uhlman, Virginia Galle served as
executive director of the Seattle Girl Scouts until she resigned to run
for Seattle City Council in 1980. She was elected easily and served two
terms.

BEER BARREL POLKA

Under the FTC's federal-state relations program, we were always on
the lookout for anticompetitive state regulations that were causing
consumers to pay more than they should. A tempting target was the
Washington State Liquor Control Board (WSLCB), a monopoly that
controlled hard-liquor retail distribution in the state through its ownership of all the retail liquor stores. It also regulated the rest of the
alcoholic beverage industry. The board had a cozy relationship with
liquor and beer distributors in the state, protecting their distribution
monopoly with a maze of anticompetitive regulations.

Following a rejection by the WSLCB of a proposal by private retail
stores to allow temporary beer and wine price cuts, we petitioned the
board in January 1977 to see if we could get some of their rules hin-
dering price competition lifted. The economic analysis by our in-house
economist, Randy Bartlett, a young economics professor—PhD,

Stanford University and on leave from Williams College for a year—
estimated that each percentage drop in the price of beer and wine
would save state consumers $17 million to $20 million annually. The
WSLCB's anticompetitive rules, we concluded, constituted "price-
fixing on a massive scale."

The WSLCB scheduled a hearing for our petition at the end of
March. We met in a large room in the legislative capitol building in
Olympia. From the moment we entered the hearing room, we knew we
were not welcome. The room was packed with industry lobbyists, attorneys, and liquor distributors. Former Washington State governor Al
Rossellini and former house speaker Robert Schaefer, both Democrats,
representing beer interests, openly questioned the FTC's right to petition the board, and a score of other witnesses also questioned our
jurisdiction. Rossellini, now a Tacoma-based beer distributor, introduced himself as "a lawyer and former state employee," and added, "I'm
sure you're not going to let [the FTC] tell you what to do. You'll treat
them courteously, but tell them to mind their own business."

In response, we argued that part of our responsibility was to act on
behalf of consumers as an advocate, especially since some members of
the industry had informed us that they were fearful of appearing before
the board as adverse witnesses. The board chairman, L. H. Pedersen,
told me to name names of those who were fearful or shut up. I refused
to do either. It seemed clear to me that Pedersen, a public official, was
acting as an industry representative rather than as a representative of
the public interest.

The liquor board announced that they would take our petition
under advisement and render a decision later. The *Seattle P-I* reported
the encounter the next day with a front-page, above-the-fold banner
headline: "U.S., State Tangle Over Price of Beer."

A few months later, we had another opportunity to address restric-
tive regulations of the WSLCB. One regulation, Rule 35, required, as
a condition of obtaining a license for beer and wine, that a restaurant
must maintain a ratio of at least 40 percent food to wine in their sales.
Twenty-nine Washington State restaurants that had failed to meet the
ratio were scheduled to lose their licenses. The restaurant owners asked
us to appear at a hearing scheduled in late April by the Washington

State House Commerce Subcommittee on Liquor Laws. The hearing would be held at the Price Is Right restaurant in Seattle, one of the restaurants adversely affected.

I testified at the packed hearing and criticized the lack of responsiveness of the liquor board to the public interest. This generated another story with an entertaining headline by the *Seattle P-I*: "FTC Man Gets Good Belt at Liquor Hearing."

If speakers at yesterday's hearing on the liquor board Rule 35 could be compared to drinks, William Erxleben was like a double martini after a lineup of slow gin fizzes.

The Region 10 director of the Federal Trade Commission came through with a good belt just when the audience needed it, a little more than halfway through the three-hour hearing, after most of the TV cameras had left and most of the media microphones had been untapped and removed from the speaker's podium. Erxleben got a sustained round of applause when he said: "If you represent small businesses or the consumer at large, you have to have a major media event like this or you have to drop a beer barrel on the toe of the liquor board to get them to be responsive to your plight."

The *P-I* noted that I had "suggested strongly that the legislature conduct a full review of the liquor board, making it one of the first agencies to be reviewed under the 'sunset laws,' which provide for the disbanding of a board or agency that has outlived its purpose."

Not surprisingly—given my record—my comments precipitated another letter addressed to FTC headquarters that questioned the propriety of my conduct (copies, of course, to the state's two US senators and the state's governor). The letter, from Pedersen, the chairman of the WSLCB, stated in part:

The Region 10 director of the FTC, William Erxleben, appeared at a legislative subcommittee hearing where he was reported by the Seattle Post-Intelligencer *to have delivered a 'rapid-fire lashing of the three-member liquor board.' . . . With the foregoing background, we would appreciate knowing whether it is the official position of the*

FTC to inject itself into state rights, and lend its weight to state legis-
lative and administrative matters.

Six weeks later, the board announced that they had denied our petition but were going to adopt several proposed rules—ones denied in December, five months earlier—that would open up beer and wine price competition among private sellers. *Advertising Age* said that the Seattle FTC office had "successfully prodded" the WSLCB to allow more competition in the pricing of beer, wine, and liquor.

We were delighted with the ruling. The *Seattle Times* heralded it with another headline—"Liquor Board Changes Rules; Savings Seen"— and quoted me saying that the changes "finally open up the door on what we felt were some of the board's most anticompetitive positions."

***

It took another forty years and the deep pockets of Costco to finally wrest the liquor monopoly from the Washington State Liquor Control Board. In 2012, with the passage of an initiative to the voters of the state of Washington—funded by a $22.5 million war chest from Costco, making it the largest single donor to a voter initiative in the state's history—the hard-liquor monopoly of the state-controlled liquor stores was completely eliminated.

THE GRINCH WHO STOLE CHRISTMAS

Christmas is a time of joy, giving, lights, and gross over-commercialization. It is also children's first experience with knowing deception by adults. But what the heck—it's a fun tradition and good training for children, teaching them not to always believe what their parents tell them is true.

There are some limits, however, to using Santa to make money: "Using Santa as the lure to take commercial advantage of parents because of the naivete of their little children seems contrary to both the Christmas spirit and Federal Trade Commission advertising standards." That's what I said in a letter to Andrew V. Smith, president of the Pacific Northwest Bell Telephone Company, in December 1978, which I attached to a press release.

The *New York Times* and the *Washington Post* jumped on the story. The *Washington Post* said, "The Federal Trade Commission is not 'ho-ho-ho-ho-ing' over a Pacific Northwest Bell promotion that had Seattle youngsters telephoning Santa Claus long-distance to New York." To Pacific Northwest Bell, offering a way for children to speak to Santa from home seemed like a great idea, certain to warm the hearts of many children. The only trouble was, the area code to be dialed from Seattle was 212, the area code for New York City, triggering long-distance charges.

To address this exploitation of children and their parents, I asked that the phone company offer refunds to customers whose children had made "unpermitted phone calls" on a special Santa line advertised by Pacific Northwest Bell in the local newspapers. According to news reports, some fifteen to twenty thousand calls were made from the Seattle area to New York to hear a one-minute recording from Santa.

Sounding like Dr. Seuss's Grinch who stole Christmas, a Pacific Northwest Bell spokesman was quoted by the *Washington Post* as saying, "We're a commercial enterprise, and one of our main sources of revenue is long-distance calls. The ad was run to see if people would make calls and to generate enough long-distance revenue to make some profit to boot."

An embarrassed Pacific Northwest Bell finally relented and discontinued the advertising, saying that it was willing to discuss refunds with parents. A few weeks later, Art Buchwald, columnist of the *Washington Post*—whom I had previously met in Washington, DC, during the Stanford Sloan Fellows Program—ran a long satirical column on the controversy titled "Next Christmas, Children, Try Calling Santa Claus Collect." He said that as a stockholder in the telephone company, he commended Pacific Northwest Bell for using some imagination toward increasing the use of its equipment. "No one knows who the genius was at Pacific Northwest Bell who thought up the idea of getting kids to call Santa long-distance," he said, "but I sincerely hope that the person involved gets the recognition he or she so richly deserves." There were endless possibilities to expand the program, he wrote, including encouraging children to call London to listen to a recorded message from the queen. "If the phone people can get pre-school children into the habit of dialing long-distance, they will generate a fantastic new market that has never been tapped before."

Never underestimate the power of the pen.

CHAPTER SIXTEEN

BITING THE HAND THAT FED ME

Benjamin Franklin was one of the earliest Americans to embrace a culture of civic responsibility in pursuit of the public good. He became an early American whistle- blower in 1773 when he exposed confidential letters showing that the king's governor in Massachusetts had misled Parliament to promote a military expansion in the colonies.

Franklin avoided retribution for speaking out, but that outcome is not the norm today. Whistle-blowers subject themselves to great risk when speaking out. We all say we want the truth, but we all know what happens to truth-tellers: they are often slain. Although our society gives great lip service to people who speak out, more often than not, they end up as sacrificial lambs, punished as transgressors by the governmental powers that be or by the businesses they expose. In Washington, DC, government truth-tellers often try to avoid retribution by leaking inside information to congressional committees or to the media. Leaking can be a powerful tool in protecting democracy and exposing wrongdoing, but it's a dangerous game, and you best not get caught.

***

If internal management reforms of the regional offices were blocked and the FTC was falling far short of being all that it could be, would I blow the whistle on the structure and management of the agency? And, if I did, would it be considered an act of ultimate disloyalty to an organization that had treated me so generously?

For me, I always felt my loyalty was to the public, not to any person or governmental institution. When I returned as Seattle regional director after my sabbatical at Stanford Graduate School of Business, I would confront the consequences of this belief.

In one of my seminar classes on organizational management, I wrote a forty-page paper analyzing the management problems at the FTC and suggested a variety of reforms, not just for the regional offices but also for the entire organization. The most important recommendation was to strengthen the office of executive director. I argued that the executive director, as the organization's chief operating officer, should have greater authority and accountability for the organization's performance. In the fall of 1976, I submitted my management critique to the FTC chairman, Calvin Collier, and the new executive director, Tim McNamar. Chairman Collier thanked me in a letter for the "thoughtful and well-written analysis," but I felt it was no more than an "attaboy" for a good memo. The memo, I feared, would be slowly walked around the FTC bureaucracy and then deposited into the institutional round file.

The election of President Carter in November of 1976 presented another opportunity for management reform. A Democratic chairman of the FTC would soon be appointed. It was expected that Michael Pertschuk would be nominated. Pertschuk, a friend of our office, was formerly a legislative assistant to Senator Maurine Neuberger of Oregon and a law clerk for US District Judge in Oregon, Gus Solomon, and now was the chief counsel and staff director of the Senate commerce committee chaired by Senator Magnuson. I was delighted with the prospect.

In January 1977, Representative Benjamin Rosenthal, Democrat of New York, the chairman of the US House Subcommittee on Government Operations—a subcommittee of the Committee on Oversight and Government Reform—began an investigation of FTC regional offices. I suspected the hand of Mike Pertschuk. Pertschuk, I believed, had triggered the investigation to air the dirty linen in the FTC's closet before he took over as chairman.

The staff of Rosenthal's subcommittee contacted all eleven of the regional FTC offices. The regional directors were asked to outline the roadblocks in the system that inhibited vigorous consumer protection enforcement and attracting talented people to the regional offices. Based upon the information submitted by the regional offices, a staff report would be written and the subcommittee would hold two days of hearings questioning Chairman Collier and other witnesses. Congressman Rosenthal asked: "Would any of the regional directors be willing to testify at the hearing in Washington, DC?"

At first glance it seemed to me like a career suicide mission—to testify before Congress and criticize your agency and its leadership for management shortcomings. All my mental alarm bells were ringing: *This is definitely not kosher in the federal bureaucracy. Bureaucrats don't believe in self-immolation. It's the antithesis of the government survival culture. Don't do it.*

I pondered the risks, and concluded that influencing the incoming chairman could be a rare opportunity to fix numerous problems that prevented many of the regional offices from performing. The Seattle regional office was effective, despite the roadblocks, because we were a maverick office and had now established a national profile. In January 1977, in a full-page article titled "FTC: For the Consumer," the *Seattle P-I* said, "Erxleben and his staff have established the Northwest as sort of the epicenter of FTC action, by finding new ways to use old FTC powers and being the first to analyze and test newer powers only recently granted by Congress." But we challenged the status quo at great risk. You really can't tolerate eleven maverick offices; you have to institutionalize necessary reforms. Was this the golden opportunity I had been waiting for? Could the Seattle office be the transformative change agent for all regional offices?

I contacted other regional directors. Many of them were willing to join me and take advantage of the opportunity to testify. We decided that there was safety in numbers. Five regional directors, from the strongest regional offices—Boston, New York, Chicago, Denver, and

Seattle—would testify. On behalf of my fellow directors, I prepared a memo for the committee with a copy to Chairman Collier detailing our concerns about the interface between the regional offices and headquarters.

The hearings began on March 15, 1977, in the main committee hearing room at the capitol in the House of Representatives. Subcommittee chairman Rosenthal, in his opening statement, announced the conclusions of the staff. It was a scathing report. Its 858 pages characterized the FTC's review procedures as "a Rube Goldberg invention gone wild." It noted that the regional offices might have to go through as many as twenty-two layers of review to win approval for antitrust matters and eight levels of review for consumer protection matters. The committee's investigation strongly suggested the need for a major restructuring of the relationship between Washington and the regions. Chairman Rosenthal concluded: "The preliminary evidence indicates that the work of the regional offices is being seriously hampered by commission attitudes and policies. I am hopeful that with new leadership, necessary changes will be undertaken."

One by one, the regional directors testified, offering multiple examples of policy changes required for the system to be efficient and effective. I concluded my own testimony by saying, "Lengthy headquarters' delay in granting investigational authority and acting on other requests and recommendations by regional offices can have a pernicious effect on employee morale and case development."

Then it was Chairman Collier's turn to testify. The situation was really awkward. The chairman of the FTC was going to be grilled by a congressional committee for historic management failings that continued on his watch. Given the recent election of Jimmy Carter as president, Collier, a Republican appointment, was a lame duck with little time left in office as chairman. He didn't look like he wanted to be there.

Collier was both defensive and aggressive in detailing FTC policy under his watch. Defending the agency's centralized control over the regional offices, Collier cited the "need to coordinate law and policy" at the federal level. He said he would advise his successor, Mike Pertschuk—who was in the hearing room observing—to make no changes in the field offices for six months. Pertschuk could then make his own decision and, if the field office personnel remained disaffected, "they can go elsewhere." Representative Robert Drinan, Democrat from Massachusetts, a well-regarded lawyer and a Jesuit priest, chided Collier, saying ruefully: "You don't tell that to your children."

Collier soon retreated, and when asked if he would like to comment on the suggestions I had made on behalf of all regional offices, he answered: "I would, I guess, because it is one of the more comprehensive memos with specifics that we received from the regional offices. One of our very talented directors, Bill Erxleben, put it together . . . I think I agree with about eighty-five percent of what that committee recommended—and not only agree with it, we're doing it." *Well, not really*, I thought, suddenly slack-jawed by his assertion.

As Chairman Collier concluded his extensive testimony, one thing became clear: no major changes were going to occur until Michael Pertschuk took office in April 1977. It remained to be seen whether going to Washington, DC, to testify was worth the risk.

FIFTEEN MINUTES

One month after the conclusion of the congressional hearings in Washington, DC, I awoke one morning and went outside to retrieve the Saturday edition of the *Seattle Times* from my driveway in front of our house. I unfolded the newspaper and looked at the front page. To my surprise, I was staring at myself. A large color head shot and an accompanying story dominated the top two-thirds of the front page. I looked like I was about twelve years old. The above-the-fold headlined blared, "Erxleben Consumes the Criticism." I thought, *Darn, this isn't going to be good.* But it was.

The story, written by the *Seattle Times'* ace consumer reporter, Debby Lowman, first detailed all the people who were calling for my dismissal, then followed with laudatory comments from Attorney General Slade Gorton and Ken Bostock, the former director of the Washington Committee on Consumer Interests. Bostock said, "As far as I'm concerned, the low-key role has been tried previously and proved ineffective. I much prefer the aggressive approach." Lowman's article continued: "Erxleben has a reputation at the F.T.C. national headquarters as one of the brightest, most imaginative and most effective of the regional directors."

Many of the Seattle office's major cases were highlighted in the article, including our current suit against the nation's three major auto manufacturers, questioning their repossession practices. Our actions, Lowman said, "upset some businesspeople who think the F.T.C. should stay out of their affairs. But Erxleben, whose close-cropped hair and clean-shaven face give him the image of an All-American boy, argues that the F.T.C. just wants to make capitalism work." (Maybe that picture was better than I thought.)

But wait, there's more!

In a companion story on the inside of the front section, there was another half-page article by Debby Lowman, with a better and even larger bold headline: "Erxleben: A Lion Where There Were Lambs." *A bit of an overstatement,* I thought, *but I like it.* Given the first headline, I needed to be rehabilitated.

The interior article recounted in detail my confrontations over the years with professional associations' state regulatory agencies and politicians. Lowman noted that, contrary to the Washington and Oregon pharmacy associations' criticism of me, my show of support for Fred Meyer's prescription drug ad campaign wasn't exactly favoritism of Fred Meyer: "In 1975, Fred Meyer paid a $200,000 settlement after the F.T.C. charged [that] the Portland-based chain used unfair methods of competition. It was the largest settlement ever obtained from a regional company."

The article noted that I was undaunted by all the criticism and had purposely chosen a high profile. I was quoted as having said, "To represent the consumer . . . you have to use the media to gain wide dissemination of the problem. . . . We believe in informing the public so they realize what is happening to their hard-earned dollars. Some are being taken away from them unfairly." I had described our enforcement style as one of "creative aggression." "We can't hope to stop all abuses," I had said, "but the alternative is not to attempt the change at all. Maybe that's why we are so aggressive—we see the task is so large."

There you have it. My fifteen minutes of fame. *No matter how brief the moment, bask in the sun. You never know when it might rain,* I thought. As one who early in life had claimed to value his anonymity, it was an odd situation for me.

***

One year after consumer reporter Debby Lowman wrote her front-page story on the controversies surrounding the Seattle regional office of the FTC, she died of cancer. She was not yet thirty years of age.

The *Seattle Times* honored her by establishing the Debby Lowman Award for Distinguished Reporting of Consumer Affairs as one of the Blethen Awards for distinguished reporting in the Pacific Northwest. The award is now given annually in her name. Her early death was a great loss to consumer journalism.

ED DONOHOE

Ed Donohoe, political columnist, pundit, and satirist for the *Washington Teamster* newspaper, had a legendary reputation as a crusty curmudgeon who mercilessly skewered every public figure within the range of his pen with his acerbic wit. Once called "the Don Rickles of the typewriter," he specialized in deflating the overblown egos of the high and the mighty. His column Tilting the Windmill, topped with a Don Quixote cartoon parody image of Donohoe on a horse using his pen as a lance, was avidly read, particularly by Washington State political figures. The venom spewing from his pen outraged many people to whom it was directed, but not me. I thought he was absolutely hilarious.

Months earlier, while I was jousting with the Washington State Liquor Control Board, Donohoe slammed me with what had become a recurrent theme: my use of the media. In his words: "Recently Erxleben mounted a white charger, which turned out to be a Sony television set, and took off against certain regulations that are the traditional domain of the state liquor control board. . . . Erxleben doesn't put his cases in press form like [Attorney General] Gorton, but why should he when all he has to do is call a television station and they come running with their creepy-peepy pencils!"

The victims of Donohoe's pen were identified with nick-names designed for maximum personal humiliation. Slade Gorton, Washington State's attorney general, was "Slippery Slade," and Chris Bayley, King County's prosecutor, was "Sugarplums." Donohoe's description of Seattle's mayor, Wes Uhlman, was that "our prematurely gray mayor is also prematurely dumb." Over the years I had had several monikers, ranging from "Dudley Do-Right" (the dim-witted but con-scientious Canadian Mountie) to "Don Quixote" (the hapless knight who loses his sanity and sets out to undo wrongs and bring justice to the world). But now, with the publication of the front-page story and picture in the *Seattle Times*, I was immediately rechristened:

> William "Front Page" Erxleben, supermouth for the local Federal Trade Commission, who tries most of his cases on the 5:30 tv news. A strong advocate of press release justice, Erxleben would have to ask the Triple "A" for directions to court. Now he claims that in the secrecy of the voting booth he may have pulled the lever for Carter. Which is another way of trying to keep his $37,500 job by putting the next four years between himself, Erlichman, Pitkin, Gorton and Sugarplums.

Ed Donohoe sure had a way with words.

By ED DONOHOE

Honoring the least among us

WILLIAM "Front Page" ERXLEBEN, supermouth for

CHAPTER SEVENTEEN

GRANNY THE NANNY

Sometimes, when surfing a populist wave, you can get too aggressive and lean too far forward on the board, and disaster befalls: you are flipped off the board and into the water before you finish your run.

For many years, the FTC possessed the authority to promulgate trade regulation rules. The scope of this authority, however, was unclear, and the FTC promulgated such rules only in narrow substantive areas. In 1974 the US Supreme Court ruled that the FTC had general rulemaking authority under section 5 of the Federal Trade Commission Act, outlawing "unfair and deceptive acts and practices." The passage of the Magnuson-Moss Warranty Act in 1975 further expanded and clarified the FTC's rulemaking authority. This legislation required a high evidentiary standard for a rule. The FTC must show "substantial evidence" to regulate "prevalent" unfair or deceptive acts. Since rules were designed to apply industry-wide, this meant that by the very nature of things, a long period of investigation would be required before a rule could be promulgated. Critics of the FTC, who worried that more rulemaking would open a floodgate of regulation with the FTC becoming the second most powerful legislature in the nation, were galvanized into action.

For the Seattle regional office, the new trade regulation authority spelled a great opportunity to dramatically affect the marketplace across an entire industry rather than proceeding on a case-by-case basis. Rising to the challenge, we began to focus on rulemaking by pursuing investigations into industries with a large number of consumer complaints, recognized safety issues, or the potential for high economic impact. Four areas were selected for investigation: used car and new car sales, residential real estate brokerage commissions, labeling of indoor and outdoor plants, and nursing homes.

The sale of used cars by dealers topped the chart for the number of consumer complaints. You never knew if the car was mechanically sound or if you were buying a lemon. A 1973 study by our office showed that more than two-thirds of used car buyers found some defect in their cars after purchase that required costly repairs.

Beginning in 1972, we started to investigate the industry for possible remedies. In 1973, in our flagship rulemaking proposal, Dave Pender and consumer protection specialist Mike Katz from our office asked the FTC to commence a used car trade regulation rule that would require a dealer to inspect a vehicle before it was sold and disclose any defects. Despite commissioner Mary Gardiner Jones praising our office as "one of the most creative planning offices we have," the proposal was voted down by the commission, but was revived in the 1975 Magnuson-Moss Warranty Act, which required the FTC to implement the act by, among other things, promulgating a rule for used car dealers. In 1978 the DC staff again recommended a similar rule as originally drafted by our office and urged its adoption by the commission.

A second investigation involved residential real estate. The purchase of a home is the biggest financial transaction most consumers make and the one they are usually least knowledgeable about. For years, economists and antitrust enforcers have puzzled over the intractability and the high cost of residential real estate brokerage commissions. Our survey with the City of Seattle showed that for 97 percent of commissions, the commission amounted to 7 percent of the sale price— one of the highest real estate fees in any city in the country, regardless of the price of the home. Was this market failure, an indication of illegal price-fixing? Because each artificial percentage rise in brokerage commissions cost American consumers $1.5 billion a year, this anomaly required closer scrutiny. In 1978 a national FTC investigation into residential real estate practices was opened, with the Seattle and Los Angeles regional offices in charge.[1]

Our third and most controversial proposed rulemaking investigation started in 1975. The FTC approved an investigation that focused on toxicity disclosures and plant care labeling for the $52-billion-a-year nursery business. How many people knew that if the leaves of the common houseplant dieffenbachia (sometimes jokingly called the mother-in-law plant) were ingested, the tongue could swell and cause you to lose the power of speech? How many Washingtonians knew that the state flower, the rhododendron, was poisonous? Each year an estimated twelve thousand children across the nation ingested plants that neither they nor their parents thought were harmful. Some common houseplants, like the peace lily, elephant ears, and the rubber plant, are toxic to pets as well.

Our investigation, headed by consumer protection specialists Ron Sims and Fran Abel, identified twenty-seven categories of houseplants as toxic. These would require a warning label at point of sale under our proposal. But when the commissioners narrowly approved the investigation on a three-to-two vote, we learned that our proposed rule would be a tempting target for ridicule: the two dissenting commissioners said they thought this investigation had "about as much usefulness to the American public as a pair of socks on a rooster."

Commissioner Elizabeth Hanford initially proposed our fourth rulemaking investigation, which led to a nationwide investigation into nursing home practices. Commissioner Hanford's primary concerns were "numerous reports of economic abuse of patients and families and wretched quality of care provided by many nursing home facilities." Our office was one of four regional offices charged with carrying out the national investigation with Elizabeth Taylor, of our office, named program director.

Courtesy of Seattle Post-Intelligencer.

MICHAEL PERTSCHUK

Befitting his seniority, and his belief in legislative activism, Senator Warren G. Magnuson was able to attract the best and the brightest lawyers to the committees he chaired and to his personal office staff. He delegated widely to his top aides, often making them de facto lawmakers.

Michael Pertschuk—now chairman of the FTC—had been the staffer entrusted with the senator's consumer protection portfolio. Pertschuk, a Yale Law School graduate, was a talented, energetic firebrand for consumer protection. During his tenure as chief of staff and general counsel of the Senate commerce committee, he had been a driving force in much of the legislation that expanded the FTC's powers during the 1970s. His appointment by President Carter in 1977 as the chairman of the FTC was a dream come true for him—and for us as well. For years he had waited patiently, on Senator Magnuson's staff, for the Democrats' return to power and his chance—with Senator Magnuson's support—to head the FTC. Ironically, just as he became chairman, congressional support for consumer protection enforcement took a nosedive as the midterm congressional elections set the stage for the Reagan Revolution.

After less than a year in office, in February 1978, Pertschuk engineered his first major policy move, a very brave and bold move given the changed environment for consumer protection initiatives. The commissioners voted to consider regulations to ban all TV advertising aimed at children younger than eight years of age. It would also ban TV advertising of heavily sugared products to children younger than twelve.

The case for regulation of children's advertising was compelling. The FTC found that the average child, age two to eleven, watched more than thirteen hundred hours of television a year, involving about twenty thousand commercials. More than half the advertising was for food, almost all of which contained large amounts of sugar and posed a problem for health generally, particularly dental health and childhood obesity.

I welcomed Pertschuk's initiative. A *Seattle P-I* story on March 5, 1978, titled "Kids Versus Sugar: One Dad's Battle," referenced my struggle to monitor the sugar consumption of our children, Jennifer and David, then six and eight years old:

> *Bill Erxleben, Seattle's young (35) regional Federal Trade Commission director, is known for his ability to muster up plenty of righteous indignation when confronted with assorted consumer abuses.*
>
> *But rarely has Erxleben been in such fine form as he was last Tuesday at a press briefing about future FTC rules, which would clamp down on TV advertising directed at children.*
>
> *"It's very difficult for parents to battle" the impact of TV ads which pitch over-sugared nutritionally unsound food products to their children, Erxleben complained, finding the ads "particularly unfair and deceptive."*

***

In 2017, Seattle passed a tax on sugary drinks to use higher soda prices to reduce consumption, improve the health of Seattleites, and raise revenues. Four months later, the beverage industry spent over $20 million to place a statewide initiative on the ballot in November 2018—I-1634—calling it deceptively the "Affordable Grocery initiative." The industry initiative, bankrolled largely by Coca-Cola and Pepsi, easily passed in Washington State, but a similar industry measure was defeated in Oregon where far less industry money was spent supporting it. The Washington initiative prevents local jurisdictions, other than Seattle, from singling out similar drinks for special taxation. Earlier in 2010 the soft drink industry, using another misleading playbook, spent $16 million to overturn a Washington State enacted carbonated beverage tax.

Erxleben family.

THE KID-VID CASE

We marched in lockstep behind Pertschuk's children's advertising enforcement parade and announced that the Seattle office would open its own industry-wide investigation into comic book publishers to determine what ads directed to children in comic books might be unfair and deceptive. Our investigation started out in high gear, receiving national publicity. The *Louisville Times* headlined a story "Comics or Conics? FTC Plans Probe of Ads That Mislead Kids." But before the FTC marching band had a chance to play for the children, the parade was stopped dead in its tracks.

The ink was barely dry on the FTC's press release announcing its foray into children's advertising when the powerful, liberal, Democrat-leaning *Washington Post*—the owner of five large-market television stations, still basking in the glow of its Watergate exposé—on March 1, 1978, hit the FTC with a devastating lead editorial headline broadside: "The FTC as National Nanny."

The editorial said the goal of children's advertising enforcement was admirable, "but the means the FTC is considering are something else. It is a preposterous intervention that would turn the agency into a great national nanny." In one fell swoop, the *Washington Post* transformed the public perception of the FTC from "the Consumers' Champion" to "the Nation's Nanny." The FTC's best friend and heretofore ally, the press, stabbed us in the front under the guise that it had to stop the agency in its tracks to prevent us from being put out of business entirely. For the second time in ten years, the FTC faced an existential threat.

The children's advertising investigation became widely and pejoratively referred to as the "kid-vid" case. The populist consumer movement, always dependent for its effectiveness on its unspoken alliance with the major media, was in trouble. If that alliance were broken, anti-regulation business vultures would soon arrive to pick the bones of the agency's carcass. Without the support of the mainstream media, and facing the loss of Congress to conservative anti-government Republicans, the granny of Pennsylvania Avenue would have her prescriptions for steroids taken away and face relocation back to her former residence in bureaucratic nursing care.

Smelling blood, the sugar lobby and the advertising industry—with buckets of campaign donations—spurred the US Congress into action. A House appropriations subcommittee voted to deny the FTC funding to carry out its planned two-year fact-finding inquiry into children's advertising to include public hearings around the country. The House of Representatives then piled on by threatening to make all FTC rules subject to veto.

If you get too far ahead of the parade, there might be no one following you. Pertschuk had underestimated the change in the national mood and ended up having the FTC's momentum slammed into reverse by its former ally, the fourth estate. One important lesson learned: don't threaten the media's golden goose by attempting to restrict advertising revenues. The media are fair-wallet friends: threaten their pocketbooks and they may abandon you.

Our comic book advertising investigation did not manage to escape the onslaught of media ridicule. In a satirical article in the *Seattle P-I* in April 1978, columnist Jean Godden, who later would become a three-term Seattle City Council member, said:

> *William Erxleben may get high marks as a public servant, but he must have flunked childhood.*
>
> *The director of the Seattle office of the Federal Trade Commission says he's going to investigate funny books. Erxleben is concerned that the ads in comic books fail to deliver what they promise. As a consequence, he fears that "the children, frustrated and disappointed, could develop a cynicism about the free enterprise system."*
>
> *If Bill Erxleben succeeds in his mission to keep comic book advertisers honest, children will be deprived of the best possible training in corporate ethics. How will they ever understand the economic facts of life?*

***

Populist waves can be two-edged swords: some promote the common good and some don't. Even if you disagree with the beneficence of a new wave, if that wave runs counter to the wave you've been riding, you may end up the victim of a wipeout.

The consumer wave of popular and media support for consumer protection had crested and was threatened as a new wave of economic and political populism started to sweep the country. It was a

Republican-based conservative movement, first fueled by Senator Goldwater, whose banner was now carried by Ronald Reagan, a celebrity conservative populist and the former governor of California. Government was no longer seen as a friend delivering on its promises of a "Great Society." Instead, government "overregulation"—particularly consumer and environmental regulation—launched a new populist political mantra: the government was now your enemy, not your friend.

By 1979, the commission was viewed as a runaway agency, and Congress, at the behest of lobbyists, took aggressive steps to rein it in. The horses, depicted by the *Man Controlling Trade* statues in front of the FTC headquarters, had broken free of FTC restraints and were sent galloping down Pennsylvania Avenue toward friendlier pastures, now seen being hand-fed some green just outside the lobbyists' meeting rooms in the United States Congress.[2]

CAMELOT FORSAKEN

Everything has an expiration date, including organizations and people.

—Michael Houston, worldwide CEO of Grey
Group

Clearly, the winds had changed. I needed to reassess the future. I had served as a regional director for seven years. One of my heroes, John W. Gardner, a former cabinet secretary of health, education, and welfare in the heyday of President Johnson's Great Society, and the founder of Common Cause, a nonpartisan public interest lobby seeking greater political transparency and accountability, described in his book *Self-Renewal* a strategy to prevent managers from staying in one position too long. He called it "repotting," a way to stay engaged and innovative. Ernie Arbuckle, a dean of the Stanford Graduate School of Business, commenting on Gardner's theory, said, "Repotting, that's how you get a new bloom . . . you should have a plan of accomplishment, and when it is achieved, you should be willing to start off again."

After only seven years, under three different presidents—two Republican and one Democrat—I was currently the longest-serving regional director in the FTC. Did I have a seven-year itch? Was it time to repot?

In an effort to zealously pursue the public interest and to reinvigorate the FTC's Seattle regional office, I played a high-stakes poker game. But as in all games of chance and skill, you have to know when to hold them and when to fold them. The cards had turned against me. It was time to cash in the chips. I told the *Bellevue Journal-American*, "I think the Camelot time is over for consumer protection and the FTC. There is a change in the national mood. People are more concerned about jobs and inflation."

Having completed my obligation to stay with the FTC for three years following the Sloan Fellows Program, late in 1978, I decided to resign from the FTC. I was resigning a job I treasured. I wasn't interested in taking the revolving door between business and government and leaving my beloved Pacific Northwest to go to New York City or Washington, DC, and join an industry highly regulated by the FTC, or a big-time law firm with regulated clients—which admittedly could be very lucrative. I had a better option, a chance to do something I had first wanted to do: teach full-time. Previously, I'd believed that without a PhD, my chances of teaching full-time for the University of Washington, long considered the biggest and best research university in the Northwest, were slim to none. Earlier in 1977, with some strong recommendations from prominent people, including the state attorney general, Slade Gorton, who said in a letter of recommendation that I ran the best FTC office in the United States, I was offered an opportunity to teach one MBA course on government regulation of business at the University of Washington Graduate School of Business. I discovered I loved teaching students. Could I convert this into a full-time opportunity?

I had an ace in the hole. Ken Walters, a classmate of mine in law school, was a full professor in the Department of Business, Government, and Society in the well-regarded Graduate School of Business. The Department of Business, Government, and Society was an interdisciplinary department combining law, economics, and the social sciences. After law school, Walters had enrolled in a PhD program in business at the University of California, Berkeley. With his doctorate in hand, he taught at several colleges and was now at the University of Washington. Importantly, he was scheduled to become the next department chairman.

Since I had been working in the intersection between business and government regulation, the department, composed of eight faculty members, was an ideal fit for me. With the department's approval, Ken invited me to try my hand full-time at teaching. I was offered an appointment for one year as a nontenured senior lecturer in the Department of Business, Government, and Society, with the pay of a full professor. I would teach antitrust law, government regulation of business, and corporate social responsibility. I was excited by the opportunity and accepted the position.

VALEDICTION

Had I accomplished what I set out to do seven years earlier? Were all the risks worth it? Had this journey been a success? Despite the rapid slide in the public image of the FTC, accolades for my tenure came pouring in from all sides, much to my relief.

The *Seattle P-I*, never to be outdone by the *Seattle Times*, ran a two-thirds-page article by Don Carter, the *P-I*'s consumer affairs writer, on my resignation, with a picture of me larger than the *Times'* front-page picture the previous year. The story, headlined "Consumer Advocate Resigns," began:

> *After eight years [sic] in the eye of a consumer cyclone he created, Bill Erxleben quietly breezed out of his office Friday afternoon.*
>
> *Leaving behind the spacious corner view office on the 28th floor of the Federal Office Building, the large polished wood desk, his interest in the federal retirement program, the $45,000 a year salary, and other perks of a regional federal executive, Erxleben says simply that it's time to "repot myself in a new career."*

The *Seattle Times* echoed the story:

> *Erxleben was a lawyer known for his aggressive, usually effective tactics against businesses he felt were cheating the public. His actions against questionable practices by auto companies, drugstores, travel agencies, comic-book advertisements, even "psychic surgeons," often grabbed headlines. He was one of a new wave of F.T.C. administrators who came into office in the early 1970s after Ralph Nader and the American Bar Association accused the agency of being overly concerned with trivialities.*

Sid Lezak, the dean of US attorneys and the US attorney for Oregon, sent me a letter shortly after my resignation, saying, "Your efforts in turning around the regional office in Seattle provide one of the best success stories that I know about in the 18 years I have been with Uncle. It proves that one man can make a difference."

But the most unexpected accolade came from a full-page article in *Seattle Business* magazine in March 1979. This was the magazine of the Seattle Chamber of Commerce, the guardian of Seattle's conservative, pro-business Republican establishment. The article headlined, "No More White Horses for FTC's Bill Erxleben," to my great surprise, was the most laudatory of all.

> *Perhaps seven years ago, one might have asked what powers of moral discernment qualified him to exercise power as director of a commission, which has been harshly criticized by Ralph Nader and the American Bar Association. But now, with this regional office transformed into one with national clout, Erxleben's record is a triumph of the idealist. Because he is an idealist, a man strangely untouched by the cynicism of the late sixties and the disenchanted boredom of the seventies, who could probably slip you a line about Truth, Justice, and the American Way without provoking a cackle of disbelief.*

But the most treasured recognition that I received was the FTC's Award for Distinguished Service, its highest award. Signed by Chairman Michael Pertschuk, the citation reads: "For your substantial contributions to the Federal Trade Commission and the consumers within the Seattle Region. Your commitment to the public will serve as an example for others." That said it all. I had left my mark. I had done my duty.

I enjoyed the accolades and my moment in the sun. In my heart of hearts, however, I knew that my success was the success of my staff. I was merely the vessel that organized their talent. They provided the passion, the creativity, the energy, and the legal and investigative skills that allowed the office to punch well above its weight in the FTC bureaucracy. I'll accept the credit for leadership, but what is a leader without a skilled team?

Valedictions are like eulogies—the praise is overdone, faults are erased, and the people who are glad to see you gone hold their tongues and fake sorrow. But to honor the truth, I didn't need to walk the valedictions back myself. I always had my ego deflator in chief, Ed Donohoe, to bring me quickly back to Earth. Ed wasn't going to let my resignation pass without sticking the lance of his pen once again into my torso:

> *Why did William C. Erxleben resign, in his own sweet time of course, from his $44,500 job as regional director of the Federal Trade Commission?*
>
> *The so-called boy wonder of instant television justice says there was no pressure for him to resign, but he felt it was time to move on to other things like teaching a course in business ethics at the University of Washington next spring. I hope Washington isn't in the kind of fat that can afford Erxleben's salary or work habits.*

A short time later, in a very long column devoted solely to me, Donohoe concluded, "Erxleben turned to teaching at the Washington Graduate School of Business, which sort of figured, since he's never been near a real business in his life."

As I have often said, Ed had a way with words.

BYE-BYE, BILLIE

The Seattle regional office never did any office social event halfway. And so it was with my farewell party in 1979. Ivan Orton, an attorney in our office and an amateur playwright, wrote a humorous play titled *Bye, Billie. Bye-Bye*. Only this time I was cast as myself, rather than as "Biff"—my last and only theatrical appearance in a play, at Batesville High School. Each member of the office had a cameo role that recounted the trials and tribulations of the office during my tenure.

Ivan rented a small downtown theater as the venue for the production. The theater was down a flight of stairs in a basement and seated less than a hundred patrons. About halfway through the play, I said a line in the script that read, "I am the real Bill Erxleben," when suddenly, from the back of the darkened theater, a man stood up and came forward, shouting, "Stop the play. I am the real Bill Erxleben." He bounded up the stairs of the stage, and, to my shock and amazement, I was looking at myself.

My double said, "Impostor, hand me the script." I did. I then retreated to a seat in the audience to watch "the real Bill Erxleben" complete the scene. This man walked, talked, and looked just like me. (I had mistakenly thought my splayfooted duck walk was unique.) I later learned that a few weeks earlier, a staff member had spotted my doppelgänger on the streets of Seattle—one of three hundred or so vice presidents at the Seattle First National Bank—and asked him to appear in the production. Gamely, he agreed. For creativity and imagination, my staff had few peers.

***

In the summer of 2015, more than thirty-five years after I left the office, a Seattle regional office reunion was organized by some of my former staff members. People came from far and wide (Hawaii, Massachusetts, California) to attend. It was great to see so many attend and to catch up on their lives.[3] Since many years had passed, I asked one staff member in attendance to explain the enthusiasm of those who had shown up.

She said, "For many, it was the best of times, the best professional days of their lives." I think it was for me too.

Looking back over the decade of my career as a public lawyer, I've never enjoyed anything as much in my professional life as serving the public in pursuit of the common good. The psychic income surpassed any possible material wealth that otherwise I might have gained. Raise a glass or two, my friends: those were days to remember.

CHAPTER EIGHTEEN

DREAMS OF THE FUTURE

(FORTY YEARS LATER: 2019)

I like the dreams of the future better than the history of the past. So good night.
> —Thomas Jefferson, in a letter to John Adams,
> from Monticello (1816)

Looking back over my decade in public service, as an idealist, as a youth of the 1960s, in my flights of fancy, I wanted to save the world. In the ensuing years the world has changed, just not wholly in the direction I intended. Strides have been made for women and minority rights, for example, the Civil Rights Act (1964), Voting Rights Act (1965), *Roe v. Wade* (1973), the Americans with Disabilities Act (1990), and *Obergefell v. Hodges* (2015), where the Supreme Court struck down state bans on same-sex marriage. There is more equality as well as more acceptance of difference than ever before. Where darkness existed in the past, the spotlight shines brightly on victims of sexual abuse, and the victims now are treated less badly—particularly those victims abused by the Catholic clergy over decades, and others abused by people in positions of corporate power or celebrity. And yet despite the progress that has been made, it seems the twin true north of my moral compass—the golden rule and the rule of law—is currently in retreat in America these days.

Sometimes I feel like the Civil War in America never ended; it just lingered as a cold war. The wounds never fully healed. Racial divisions and gaping income inequality are open sores that still divide American society today. In 2017, the United States had the sharpest increase in suicides in nearly a decade, causing life expectancy in the country to fall. Declining social mobility, crumbling infrastructure, a shrinking middle class, political gridlock, and ever-increasing personal gun ownership are all signs of a country in disarray and decline, increasingly sinking into a Hobbesian world of "all against all."

Alexis de Tocqueville believed that liberal optimism about the future needed to be tempered by a dose of pessimism. I have more than a dose of Tocqueville's recommended dose of pessimism. I struggle to be optimistic, which is understandable, I suppose, since pessimism about the future seems to come easily to those of German descent. After all, Wagner's Ring Cycle does end with Valhalla in flames.

Perhaps the biggest current threat to our country and to my quest to become an optimist resides in the Oval Office. To my surprise and great disappointment, Donald J. Trump—a vulgar, egomaniacal man who remade the Republican Party in his own image, leaving former principled Republicans cowed before him shorn of their moral fiber like sheep—captured the hearts and minds of evangelical Christians, the non–college educated, and most white rural residents and blue-collar workers with a false promise to "Make America Great Again." Trump is a climate-change denier who rejected the Paris climate agreement, signed by 195 nations, to join two nations, Syria and Nicaragua, in rejecting it; who governs from bed in early-morning ill-informed tweets; who, with aid from Russia hacking, the electoral college, Hillary's emails, and hush money payments to a porn star and Playboy Playmate, was elected in 2016 as the forty-fifth president of the United States, despite losing the popular vote.

Since Trump's election, the rule of law has been rent asunder, the truth Orwellian, and bullying has replaced the golden rule. Who would have thought we'd have a president who would berate Mexico,

Canada, and the European Union while carrying on a bromance with Russia's Vladimir Putin and North Korea's Kim Jong-un? (Trump said he fell in love with the notoriously cruel dictator from North Korea.) In a country founded on the principle of free speech, who would have thought the president of the United States would call his own country's media the enemy of the people?

The Sturm und Drang produced by Trump has created a White House full of obsequious staffers, many plagued by their own ethical lapses, that fall in and out of favor at the whim of this former reality-TV star. He governs from the Oval Office like a deranged New York City crime family don who believes that if he pardons himself he will be immune from any threat of criminal prosecution. I bet even the novelist Franz Kafka—one of the main fixtures of twentieth-century literature, who wrote about the bizarre and absurd—is rolling over in his grave at this metamorphosis of the American presidency.

The Democrats must assume their fair share of the blame for our current malaise as well. They dropped the ball with their myopic focus on diversity, gender politics, and political correctness, while ignoring programs to ameliorate the negative economic effects of globalization, which created unemployment and income stagnation in the flyover, rust belt, and rural areas of the interior. And both major political parties, through gerrymandering, which often favor the most liberal or most conservative candidates, have exacerbated the political divide and destroyed the chances of voters to elect moderate, unifying voices to craft bipartisan sensible solutions while critical issues like campaign financing reform and immigration and border control remain unresolved.

***

Looking at the headlines today, our current fears include nuclear destruction, potentially catastrophic human-exacerbated climate change, disease pandemics, and even a possible takeover by the intelligent machines that we are now creating. Do we face a dystopian future like this? As the eminently quotable Yogi Berra once said, "The future ain't what it used to be."

What does the future hold for our planet? Although his solution appears rather draconian, Elon Musk—billionaire and cofounder of Tesla and founder and owner of privately held rocket company, SpaceX, America's current preeminent technological visionary and serial entrepreneur—is not wasting time to find out. He wants to colonize Mars as a refuge should planet Earth become uninhabitable. In the advent that artificial intelligence goes rogue and turns on humanity, we may need a bolt-hole, he posits. Musk's apocalyptic vision reflects a dictum from Ayn Rand's *Atlas Shrugged*. "Man has the power to act as his own destroyer—and that is the way he has acted through most of history."

Jeff Bezos, the nation's current preeminent business entrepreneur, another rocket aficionado and the founder and owner of the privately held rocket company, Blue Origin, shares Musk's concern about the sustainability of life on Earth. He speaks with urgency about humanity running out of resources and hitting the limits of sustainable population growth.

And yet, there are many voices taking a decidedly more optimistic position. Harvard psychologist and author Steven Pinker posits in his popular 2018 book, *Enlightenment Now: The Case for Reason, Science, Humanism, and Progress*—a book described by Bill Gates as "my new favorite book of all time"—that reason and science have worked. People are systematically too pessimistic, he says, because they don't know the facts. He uses fact-based arguments to prove that on almost every measure life is improving for human beings, not only in the United States but worldwide. For the first time, 50 percent of the world's population—mostly Asian—is now considered middle class. Gross world product and incomes, calories consumed, life expectancy, and happiness are increasing, while extreme poverty, deaths from war, and infant and maternal mortality are decreasing. The economy is booming, and the stock market is near an all-time high. The world is in fine fettle, Pinker believes.

So which camp is right? Musk and Bezos, or Pinker and Gates?

My guess is that the choice is not so binary, and the truth probably lies somewhere in the middle. The greatest risk, however, is due to economic and political inertia; we muddle through in the middle until it is too late to avoid catastrophic damage to the planet.

There is an old story—one Abraham Lincoln once recounted in a speech—about an Eastern monarch who asked his wise men to invent a sentence that should be true in all times and all situations. The wise men presented the monarch with these words: "And this too shall pass away." The American dream is not gone; I believe it's just stalled. None of America's ills are irreparable. The arc of history bends toward justice and the betterment of people's lives; most woes and troubles pass as civilization advances. People are predisposed to think that things are worse off than they are.

I am not Nostradamus, and my predictions about the future like anyone's are as likely to be wrong as right. And, by definition, so-called unforeseen black swan events can radically alter any educated guess. But attitude matters. Problems should be seen as a call to action.

Should you believe the glass is half-full or half-empty? Your choice has consequences. The polls tell us that most people in America believe the glass is half-empty and are pessimistic about the future. But optimism, I believe, is preferable for good reasons. It really does make a difference in outcomes. If people believe they can't make a difference, undue pessimism can be self-fulfilling. Optimism is necessary for success because pessimism produces apathy, paralysis, and despair. Nothing will get done. It is also bad for your health. Studies show that a pessimistic outlook significantly increases the risk of death from heart disease, cancer, stroke, respiratory disease, and infections. Amos Tversky is quoted in Michael Lewis's 2016 book *The Undoing Project* as saying, "When you are a pessimist and the bad things happen, you live it twice. Once when you worry about it, and the second time when it happens."

Jim Mattis, a retired four-star marine corps general and former visiting fellow at the Hoover Institution at Stanford University, and from 2017–2018 the US secretary of defense, was the brightest light in the Trump administration, until he resigned in protest of the president's conduct of foreign affairs. He grew up in Washington State along the Columbia River and graduated from Central Washington University. In a 2017 interview with a reporter for Mercer Island's high school student-run newspaper, he gave the following advice to graduating seniors, "If you can help the larger community in the world, you won't be lying on a psychiatrist's couch when you're forty-five years old, wondering what you did with your life."

The path to improvement will not be linear; it will require a new populist wave that demands integrity and transparency in government, a respect for science and objective truth, and the rule of law, and it will take time. We all need to show greater empathy for the plight of those less fortunate and a willingness to listen to other points of view despite our differences. It will require people of good judgment, intelligence, and goodwill—people of moral courage—to stand up for the common good. Speaking out in pursuit of the common good is at the core of a vibrant democracy. Silence and inaction are unacceptable. We can't take democracy for granted; it requires constant vigilance. We must cherish our hard-won freedoms and en masse become politically active and provide societal leadership where we can. We must restore the country's reputation for decency, integrity, and the rule of law. A successful democracy can never be a spectator sport. We should strive to make America good again.

***

Just as one must muse about the future and the meaning of existence, one must muse about its absence as well. In a Faustian bargain we gain life in exchange for death. To be born is to live in the shadow of death, a final and literal repotting. But dying is not the problem; we will not fail. Living is the problem, and the opportunity. The key to success in life is not the key to one's own executive private bathroom; the key is finding purposeful work. There is a difference between being alive and living. We should all strive for a good life full of meaning with few regrets.

Forty years ago, in 1979, I articulated my vision for a purposeful life in *Seattle Business* magazine: "To be able, when I am old, to look directly into the eyes of my children, and say, 'I've lived a good life, I've tried to make the world a better place to live in, and I've sampled fully what life has to give.'" Today, I wouldn't change a word. This is the legacy I want to leave: a life well lived, infused with purpose, and filled with laughter. What more is there, really?

EPILOGUE

AFTERMATHS

(AFTER THE *COOK* TRIAL)

Based upon his admission at trial that he took payoffs, Major David Jessup, the biggest police hero of the *Cook* trial, was fired from the Seattle Police Department for "unofficerlike conduct." Stan Pitkin came to his rescue and convinced the Justice Department to hire him as a special investigator for Seattle's US attorney's office. In contrast, Major Neil Moloney—one of the "honest" officers who testified as defense witnesses for Cook, knew about the payoff system and refused to participate, but didn't investigate it—was promoted to assistant chief of police. Later, Republican governor John Spellman, a friend of Prosecutor Charles Carroll, after the trial named Moloney chief of the Washington State Patrol.

Success for the US attorney's office was not defined by the conviction and imprisonment of Buzz Cook. Only through a change in control of the King County prosecutor's office would there be any hope of long-term success in stamping out widespread corruption and shakedowns in the Seattle Police Department. Real success came when Chris Bayley challenged the incumbent King County prosecutor, Charles O.

Carroll, in the Republican primary, two months after the *Cook* trial began.

A thirty-two-year-old Harvard-educated lawyer, with blue-blooded Seattle roots and strong Republican connections, Bayley was a protégé of Attorney General Slade Gorton and served as chief of the attorney general's office of consumer protection. Bayley had even less litigation experience than Stan Pitkin did. In fact, he had no trial experience at all. Carroll was expected to easily win the primary and continue his twenty-two-year dominance of the prosecutor' office—until the daily front-page publicity from the *Cook* trial forever changed the public's perception of him. Bayley won easily in the Republican primary and later squeaked through the general election in a race against Democrat Ed Heavey. The *Cook* trial was clearly the catalyst that got Bayley elected as King County prosecutor in 1970. In his 2015 memoir, *Seattle Justice*, Bayley acknowledges his debt to Stan Pitkin for his election as prosecutor in a section titled "Providence Provides Pitkin."

In July 1971, seven months after his election as King County prosecutor, Bayley instituted a flurry of indictments. A King County grand jury indicted twenty-eight police officers and political leaders, including the former King County sheriff and Charles O. Carroll, the former King County prosecutor. In the end, fifty-four public officials would be charged with graft, perjury, bribery, and contempt. Most of the cases were dismissed and did not result in convictions. A number of officers fled the country to avoid prosecution. Carroll and the former King County sheriff were acquitted, but the backbone of the payoff system was broken.

Defense attorneys Thomas P. Keefe and Emmett T. Walsh appealed Cook's federal perjury conviction to the Ninth Circuit Court of Appeals. The conviction was upheld in August 1971 in a two-to-one decision by a three-judge panel. The majority opinion stated that there were "great volumes of direct testimony" that policemen had taken payoffs; that Cook had "direct and circumstantial knowledge of the payoffs"; and that "the evidence leaves little room for doubt that there had been widespread corruption in the Seattle Police Department." But several months later, the full nine-member appeals court reheard the case. The court then reversed its previous decision that had upheld the perjury conviction, based upon a recent decision by the US Supreme Court redefining the standard for perjury convictions. This decision led to Cook's release from federal prison.

Cook's freedom from incarceration didn't last long. He was indicted again—this time by a King County grand jury on state charges alleging his involvement in a police gambling, bribery, and vice conspiracy. In May 1973, Cook was again convicted and sentenced to three years in prison. Despite his prison sentence, former assistant chief of police Milton "Buzz" Cook was allowed to take early retirement from the police force. Now in his nineties, he still draws a generous public retirement pension.

Thomas P. Keefe and Emmett T. Walsh, Cook's defense attorneys, continued their law partnership. Walsh was suspended from Washington State law practice in 1997 for conflicts of interest and excessive attorney's fees charged to clients.

After failing to be reelected as prosecutor in 1970, and then being acquitted on state charges of corruption, former King County prosecutor Charles O. Carroll retired from politics. He counted among his friends and lunch companions former governor John Spellman (Republican), former governor Al Rossellini (Democrat), and former Seattle mayor Wes Uhlman (Democrat). He died in 2003 at age ninety-six, and in a front-page positive eulogy in the *Seattle Times*, scant mention was made of Carroll's role in failing to investigate and prosecute widespread corruption in Seattle government. The *Seattle P-I* obituary was marginally less effusive, noting that the end of Carroll's career was engulfed in a "cloud of controversy." Was Carroll's conduct in office malfeasance, an act by a public official that is wrongful or unlawful, or misfeasance, the failure to act when he was under a duty to do so? Under either theory, I believe, he failed the public miserably.

Tim Oliphant, my investigative partner, left Seattle after the *Cook* trial. He returned to the Virgin Islands to serve as chief of the criminal division, Department of Law, and then as a member of President Nixon's impeachment inquiry staff. He later returned to Colorado to practice law privately in Steamboat Springs.

AFTER THE SEATTLE SEVEN TRIAL

After the Seattle Seven trial, a radical women's collective within the Seattle Liberation Front denounced the six male defendants for male chauvinism. Succumbing to internal dissent, the SLF was disbanded. The trial put a damper on radical organizing overall; only a few collectives survived, and as the Vietnam War wound down, large-scale, violent anti-war protests in Seattle came to an end.

Defendant Michael Lerner, the Marxist founder of the SLF, became a rabbi. Michael Paley, a former chaplain of Columbia University, has described Lerner as "America's preeminent Jewish intellectual." Lerner is the editor in chief of *Tikkun*, one of the most influential progressive Jewish journals, and is one of the few prominent Jewish intellectuals who have had the courage to speak out in favor of the Palestinians. During the first Clinton administration, he was an advisor to Bill and Hillary Clinton. At one point, the *Washington Post* described him as "the guru of the White House." Muhammad Ali, the heavyweight boxing champion, collaborated with Lerner on several Vietnam anti-war issues. Upon Ali's death at age seventy-four in 2016, Lerner was one of the speakers at Ali's memorial service.

Defendant Jeffrey Dowd went to Hollywood and became a screenwriter and producer. As a passionate cineaste, in 1976, he helped found the Seattle International Film Festival. He is best known as the inspiration for "The Dude," the fictional stoner character played by Jeff Bridges in the Coen brothers' cult classic *The Big Lebowski* (1998). In the movie, The Dude says, "Did you ever hear of the Seattle Seven? That was me . . . and six other guys." The movie inspired a two-day annual festival in Seattle's Fremont neighborhood and even spawned a pseudo-religion called Dudeism.

Defendant Susan Stern, after her release from prison, became a heavy drug user, addicted to cocaine. She resumed topless dancing to support her habit. She died in 1976, at age thirty-three, from drug-related heart and lung failure. Her ex-husband, Robby Stern, a Seattle SDS founder and leader, graduated from the University of Washington Law School in 1974, and from 1993 until his retirement in 2008 was the lead lobbyist and special assistant to the president of the Washington

State Labor Council. Upon Robby's retirement, Washington State governor Christine Gregoire declared May 2, 2008, "Robby Stern Day" for his "lifelong commitment to labor and families" in the state of Washington.

Defendant Chip Marshall remained active in Seattle politics, running twice unsuccessfully for the Seattle City Council. Surprising many, the former revolutionary became a full-throated capitalist—a land developer, no less. As vice president of a Los Angeles–based real estate developer, he participated in a number of real estate projects, including the large suburban Klahanie development in Issaquah, Washington. Later he moved to China, where he continued to work in building and land development. At last report he is retired and lives in Malta. One of the smallest and most densely populated countries in the world, Malta, a tax haven for expatriates, has a reputation as a place of intrigue and dodgy financial transactions.

Defendant Joe Kelly worked for the Alaska Department of Fish and Game and later as a fish biologist in eastern Washington for the US Bureau of Land Management.

Defendant Roger Lippman worked in energy conservation, including coordinating a solar development project in Nicaragua; he is a frequent internet blogger.

Defendant Michael Abeles worked as a tile setter and painter in Seattle. He died in 2016.

Co-lead defense counsel Michael Tigar enjoyed a noted career as a teacher, author, and lawyer. He taught law at several law schools, including Texas, UCLA, Duke, and American University. In 1997 he represented Oklahoma City bombing codefendant Terry Nichols, helping him to avoid the death penalty. In his 2002 memoir, *Fighting Injustice*, Tigar speculated on the reason why he was never charged for an assault on a federal officer in the December 10, 1970, Seattle Seven courtroom melee: "Maybe they concluded that since I was out for the count ten seconds in the first round, it was not worth pursuing."

Co-lead defense counsel Carl Maxey, after a long and distinguished legal career in Spokane, where he became one of that city's power elite, died in 1997, at age seventy-three. A *New York Times* obituary described him as "a scrappy civil rights lawyer credited with virtually singlehandedly desegregating much of the inland Northwest." Maxey died from a self-inflicted gunshot wound. Some said he was despondent about his law career coming to an end.

Judge George Boldt temporarily left the federal bench eight months after the mistrial of the Seattle Seven—to become the nationally prestigious, high-profile "Pay Czar," the chairman of the Federal Pay Board, established by Congress at the request of President Nixon to fight inflation with wage and price controls. It was reported that Air Force One flew to Tacoma to pick up Judge Boldt and whisk him away to Washington, DC, for the announcement of his appointment. Some publicly wondered (including defendant Jeffrey Dowd) why an obscure judge from Tacoma, Washington, without any background in economics, was picked for such an important post. My prosecutorial nose said, by any standard the timing was most curious. Was it a reward for his handling of the trial of the Seattle Seven? Nixon's wage and price controls, initially greeted with great fanfare, later proved to be disastrous for the American economy, and most of the system was abolished in April 1974, four months before Nixon resigned as president.

Judge Boldt returned from Washington, DC, to the federal bench in Tacoma in 1974 to decide a famous and controversial Indian fishing rights case, commonly called the Boldt Decision. The court decision affirmed the treaty rights of Washington's Indian tribes and gave them a fifty-fifty "fair share" of the harvest and the right to comanage the salmon fishery alongside the State of Washington. This landmark case was filed in 1970 by Stan Pitkin for the federal government and opposed by Slade Gorton, who represented the State of Washington as attorney general. Judge Boldt died in Tacoma in 1984 at age eighty.

Weathermen Bernardine Dohrn and Bill Ayers remained underground for eleven years. During this time, the Weather Underground was responsible for thirty bombings around the United States, including at the US Capitol, the Pentagon, several police stations in New York, and a Greenwich Village town house, where an explosion killed three Weathermen who were preparing bombs for the Underground.

While on the run, Dohrn and Ayers had two children. They finally surrendered to authorities in 1980, but most of the charges were dismissed because of a 1973 US Supreme Court ruling that barred electronic surveillance without a court order. Since the evidence supporting the main charges against the couple was illegally obtained by electronic means, Bill Ayers was soon released and never served jail time. Regarding his good fortune, he said, "Guilty as sin, free as a bird. America is a great country."

Bernardine Dohrn wasn't quite as lucky. Although prior charges against her also were dismissed, she served seven months in jail in 1982 for contempt of court for refusing to testify against Weatherman Susan Rosenberg in a bank robbery case. While reflecting on her life in jail, Dohrn decided to drop her long-held opposition to marriage and marry Bill Ayers. From 1991 to 2013, she was a clinical associate professor of law at Northwestern University.

In the 1980s, Bill Ayers returned to school and earned a doctorate in education at Columbia University. Upon his return to Chicago, he was hired as a professor of education at the University of Illinois. For his work in public education, Bill Ayers was named the 1997 Chicago Citizen of the Year.

While in Chicago, Bernardine Dohrn and Bill Ayers became longtime casual acquaintances of Barack and Michelle Obama, something that John McCain tried to make hay of in the 2008 presidential election campaign.

Because of internal discord, the Weather Underground organization splintered and was largely defunct by 1977.

Guy Goodwin, the head of the US Department of Justice's internal security division, became a traveling prosecutor for the Justice Department. He supervised federal grand jury investigations that returned more than four hundred indictments, but fewer than 25 percent of his indictments resulted in convictions. The Vietnam Veterans Against the War filed a $1.8 million civil suit against him. In 1998 he retired from the Justice Department, believing that his work had disrupted terrorism and saved lives. Upon his retirement, he was awarded the John Marshall Award by the Justice Department for excellence in service.

Ironically, Attorney General John Mitchell, who never won substantive convictions against either the Seattle Seven or the Chicago Seven "conspirators," was himself charged with conspiracy and other crimes for his role in the Watergate scandal of the 1970s. He was sentenced to prison in 1977 and served nineteen months.

AFTER THE KID-VID DEBACLE AT THE FTC

The subsequent retrenchment of the FTC in 1980 to the Little Old Lady of Pennsylvania Avenue again was finally too much even for the *Washington Post*. In a 180-degree turn, the ever-fickle newspaper went from calling the FTC the "National Nanny" in 1978 to, in 1983, the "Great Wimp of Pennsylvania Avenue," but this time the FTC was criticized for not pursuing consumer protection aggressively enough.

By 1980, industry lobbyists—rubbing their hands with glee—were ready to pounce and convince Congress to rein the FTC in. A new myth was perpetuated: that the FTC was a threat to individual and corporate freedom. The FTC was publicly chastised in Senate hearings in 1979, the kid-vid rulemaking was halted, and curbs were placed on the most controversial investigations. The Seattle regional office's rulemaking investigations all met quixotic defeats: the proposed used car rule was decimated, sent to the DC chop shop, and eventually enacted only as a mini-rule (the new car rule never made it out of the DC bureaucracy); the investigation into real estate brokerage practices produced an exhaustive 1983 regional staff report that was published but not adopted by the commission and is still gathering dust; the proposed houseplant rule was referred back to the Consumer Product Safety Commission, where it was promptly composted; and the proposed nursing home rule was declared dead on arrival and cremated as "not needed."

***

With the election of President Ronald Reagan, the Republicans regained the Senate, and in 1981 President Reagan appointed a conservative Republican as chairman of the FTC, James Miller III. Miller, an economist, was the first nonlawyer to head the FTC. One of his first acts was to propose to the Congress a reduction in the number of regional offices by one-third, including the closure of the Seattle regional office.

In 1982, five years after I had appeared before the Congress and three years after I had left the FTC, the House Subcommittee on Government Operations, still chaired by Congressman Benjamin Rosenthal, again convened in Washington, DC. This time it was to investigate the FTC's proposed closing of four of the FTC regional offices, including the Seattle regional office. The subcommittee issued a 580-page report that carried a strong recommendation not to close the offices, concluding: "Regional Offices are the most productive aspect of FTC operations." The Seattle office remained open, but, with the concurrence of the appropriations committees of the House and Senate, in 1983 the number of regional FTC offices was reduced from eleven to seven, and new directors were appointed to head them. The former Seattle regional office, effectively corralled, now known as the Northwest Region—with Wyoming added as a sixth state, now carries a low profile in the Pacific Northwest.

***

Over its hundred-year history, the FTC has gone through several reincarnations. In its latest rebirth, the FTC has reinvented itself as the nation's most powerful technology cop.

"The Federal Trade Commission is becoming, for better or worse, the Federal Technology Commission," said Geoffrey Manne, executive director of the International Center for Law and Economics, in 2014. Is big tech an existential threat? Are superstar new-age monopolies like Amazon, Facebook, and Google so powerful that they need to be broken up? These data-driven technology companies—whose leaders often worship at the fountainhead of Ayn Rand—too often seem to lack a corporate soul, a sense of corporate responsibility, consistent with their monopoly of power.

New frontiers for antitrust enforcement and consumer protection are waiting to be mined: unfair dissemination of personal computer data; the use of price bots—sophisticated algorithms used to set prices; exploitation of deep learning algorithms from dominant deep data gathers; and market distribution dominance. These technology-based business practices are all in the crosshairs of the FTC's twenty-first-century enforcement program.

Today the FTC still has about 1,100 employees, about the same number it had when I joined the agency in 1972. It is severely under-staffed given the public expectation of its new role as the policeman of the country's technology behemoths. Will the FTC be properly funded and empowered by the Congress and the president to perform its new role? Only time will tell. The jury is out and the public is waiting.

SELECTED BIBLIOGRAPHY

BOOKS

Anderson, Rick. *Seattle Vice: Strippers, Prostitution, Dirty Money, and Crooked Cops in the Emerald City*. Seattle: Sasquatch Books, 2010.

Bakke, Kit. *Protest on Trial: The Seattle 7 Conspiracy*. Pullman: Washington State University Press, 2018.

Bayley, Christopher T. *Seattle Justice: The Rise and Fall of the Police Payoff System in Seattle*. Seattle: Sasquatch Books, 2015.

Kershner, Jim. *Carl Maxey: A Fighting Life*. Seattle: University of Washington Press, 2008.

Pertschuk, Michael. *Revolt Against Regulation*. Berkeley, CA: University of California Press, 1982.

Stern, Susan. *With the Weathermen: The Personal Journal of a Revolutionary Woman*. New York: Doubleday, 1975.

Tigar, Michael E. *Fighting Injustice*. Chicago: American Bar Association, 2003.

US CONGRESSIONAL HEARINGS

Protecting America's Estuaries: Puget Sound and the Straits of Georgia and Juan de Fuca: Hearing Before a Subcommittee of the Committee on Government Operations, House of Representatives, 92nd Congress (1971).

Federal Trade Commission Regional Office Operations: Hearings Before a Subcommittee of the Committee on Government Operations, House of Representatives, 95th Congress (1977).

Proposed Closing of Four FTC Regional Offices: Hearing Before a Subcommittee of the Committee on Government Operations, House of Representatives, 97th Congress (1982).

FTC PUBLICATION

Federal Trade Commission, Seattle Regional Office. *Consumer Problems of the Klamath Indians: A Call for Action.* Seattle: FTC Regional Office, 1974.

CASES

Bronston v. United States, 409 U.S. 352 (1973).

United States v. Charles Marshall III et al., Case No. 51942 (1970), US District Court for the Western District of Washington (Tacoma); United States v. Charles Marshall III et al., 451 F. 2d 372 (9th Cir. 1971).

United States v. Milford E. Cook, 497 F. 2d 753 (9th Cir. 1972), reversed, 489 F. 2d 286 (9th Cir. 1973).

ARTICLES

Berger, Knute. "Blown Coverage." *Seattle Weekly.* October 9, 2006.

Crowley, Walt. "Seattle Liberation Front." HistoryLink.org. Last updated July 24, 2012. http://www.historylink.org/File/2131.

Fung, Brian. "The FTC Was Built 100 Years Ago to Fight Monopolists. Now, It's Washington's Most Powerful Technology Cop." *Washington Post.* September 25, 2014.

Lieb, Emily. "Uhlman, Wesley Carl (b. 1935)." HistoryLink.org. Last updated October 27, 2013. http://www.historylink.org/File/7854.

New York Times. "Perjury Conviction of Assistant Chief Discloses a Police Shakedown and Bribery Scandal." July 20, 1970.

New York Times. "'Seattle 7' Echo of Chicago Trial." November 1, 1970.

Wall Street Journal. "Seattle Is the Latest City to Find Police Graft; Is the Problem Solvable?" August 21, 1970.

Washington Post. "The FTC as National Nanny." March 1, 1978.

Wilma, David. "The *Seattle Times* Documents Payoffs to Police on January 13, 1967." HistoryLink.org. Posted May 26, 2001. http://www.historylink.org/File/3292.

NOTES

CHAPTER ONE

1   As of 2018, an estimated 128 countries have banned corporal punishment, including Germany, but it is still technically legal in all fifty of the United States.

2   Today Batesville is no longer a tale of two cities, nor has it become part of the midwestern Rust Belt decimated by the loss of factory jobs. Although the furniture industry is largely gone, the casket business and the hospital supply business are both healthy. The casket company remains the main employer, although the market for caskets—if not the size of caskets—is slowly shrinking because of the increased preference for cremation. But caskets still remain a very profitable business, a luxury enjoyed by a related Batesville company, Hill-Rom, that is a leading manufacturer of hospital beds and other health-care supplies. Both the Batesville Casket Company and Hill-Rom are listed on the New York Stock Exchange. The Batesville Casket Company's dynastic family, the Hillenbrands, ranks among the richest families in America.

3   Batesville's population has nearly doubled in size, nearly seven thousand in 2017, and minorities are welcome, but the town is still 95 percent white. A winery with a trendy upscale restaurant opened nearby in the countryside. The town sports newer public elementary and high school campuses. When I attended my

fiftieth Batesville High School graduation reunion in 2009, my high school football coach and my favorite teacher joined the gathering. The teacher, a lifelong bachelor, now retired, came with his male partner. Things have changed in Batesville, much for the better.

CHAPTER TWO

1   In a widely read manifesto posted on his survival blog in 2011, James Wesley Rawles, a survivalist and author of the best-selling Patriots novels, referred to rural areas in Idaho, Montana, Wyoming, and eastern Oregon and Washington as the "American Redoubt," a haven for strongly religious people, libertarians, and survivalists.

CHAPTER THREE

1   My Amaranta Five roommates went on to distinguished careers in law and public policy. We teased Darryl Wold, a political conservative, about his enthusiastic support of the archconservative senator Barry Goldwater and the actor who starred in *Bedtime for Bonzo*, California's soon-to-be-elected governor Ronald Reagan. Darryl became an election-law specialist and his fealty to the emerging conservative movement paid off when President Bill Clinton named him to a Republican opening on the Federal Elections Commission, where he later served as chairman. After a two-year battle with cancer, Dick Stall died in 2018. As our class correspondent for thirty-one years, he will be missed.

2   I had many law professors that I really admired. But the only professor I got close enough to ask for a job reference was Joseph Sneed, a tax professor, who earlier in his career had been a law professor at the University of Texas and Cornell Law School. After I graduated from law school, Sneed was appointed deputy attorney general under President Nixon; he

then served as a judge on the Ninth Circuit Court of Appeals in San Francisco. He was a great teacher and an absolutely delightful human being. His only child, a daughter, Carly Fiorina, has been the CEO of Hewlett-Packard and a Republican candidate for the United States Senate in California; she ran for president of the United States in 2016. After she graduated from Stanford as an undergraduate, her father encouraged her to attend law school. She did, for one semester at the University of California, Los Angeles, and then dropped out. Law school gave her blinding headaches, she said.

3   My classmate Michael Wilson had the most interesting career after law school. After a few years practicing law, Mike, the stepson of Albert Broccoli, the cofounder of the James Bond film franchise, along with his half-sister, Barbara Broccoli, inherited the franchise. On every Bond film since *Moonraker*, Mike has coproduced with Barbara or acted as screenwriter, or both. Like Alfred Hitchcock did in his films, Mike has made many cameo appearances in Bond films.

CHAPTER SIX

1   The greater Seattle area is now a capitalist's paradise, a world-renowned center of innovation. It hosts the headquarters of Microsoft, Amazon, Costco, Starbucks, REI, and, until 2001, Boeing. In 2001, Boeing's top executives, harassed by continuing harsh criticism from the local machinists union and recognizing the loss of Washington's politically powerful senior senators, Magnuson and Jackson, flew the coop for Chicago.

CHAPTER SEVEN

1   After the *Cook* trial, Captain Corning received multiple contempt citations from the grand jury for noncompliance with grand jury and trial subpoenas. Most ominously, Corning was also cited for contempt for threatening to intimidate Dr.

Paine—the court-ordered cardiologist who had examined
Corning and said he could testify. Dr. Paine testified in the contempt trial that after the examination, Corning showed up at
his office without an appointment: "He wanted to speak to me
as though in a parable," Dr. Paine said, "that if he was forced to
testify and dropped dead on the witness stand [that perhaps] he
had made arrangements for someone to shoot, injure, or kill me
so I would be hospitalized for some time. He wanted me to have
this parable in mind as I made my report."

2   The Seattle Police Department still has problems today. In a
       2012 consent decree, signed with the Justice Department, the
       SPD is required to address excessive force and biased policing.
       The decree will remain in effect until 2020.

CHAPTER EIGHT

1   According to a 2018 report of the Economic Policy Institute,
       executive compensation has risen about 1,000 percent since
       1978, while real wages are up about 11 percent. Bill Gates, Jeff
       Bezos, and Warren Buffett together have more wealth than the
       bottom 50 percent of the population in the United States. Many
       people feel they are getting screwed because most of the bounty
       of our capitalist system flows to the top. The golden rule fol-
       lowed in America is increasingly seen as "he who has the gold
       rules."
          Seattle-area residents Gates and Bezos play musical chairs
       in a game of thrones as the title swings, pendulum-like, back and
       forth between them to determine which will wear the crown
       as the world's richest man. Before a pre-divorce settlement, in
       January 2019, Bezos was in the lead with a fortune estimated at
       $140 billion—although if you were to add back to Bill Gates's
       net worth of $90 billion the more than $40 billion in charitable
       contributions he's made to the Bill & Melinda Gates Foundation
       that he and his wife control, it is a closer race. Where char-
       itable contributions are concerned, at times, Jeff Bezos and

fellow Seattle billionaire Steve Balmer have been labeled as a parsimonious, given their massive personal wealth. Although it should be noted that big philanthropic donations to widely praised family-controlled charitable organizations, like the Bill & Melinda Gates Foundation, have been criticized by some for the outsize, and often multiple, federal tax deductions involved in their formation, as well as the anti-Democratic implications of converting immense private wealth into public influence through a tax-exempt foundation.

2 Although in absolute terms, incomes have risen, inequality in Seattle in 2018 was even greater than it was during the riots of the early twentieth century: Seattle is a place of haves and have-nots. More than 560 billionaires live in the United States, and a disproportionate number live in the Seattle area. Yet, as in many cities, widespread homelessness is an endemic condition in the area; because of a failure to create affordable, decent housing for those in distress, exacerbated in recent years by a toxic mix of slow wage growth and skyrocketing rents, Seattle has one of the nation's worst homelessness problems, surpassed only by Los Angeles and New York, with an official state of emergency spanning more than two years and a record 160 deaths in 2017. In the Puget Sound area no one appears to be in charge of the problem, unlike Portland, which, in the 2018 elections, passed a measure to raise $650 million for affordable housing.

3 After fleeing Seattle, Michael Justesen lived in a Weathermen collective in California until he was arrested in 1977 and charged in a conspiracy and bombing plot against a California state senator. He was convicted and served two years in prison.

CHAPTER NINE

1 Michael Tigar, *Fighting Injustice* (Chicago: American Bar Association, 2003), 184.

2   United States v. Charles Marshall III et al., Case No. 15942
      (1970), US District Court for the Western District of
      Washington (Tacoma) at 1648.

CHAPTER TEN

1   Because corporate misconduct is hard to detect, many nations
      have historically relied upon citizens to report violations. The
      basic idea of the early statutes was to reward individuals with
      a portion of the money recovered from the violator. The False
      Claims Act—enacted during the US Civil War—is one early
      example where the government offered a bounty to anyone who
      exposed people or companies that tried to defraud the govern-
      ment. After World War II, the False Claims Act was amended
      to eliminate the bounty, and the use of bounty whistle-blower
      statutes lost favor, only to be revived in 1986, when the bounty
      program was restored. Today, several new whistle-blower
      statutes have expanded federal bounty programs. In 2012 the
      Internal Revenue Service paid $104 million to a whistle-blower
      for revealing the secrets of the Swiss banking system.
           One interesting approach to using unpaid, ordinary citizens
      to monitor waterways is found in China. More than one mil-
      lion "chiefs" have been recruited to monitor the nation's rivers
      and waterways, keeping an eye out for polluters and reporting
      infractions to authorities.

2   New scientific tools, including mobile applications for smart-
      phones and tablets, are making it easier for citizens to gather
      environmental data that governments are ignoring—thus offer-
      ing citizens a way to help the environment and express their
      commitment to others.

CHAPTER ELEVEN

1   Hugh Hefner, the founder of *Playboy* magazine, died in 2017 at
      age ninety-one. He never met Marilyn Monroe or paid her for

the photographs that launched her career and his magazine. In a bizarre homage to her, Hefner paid $75,000 to get a crypt in Westwood Cemetery in Los Angeles next to hers, allowing him to spend eternity beside her.

2   The purveyors of pornography continue to innovate. Virtual reality experiences and sex robots are a new frontier for privacy and obscenity law. Adult film is now one of the most common forms of media on the planet. The effect on the culture is widely controversial, but the impact is likely to be huge the more lifelike these mediums become when fused with interactive artificial intelligence. According to the *New York Times*, the possible uses of virtual pornography are daunting: revenge and stalking porn; sex dolls that look exactly like people you know; and disputes between partners about whether virtual reality sex constitutes cheating. According to the *Huffington Post*, 30 percent of all data transferred across the internet is porn.

CHAPTER TWELVE

1   In 1972 the movie *Deep Throat* became a classic, mainstream pornography movie, epitomizing the post-sexual revolution of the 1970s. It was one of the first pornographic films to have an actual plot. A mob-financed movie, it made more than $800 million, more than any other film released during the decade, including *Star Wars*. The film was the best-known hard-core pornographic film of the 1970s. Intended to be a comedy, it earned mainstream attention and launched the "porno chic" trend.

2   Unlike federal criminal statutes that are strictly construed, section 5 of the Federal Trade Commission Act—the primary jurisdictional statute for the agency in consumer protection— is amorphous and subject to wide-ranging interpretations; therefore, it requires more coordinated review than for criminal cases in the US attorney's office, at least for other

than run-of-the-mill consumer protection deception cases.
Following a consumer symposium on the developing law of
consumer protection at Gonzaga Law School—which I participated in with Ralph Nader in 1974—to simplify the commission's review process, I suggested additional guidelines
in a *Gonzaga Law Review* article, "The FTC's Kaleidoscopic
Unfairness Statute: Section 5" (1975). The absence of a clear
standard for unfairness would contribute to the agency's downfall four years later.

3   Senator Warren "Maggie" Magnuson was a man of humble
beginnings who never knew his birth parents. He was soon
adopted and later graduated from the University of Washington
and its law school. After serving briefly as an assistant US attorney, Magnuson was elected King County prosecutor and then,
in 1944, US senator. He served in the Senate for thirty-
six years, until Slade Gorton defeated him in 1980. Senator
Magnuson was widely recognized as one of the most powerful
men in the United States Senate, and as the consumer's champion. The senator demonstrated his consumer protection clout
by cosponsoring the Magnuson-Moss Warranty Act in 1975 to
expand the FTC's enforcement powers.

4   Washington State's other, equally powerful, senator, Henry
"Scoop" Jackson, was a graduate of Stanford University and
received his law degree at the University of Washington, where
he was a member of the Delta Chi fraternity. He practiced
law in Everett, Washington, and later was elected Snohomish
County prosecutor, where he made a name for himself prosecuting gamblers and bootleggers. Elected to Congress in 1940,
he joined the Senate in 1953, where he served for thirty years.
He was twice an unsuccessful candidate for the Democratic
nomination for president. An unusual Cold War warrior/neo-
conservative, he supported Boeing, the Vietnam War, labor
unions, civil rights, Israel, and the environment. He also significantly strengthened the FTC's enforcement powers in 1973 by

attaching an amendment to the Alaska pipeline bill (the Trans-Alaska Pipeline Authorization Act) to give the FTC the ability to pursue injunctions in federal court. President Nixon called Jackson's amendments ill-advised but signed the bill anyway, because to do otherwise would slow the development of the Alaska pipeline.

CHAPTER FOURTEEN

1   For a summer job while in college, our daughter, Jennifer, was a seasonal climbing ranger at Mount Rainier for four years, where she participated in a number of hazardous climbing and helicopter rescues of climbers in distress. She summited the mountain more than twenty-five times and later spent eight years as a snow and ice safety instructor in Antarctica during the summer season, participating in a number of scientific expeditions to the interior of the continent. Her other exploits include mountaineering treks to the Andes and Himalayas, a footrace traversing the Grand Canyon, hiking the Pacific Crest Trail from California to Canada, and acting as a backcountry guide in Grand Canyon and Yellowstone National Parks. This acorn also didn't fall far from the tree, but my outdoor adventures pale next to hers.

2   FTC commissioner Elizabeth Hanford would later achieve national prominence in a series of White House cabinet posts and then as the first woman United States senator from North Carolina. From 1991 to 1999, she was the president of the American Red Cross, leaving the position to pursue her own unsuccessful shot at the presidency of the United States.

CHAPTER SEVENTEEN

1   Despite growing consumer savvy and greater competition among brokers, in 2018 the US remains one of the most expensive nations in the world in which to sell a home. Since 1979,

commissions are trending slightly downward due to the internet and increased broker competition—but are still averaging from 5 percent to 6 percent—despite soaring house prices in many areas causing total average broker transaction costs to soar as well.

While teaching at the University of Washington, I wrote a law review article, *In Search of Price and Service Competition in Residential Real Estate Brokerage: Breaking the Cartel*, 56 Wash L Rev 179 (1981), where I argued that "because of special industry conditions, collusion among brokers offers a convincing explanation for the standardization of consumer rates and services in the residential real estate industry." I urged antitrust remedies that would treat the Multiple Listing Service as an essential facility, breaking the tying arrangement with brokers and opening the system on a fee basis to all. I chastised the commission for its failure to stand up to the National Association of Realtors—one of the most powerful industry lobbies in the nation—and to use the antitrust laws to accomplish a structural reform of the brokerage industry. Despite numerous studies and reports and individual cases brought by the FTC and the Justice Department over the intervening years, the residential brokerage industry (along with title insurance) remains one of the most distorted and least competitive consumer markets in the United States.

2   Michael Pertschuk's effort to carry the FTC to new heights was effectively curtailed by the kid-vid debacle. He remained chairman of the commission until 1981 and left the FTC in 1984. After leaving the FTC, Pertschuk continued his fight for consumers as a cofounder and codirector of the Advocacy Institute, and founder of the Smoking Control Advocacy Resource Center, a group dedicated to fight the tobacco industry.

3   After 1980 a few of my former staff stayed with the regional FTC office, and some migrated to FTC headquarters, but the majority went into the world of private law, business, or other public service. After I resigned from the FTC, many of the staff

became prominent attorneys, founding-name partners in law firms, law professors, high-level federal officials, or were elected to public, professional, or public interest offices. Here is a list of some staff members who continued their service to the public in leadership roles, taught, or just did something unusual that struck my fancy.

Tom Armitage, professor of law, University of Washington; senior VP and general counsel, Children's Hospital, Los Angeles

Sharon Armstrong, judge, King County Superior Court

Barry Barnes, restaurateur

Randy Bartlett, professor of economics and director of the Urban Studies Program, Smith College

Deandra Bishop, president, Swan Computers

Dave Bricklin, past president and director of the Washington Environmental Council; former cochair, Washington Conservation Voters

Bruce Carter, assistant US attorney, Western District of Washington

Greg Colvin, Outstanding Nonprofit Attorney Award, American Bar Association

Dan Gandara, president, King County Bar Association; King County Bar Association Outstanding Lawyer Award; founder, Hispanic Bar Association

Rachel Garson, Sea-Tac media officer and manager of community relations, Port of Seattle

Craig Heyamoto, senior counsel, Boeing; appearances on *Jeopardy* and *Who Wants to Be a Millionaire*; stats crew chief for the University of Washington Huskies, the Seattle Storm, and the Seattle Sounders

Sarah Hughes, professor of law, Indiana University

Mike Katz, sculptor

Steve Kikuchi (deceased), branch chief for the US Department of Education's Office of Civil Rights; deputy director of the King County Human Resources Division

Mike Kipling, chair, Legal Committee, ACLU-WA

David Middaugh, president, Washington State Trial Lawyers; attorney, Projects Abroad, South Africa Human Rights Law Office

Sylvia Miller, assistant director for administration, FTC, Washington, DC

Ivan Orton, senior deputy, King County Prosecuting Attorney's Office

Will Patton, senior attorney, Seattle City Attorney's Office

Dave Pender, deputy acting assistant director and deputy assistant director, Bureau of Competition, FTC, Washington, DC; resident US advisor, ASEAN; consultant, OECD

Ron Sims, King County executive and council member; deputy secretary, HUD, Washington, DC; Board of Regents, Washington State University

ACKNOWLEDGMENTS

To my editors, Barbara Sjoholm and Kyra Freestar, and the excellent production staff at Girl Friday Productions, to whom I am forever grateful for their guidance and wisdom to help me craft a coherent and polished product and to bring this book to fruition.

To my wife, Gayle, who on numerous occasions corrected my sometimes-errant memory and endured the torture of reading some early drafts of my book.

To federal, state, and local public servants, the armed forces, citizen activists, and community volunteers, whose dedication is too often overlooked, poorly rewarded, and sometimes wrongly disparaged. Without the dedication of these unsung stalwarts, our democracy could not function, and we would not be safe.

And finally, to the "little ones," who will forever motivate me to follow the quest and seek justice and redress for those less fortunate. Let them never be forgotten.

INDEX

A

Abel, Fran, 271
Abeles, Michael, 128, 134, 141, 144, 152–53, 155, 295
Abzug, Bella, 242
Addams Family, The, 140
adventure travels, 35
advertising
   children's television, 273–76
   comic book, 274–76
   exploitative, 258–60
   false, 204, 222
   by lawyers, 245–46
   of prescription drug prices, 246–52, 266
Advertising Age, 222, 224, 247, 258
advertising enforcement program, 205
Advocacy Institute, 316n
Aeschylus, 52
"Affordable Grocery initiative," 274
Afghanistan, 70–71
AFL-CIO, 250
Agent Orange, 52
Alaska, 18

Alaska Department of Fish and Game, 295
Alaska pipeline bill, 315n
Alaska Teamsters, 204
Ali, Muhammad, 294
Alioto, Joseph, 76
Aloysius, Father, 17
"Amaranta Five," 45–47, 53, 308n–309n
Amazon, 299, 309n
American Bar Association, 189
American Institute of Architects, 203
American Pharmacists, 251
Americans with Disabilities Act, 285
Anderson, Jack, 127
Anderson Hall, 19
Animals, the, 69
anti-war protests, 122, 132
anticompetitive state regulations, 255–58
antitrust actions, 204, 299
antitrust law, 245
arbitration program, 205
Arbuckle, Ernie, 277
Aristotle, 243

Armitage, Tom, 239, 317n

Armstrong, Sharon, 317n

Army Corps of Engineers, 167–70, 200

Art of War, The, 71, 178

Ash Council, 198

Asotin County Republicans, 223

assimilation policy, 208

assistant attorney general, 69, 75–76, 78, 80, 190

Atlas Shrugged, 288

Auerbach, Richard, 94

Avril, Jack, 174

Award for Distinguished Service, 280

Ayers, Bill, 122, 124, 296–97

Azar, Alex, 252

B

Ballmer, Steve, 311n

baptism, 12

bar examination, 66

Barnes, Barry, 317n

Bartlett, Randy, 255, 317n

Batesville

  black people in, 15

  businesses in, 307n

  Casket Company of, 12–13, 307n

  population of, 13, 307n–308n

  prejudices in, 14–15

Bavaria, 14

Bayley, Chris, 117, 291

Bedtime for Bonzo, 308n

Bellevue, 191

Bellevue Journal-American, 278

Bellingham, 81

Bergman, Ingmar, 20

Best and the Brightest, The, 70

bestiality, 187

Beta Theta Pi fraternity, 16

Better Business Bureau, 205

Bezos, Jeff, 288, 310n

Big Lebowski, The, 294

Bill & Melinda Gates Foundation, 310n–311n

Billinghurst, Charles "Chuck," 132–33, 137, 142

Bishop, Deandra, 317n

Bitterroot Mountains, 30

Black Panther Party, 27, 115, 125

black people

  in Batesville, 15

  law enforcement prejudice against, 26–27

Blue Origin, 288

blue wall of silence, 104–5

Boalt Hall Law School, 135

Boeing, Bill Jr., 94, 106

Boeing Company, 34, 67, 90, 238, 240, 309n

Bogle and Gates, 85

Boldt, George, 132, 134–36, 138, 141, 143, 148–51, 153–54, 296

Boldt Decision, 296

Bostock, Ken, 265

Bothell, 108

Braman, Dorm, 113

Braman, J. D., 94–95

Brandeis, Louis D., 211

Brennan, William J. Jr., 135, 185

bribery, 92–95, 292–93

Bricklin, Dave, 317n

Bridges, Jeff, 294

Broadmoor, 106

Broccoli, Albert, 309n
Broccoli, Barbara, 309n
Brownson, Charles, 169
Buber, 21
Buchwald, Art, 242, 259
Budd Inlet, 75
Buffett, Warren, 71, 310n
bully pulpit, 243–45
Bureau of Land Management, 295
Burlington, Colorado, 29
business career, 17
business school sabbatical, 238–40
Butch Cassidy and the Sundance Kid,
     128
Butch Cassidy and the Sundance Kid,
     129, 160
Bye, Billie. Bye-Bye, 282

C
Camp Muir, 228–29
campaign contributions, 79
Campbell, Joseph, 21
camping, 33
Camus, Albert, 21
Canlis, 67
Capital Journal, 249
capitalism, 130, 196, 266, 309n
Capitol Hill, 33, 93
Capitol Lake, 75
Carmen Bridge, 30
Carroll, Charles O., 94–95, 102, 104, 106,
     291–93
Carson, Rachel, 164
Carter, Bruce, 317n
Carter, Jimmy, 191, 262, 264, 272
Casbah Tavern, 110

Cascade Mountains, 32
caskets, 12–14
Catch-22, 55, 57–59, 66
Catch-22, 55, 62
Catholic Church, 10–11
Catholics
     in Batesville, 14–15
     on US Supreme Court, 241
cease-and-desist orders, 199–200
Central District, 93–94
Central Drugs, 248–49
Chicago, 7–9, 13
Chicago circus, 125–26
Chicago Seven, 125–28, 133, 141
Chicago World's Fair, 35
children's advertising, 273–76
China, 12
Chinook salmon, 180–81
Christian, Mr., 12
Christianity, 12
Chrysler, 204
CIA, 144
Cincinnati, 13
civic responsibility, 261
civil rights, 26
Civil Rights Act of 1964, 285
Civil Rights Act of 1968, 125, 128
Claremont McKenna College, 45
Clark, Ramsey, 125
Clean Air Act, 163
Clinton, Bill, 40, 233, 294, 308n
Clinton, Gordon, 94
Clinton, Hillary, 294
Clinton, Michigan, 27
Coca-Cola, 274
Cole, Bert, 77–78

College Club, 103

college major, 17–18

College of Great Falls, 61

College of Wooster, 45

Collier, Calvin, 217, 237, 262, 264

Collier, Peter, 123

Columbia Law School, 77, 99, 189

Columbia River, 166

Columbia University, 297

Colville, 221

Colvin, Greg, 217, 317n

comic book advertising, 274–76

Common Cause, 277

competition, 196

competitive market restraint cases, 246

consumer abuse

  of Klamath Indians, 211–12

  psychic surgeons, 212–22

consumer arbitration program, 205

consumer education programs, 205

consumer fraud, 201

*Consumer Problems of the Klamath Indi-
  ans: A Call for Action,* 212

consumer protection

  new frontiers for, 299–300

  populist demand for, 190

  prescription drug price abuses,
    246–52, 266

Consumer Protection and
  Antitrust Act, 76

Consumer protection
  specialists, 202, 204

"Consumers' Survey Handbook on Prescription Drug Prices," 251

Cook, M. E. "Buzz," 92–117. *See also
  Cook* case

Cook, Tim, 73

Cook case

  appeal of, 292

  blue wall of silence, 104–5

  conclusion of, 115–16

  criminal payoffs, 95

  defense in, 113–14

  grand jury involvement, 100–101

  judge in, 102, 111

  media coverage of, 110

  opening day of, 110

  perjury indictment, 92, 96–97, 99, 110

  prosecution in, 99, 103, 113, 116

  retired police officers in, 105–9,
    112–13

  sentencing after, 116

  testimony in, 112–13

  trial of, 110–16, 131, 292

  verdict of, 116

  witnesses in, 101–3, 110–13

cookies, 45

cooking, 46–47, 49

Corning, Edgar True, 108–9, 113,
  309n–310n

corporal punishment, 307n

corporate misconduct, 312n

Corr, Eugene, 101

Corr, Gene, 117

corrective advertising orders, 201, 204,
  222–26

corruption, in Seattle Police Department, 92–117, 291–92

Cortese, Al, 227–30, 235

Costco, 258, 309n

courtroom law, 80

Crawford, Dan, 45, 48, 53

Crazy Horse, 207

creative aggression, 266

"creative destruction," 196

criminal justice system, 91

crisis, 198

Crothers Hall, 38–39

Crow, The, 191

Cunningham, Ross, 104

D

Daily Chronicle, 169

Daley, Richard, 130

Damocles, 38

Dartmouth College, 77

dating, at Miami University, 19–20

Davis, Rennie, 125, 141

"Days of Rage" demonstration, 130

DDT, 164

death of father, 15–16

Debby Lowman Award for Distinguished Reporting of Consumer Affairs, 267

Debs, Eugene, 121

deceptive advertising, 205

Deep Throat, 313n

Deliverance, 31

Delta Chi fraternity, 16, 314n

Democracy in America, 50

Democratic National Convention, 125–26

Democrats, 8, 287

Department of Ecology, 163

Department of Health and Human Services, 252

Department of Natural Resources (DNR), 77–78, 83

Destructive Generation: Second Thoughts about the Sixties, 123

Detroit, 8

Devine, Ed, 113

direct-to-consumer advertising of prescription drugs, 252

Disappointment Cleaver, 229

discipline, 8–9

doctrine of discovery, 208

dog tags, 56

Dohrn, Bernardine, 122–24, 129, 296–97

Dole, Bob, 236

Donohoe, Ed, 267–68, 281

Dostoevsky, 21

Douglas, Richard, 218

Douglas, William O., 43, 239

Dowd, Jeffrey, 128, 134, 138–39, 141, 145, 149, 152–53, 294, 296

draft, 51

Drinan, Robert, 265

dudeism, 294

Dudley, John, 48

Duke Law School, 43

Duncan, Don, 115

Durning, Marvin, 177–80

Duwamish River, 167

Duwamish Waterway, 167, 169

Dyes Inlet, 171, 173

Dylan, Bob, 128

E

Earth Day, 165

Economic Policy Institute, 310n

Economics and Antitrust Law Journal, The, 247

Ehlert, Charles, 252

Eisenhower, Dwight, 135, 209

Eld Inlet, 79

Elliott Bay, 167, 187, 203

Ellis, James, 164

Ellsberg, Daniel, 52

Ellsworth, Marjorie, 145

Elman, Philip, 197

Elrod, Richard, 130

empathy, 22

Engman, Lewis "Lew," 237–39, 249–50

enlightenment, 20–22

Enlightenment Now: The Case for Reason, Science, Humanism, and Progress, 288

environmental movement
  description of, 165
  landmark cases in, 166

environmental protection
  Carson's contribution to, 164
  federal regulations, 165
  landmark environmental cases, 166
  PCBs, 181
  pesticides and, 164
  populist support for, 165
  salmon, 180–81
  water pollution, 165

Environmental Protection Agency
    (EPA), 163, 165, 169

environmentalism, 163–64

Erxleben, David, 75

Erxleben, Dorothy, 9

Erxleben, Gayle
  dating of, 19–20
  engagement to, 47
  at Malmstrom Air Force Base, 60

marriage to, 48–49
  at Stanford Children's Convalescent
    Hospital, 46

Erxleben, Jennifer Renee, 170, 315n

Erxleben, Johann Polycarp, 9

Erxleben, Richard (Dick), 9, 64

Erxleben, Sara Louise
  education of, 9
  personality of, 10
  physical characteristics of, 9

Erxleben, Terry, 9, 64–65

Erxleben, Walter, Jr., 9, 17, 50, 64

Erxleben, Walter, Sr., 8–9, 13, 15, 50

Erxleben, William Charles
  in Batesville, 16–17
  birth of, 7
  childhood of, 8
  children of, 75, 170, 274
  college education of, 16–18, 21–23, 25
  disciplining of, 8–9
  early temperament of, 7
  education of, 11–12
  family of, 274
  graduate education of, 23
  parents of, 7–9
  praise for, 86–87, 279–80
  promotion of, 175
  religion of, 11, 20–22
  siblings of, 9

Estes Park, Colorado, 29

estuaries, 175

eugenics, 10

Europe, 27–28

Evans, Dan, 76, 81, 163

Everett Massacre, 121

Evergreen State, 79

existentialism, 21

expressive dysphasia, 43

F

Facebook, 299

faith healing, 215

false advertising, 204, 222

False Claims Act, 312n

Fanny Hill, 185

Farley, Jim, 121

"Farm, the," 37–38

Farwest Capitol, 167, 177

Father

    at Batesville, 13–16

    death of, 15–16

    discipline by, 8–9

    life of, 8

    occupation of, 8, 13

    physical characteristics of, 8

    religion of, 10

    residency by, 13

FBI, 53–54, 99, 144

Federal Elections Commission, 308n

Federal Pay Board, 296

Federal Trade Commission Act, 269,
    313n–314n

Federal Trade Commission (FTC)

    advertising and, 204, 222, 246

    advertising enforcement program, 205

    Alaska Teamsters antitrust
        actions, 204

    anticompetitive state regulations,
        255–58

    antitrust law, 245–46

    Award for Distinguished Service, 280

    building of, 193

    bully pulpit use of, 243–45

    Bureau of Economics, 201

    bureaucracy of, 200–201, 262, 281

    case management strategy, 202

    cease-and-desist orders from,
        199–200

    children's advertising bans, 273–76

    civil cases by, 207

    collection practice orders, 205

    Collier at, 237, 262, 264

    commissioners' weekly meeting at,
        235–36

    competitive market restraint cases,
        246

    congressional hearings on, 263–65,
        299

    consumer arbitration program, 205

    consumer education program of, 205

    consumer protection specialists at,
        202, 204

    corrective advertising orders, 201,
        204, 222–26

    creation of, 197

    criticisms of, 198–200, 298

    employees of, 300

    Engman at, 237–39

    false advertising orders, 204

    golden rule and, 194

    in Henry M. Jackson Federal Building,
        203–4

    inefficiency of, 197

    job offer at, 189

    job performance meeting at, 234–35

    Kirkpatrick at, 189–90, 194–95,
        197–98, 237

Federal Trade Commission (FTC) (*cont.*)
   Klamath Falls hearings by, 211–12
   lack of prices in prescription drug
      advertising, 246–52, 266
   Lola McClintock at, 203, 234, 237
   management problems at, 262
   media involvement by, 201
   Nader Report on, 197–98
   new attorneys at, 202, 204
   nursery business investigations, 271
   nursing home investigations, 271, 298
   Pertschuk at, 272–74
   praise for, 234
   psychic surgery/surgeons, 212–22
   purpose of, 197
   reforms in, 238
   regional director of, 195–96, 235
   regional directors' testimony before,
      263–64
   regional offices of, 198–201, 203–5,
      233, 251, 262, 299
   residential real estate investigations,
      270–71
   resignation from, 278–80, 316n
   revitalization strategy for, 198,
      200–202
   Roosevelt and, 193
   rulemaking authority of, 269–71, 298
   Seattle regional office of, 198–201,
      203–5, 233, 251, 263, 270,
      282–83, 299
   staffing of, 194, 201
   structure of, 194, 238
   technology oversight by, 299–300
   trade regulation authority of, 269–70
   understaffing of, 300

   US attorney's office versus, 200
   used cars, 270, 298
   Washington DC office of, 227–33
Fighting Injustice, 159, 295
Fiorina, Carly, 309n
First Amendment, 131, 215
Flo Villa Corporation, 83, 85, 189
Floating Homes Association, 83
Folley, Nick, 48
Fonda, Jane, 126
Food and Drug Administration
   (FDA), 223
football games, 38–39
Ford, Christine Blasey, 241
Ford, Gerald, 191, 237
Ford Motor Company, 204
foreign language, 17
Fortress, 144
Franklin, Benjamin, 28, 261
fraternities, 16, 22
fratricide, 65
Fred Meyer, 248, 266
free markets, 196
Free Speech Movement, 129
Freedom Riders, 26
French Quarter, 25
Freud, Sigmund, 7
Friendenthal, Jack, 40–44
fuel spillage, 166

G

Gain, Charles, 116
Galle, Virginia, 252–53
gambling, 93, 95, 213
Gandara, Dan, 317n
Gardner, John W., 277

Garson, Rachel, 317n

Gates, Bill, 288, 310n–311n

General Motors, 204

George Washington University, 43

Georgia-Pacific, 166, 204

gerrymandering, 287

Githens, Sara Louise. *See* Erxleben, Sara Louise

Givens, Sergeant, 60

Godden, Jean, 276

gold panning, 29–30

golden rule, 22, 194, 310n

Goldfarb v. Virginia State Bar, 245

Goldwater, Barry, 277, 308n

Gonzaga Law Review, 314n

Gonzaga Law School, 314n

Goodwin, Guy, 127, 131, 297

Google, 299

Gorsuch, Neil, 241

Gorton, Slade, 76–77, 79, 86, 90, 130, 177, 265, 267–68, 278, 292, 314n

graduate education, 23

graduation, 50

Graham, Bob, 85, 189

Grand Canyon, 49

grand jury

lying to, 96–97, 100

proceedings of, 101

purpose of, 100

subpoenas for, 108

TDA investigation, 127

witness testimony before, 101, 115

grandstanding, 116

Great Depression, 8

Great Falls, Montana, 58–61

Great Falls College, 61

Greeley, Horace, 29

Green River, 167

Gregoire, Christine, 295

groupthink, 18, 20, 70

Grove, Beverly, 110–11

Guevara, Che, 130

Gurtler, Robert, 220

Gustin, Tony, 112

Guzzo, Lou, 104

H

Haig, Alexander, 250

Halberstam, David, 70

Hamlet, 186

Han Empire, 53

Hanford, Elizabeth "Liddy," 236, 271, 315n

Hanover College, 29

Harbor Island, 167

Harbor Line Commission, 83–84

Hartman, Stanley, 250

Harvard Law Review, 41–42

Harvard Law School, 41, 236

Hayden, Tom, 122, 125–26

Heasty, Bob, 29–31, 34

Heavey, Ed, 292

Hefner, Hugh, 184, 312n–313n

Heller, Joseph, 55, 58, 62

Helsinki Youth Festival, 135

Henry M. Jackson Federal Building, 203

Heyamoto, Craig, 317n

Hicks, Floyd, 178

Hislop, Ian, 20

Hitchcock, Alfred, 309n

hitchhiking, 27–28

Ho Chi Minh, 53, 130

Hoey, Marty, 229–30, 232
Hoff, Neil, 246
Hoffman, Abbie, 125–26
Hoffman, Julius, 126, 135
Holley, Lee, 133, 151
Holocaust, 10
Home Frozen Foods, 33
homelessness, 33, 35, 311n
homosexuals, 15
Hoover, J. Edgar, 95, 99, 135, 234
Hoover Institution, 289
Horowitz, David, 123
Houger, Bill, 171
Houger, Garvey and Schubert, 171
House Subcommittee on Government
    Operations, 262, 299
Houston, Michael, 277
Huffington Post, 313n
Hughes, Palmer M., 112
Hughes, Sarah, 317n
humiliation, 41
Humphrey, Hubert, 242
Humphrey's Executor v. United States,
    241
Husky Union Building, 144

I

Idaho, 30, 32
immigrants, 8
In Search of Price and Service Competi-
    tion in Residential Real Estate Bro-
    kerage: Breaking the Cartel, 316n
income inequality, 311n
Indian Child Welfare Act, 208
Indian reservations, progressive termi-
    nation policy against, 209

Indiana, 29
Indianapolis, 13
industrial pollution
    bounty program for violators of,
        168–69
    in Duwamish River, 167
    by Joseph Mentor, 170–74
    landmark environmental cases involv-
        ing, 166
    public reporting of, 168–69
    in Puget Sound, 166
Industrial Workers of the World (IWW),
    121
Ingraham Glacier, 229
innovation, 196
International Center for Law and Eco-
    nomics, 299
Into the Strange Unknown, 214
investigative reporters, 104
"invisible hand" theory, 196
Invisible Man, The, 41
Iraq, 70
Issaquah, 295
Ithaca Four, 128
ITT Rayonier, 166
Ivar's Acres of Clams, 67

J

Jackson, Henry "Scoop," 134, 200, 234,
    253, 309n, 314n
Jackson, Mississippi, 25
Jacobellis v. Ohio, 185
JAG Corps, 53, 62
Jeffers, Richard, 86
Jefferson, Thomas, 285
Jencks Act, 147

Jesse James Gang, 122

Jessup, Dave, 101, 113, 291

Jesuit priests, 213

Jews

in Batesville, 15

Luther's antagonism toward, 11

John Birch Society, 223

Johnson, Lyndon, 52, 70, 189

Johnson Products, 205

Jones, Mary Gardiner, 270

Justesen, Michael, 128, 144, 311n

justice, 160

K

Kagan, Elena, 241

Kaplan, Bernard, 249

Katz, Mike, 317n

Kaufman, Andy, 221–22

Kavanaugh, Brett, 241

Keefe, Thomas P., 102, 292

Kelly, Joseph, 128, 134, 144, 157, 295

Kennedy, John F., 38, 52, 121

Kennedy, Robert, 121

Kent State, 122

"kid-vid" case, 274–76, 298, 316n

Kierkegaard, Soren, 21

Kikuchi, Steve, 317n

Killion, Dean, 250

Kim Jong-un, 287

King, Martin Luther Jr., 121

King County Bar Association (KCBA), 245

King County Metro agency, 164

king salmon, 180–81

KING-TV, 95, 104, 176, 178, 183, 187–88

Kipling, Mike, 318n

Kirkpatrick, Miles, 189, 194–95, 197, 237

Kitsap County, 170

Klamath Falls

description of, 209

FTC hearings at, 211–12

Klamath Indians/Klamath Indian Reservation

consumer abuse of, 211–12

description of, 207–8

FTC hearings, 211–12

progressive termination policy against, 209

sale of, 209

termination payments to tribal members after sale of, 209

unfair and deceptive business practices against, 211

Krinhop, Kenny, 20

Kunstler, Bill, 133, 152

L

labor history, 121

Lackland Air Force Base, 54, 58

Lake Union, 83

Lake Washington, 106, 164, 191

landfills, 170

Larkin, Wayne, 112, 253

Lavoie, Robert, 113

law enforcement, 26–27

law firms, in Seattle, 68–69

Le Havre, 27

Lee, Brandon, 191

Lee, Bruce, 191

Lee, Linda, 191

Lee, Shannon, 191

Lee, Tom, 165, 172

legal profession
    assistant attorney general position, 69,
        75–76, 78, 80, 91, 190
    bar examination for, 66, 69
    in Bellingham, 81
    courtroom law, 80
    first job in, 75–79
    Harbor Line Commission, 83–84
    public sector, 68
    success in, 41
legal writing, 44
Leib, Emily, 115
Leland Stanford Junior University, 37
Lerner, Michael, 128–29, 133–34, 141,
    150, 152, 155, 294
Lewis & Clark College, 143
Lewis, Michael, 289
Lewis and Clark Expedition, 60
Lewis and Clark National Historic Trail,
    29–30
Lezak, Sid, 249, 280
Libya, 70
Life of Reason, The, 71
Lincoln, Abraham, 289
Lincoln Memorial, 234
Lincoln Park Zoo, 9
Lindberg, William, 102, 104, 108–9, 111,
    116, 173
line of mean high tide, 171–74
Lippman, Roger, 128–29, 134, 140, 295
liquor distribution and sales, 255–58
liquor licenses, 256
Little Egypt, 35
"Little Red Book," 130, 143
Louisville, 19, 48
Louisville Times, 275

Lowman, Debby, 265–67
Luther, Martin, 11
Lutheran Church
    description of, 11
    dogma of, 11
    missionary work of, 12
    religious conversions, 12
Lutheranism, 12

M

Mac and Joe's, 17, 19
mafia, 107
Magnuson, Warren, 200, 234, 253, 262,
    272, 309n, 314n
Magnuson-Moss Warranty Act, 269–70,
    314n
"Make America Great Again," 286
Malmstrom Air Force Base
    life at, 58–60
    military discipline at, 62–63
    sport competitions at, 63
    volleyball team at, 63–64
Malta, 295
Man Controlling Trade, 193
Manhattan, Kansas, 29
manifest destiny, 208
Manne, Geoffrey, 299
Manning, Bayless, 44–45
Mao Tse Tung, 130, 143, 145
Marcos, Ferdinand, 216
marriage, 48–49
Marshall, Charles "Chip" III, 128, 133,
    140–42, 146, 150, 157, 159, 295,
    312n
Marx, Karl, 143, 145
Mason-Dixon Line, 14

Mattfeld, Mr., 60, 62

Mattis, Jim, 289–90

Maxey, Carl, 134, 138–39, 141, 149, 151, 161, 295–96

Mayflower Hotel, 234

McBroom, Dick, 99, 117, 119

McCain, John, 297

McCausland, Bob, 254

McClintock, Lola, 203, 234, 237

McConnell, Richard, 167

McGaffin, Don, 104

McGill, Ormond, 214

McGovern, Walter, 173–74

McGrath, Lindsey, 250

McNamar, Tim, 262

McNamara, Robert, 70, 241

meaning of life, 21

medical tourism, 214

Meeds, Lloyd, 81

Memoirs v. Massachusetts, 185

Mentor, Joseph, 170–74

Mercator, 168

Mercer Island, 106, 112

Mercury, 166

Mezines, Basil, 234–36

Miami University

  Bernardine Dohrn at, 124

  dating at, 19–20

  fraternities at, 16

  graduation from, 27

  jobs after, 29

  majoring at, 17–18

  prejudice at, 22

  social life at, 19

  Stanford University versus, 38–39

  women at, 19

Michigan State University, 9

Microsoft, 309n

Middaugh, David, 318n

middle class, 288

migrant laborers, 31–32, 35

Miller, Floyd, 95

Miller, James III, 298

Miller, Sylvia, 318n

Millionair Club, 32

minorities

  in criminal justice system, 91

  rights of, 285

Minot Air Force Base, 64

misleading advertising, 205

Mississippi River, 29

Missoula, Montana, 30

Missouri River, 60

Missouri Synod Lutheran, 11

mistrial, 150–51

Mitchell, John, 120, 125, 127, 297–98

Mogen David, 14

Moloney, Neil, 113, 291

Monroe, Marilyn, 185–86, 312n

Montgomery Ward, 204

Montreal, 27

Moore, Frank, 127

Moore, Wesley, 106–7, 112

Morgan, Lewis, & Bockius, 194

Mormon missionaries, 13

Morris, Maribeth, 104

mother. *See* Erxleben, Sara Louise

Mount Baker, 32, 80

Mount Craig, 29

Mount Everest, 232

Mount Rainier, 315n

  Camp Muir at, 228–29

Mount Rainier (*cont.*)
  climbing expedition on, 227–33
  description of, 32, 105, 203
  Disappointment Cleaver, 229
  Ingraham Glacier, 229
  summiting of, 232
  weather on, 229, 232
Mount Tahoma, 227
Mountain Room, 33
Mountain View, 45
Musk, Elon, 288
Myrtle Edwards Park, 103

N
Nader, Ralph, 190, 197, 244, 314n
National Association of Realtors, 316n
National Geodetic Survey, 173
National Ocean Service, 173
National Oceanic and Atmospheric
  Administration (NOAA), 191
National Women's Political Caucus, 242
Native American Rights Fund, 210
Native Americans
  assimilation policy against, 208
  boarding schools for children of,
    208–9
  children of, 208–9
  Indian Child Welfare Act, 208
  Jesuit priests and, 213
  peace treaties with, 208
  progressive termination policy
    against, 209
  racial discrimination against, 210
Naval ROTC, 134
Nazis, 11, 153
Neuberger, Maurine, 262

New Deal, 8
New Orleans, 25–26
New York Times, 52, 259, 295
Newman, Paul, 160
newspapers, 104
Nez Perce Trail, 30
Nichols, Terry, 295
Nietzsche, 21
1960s culture, 129
Ninety-Five Theses, 10
Nixon, Richard, 52, 77, 82, 89, 115, 120,
    127, 129, 163, 173, 250, 296, 308n
North Korea, 287
North Vietnamese, 52
Norton, Dee, 104
Norwood Park, 8, 11
nursing homes, 271, 298
nutritional supplement market, 222

O
Obama, Barack, 297
Obama, Michelle, 297
Obergefell v. Hodges, 285
obscene pornography, 183–88
O'Connell, John J., 75–76
Office of Special Investigations, 54
Officer Training School, 54, 61
Ohrnstein, Bernardine, 124
Oklahoma City bombing, 295
"Old Blue," 37–38, 49
Oliphant, Tim, 103, 293
Olympia, 69, 75, 79
Olympic Mountains, 203
optimism, 289
orcas, 180–81
Oregon, 67

Oregon Board of Pharmacy, 246, 248, 250

Oregon Journal, 212, 249

Oregon Office of Indian Education, 210

Oregon Students Public Interest Research Group, 250

Organization Man, The, 17

organized crime, 95, 107

Ormond, Ron, 214

Orton, Ivan, 282, 318n

Oslo, 27

Our Savior Lutheran School, 11

Oxford, Ohio, 16–17, 25, 27

P

Pacific Northwest Bell, 259

Pacific Science Center

  description of, 34

  environmental hearings at, 175–76

Paine, Robert, 109, 310n

Paley, Michael, 294

Palitayan, Placido, 221

Pan-Alaska Fisheries, 168

Pan American Airways, 213

Panama Canal Zone, 64

Parker, Horace "Red," 143–49, 158–60

Patton, Will, 318n

Pay 'n Save, 204

PCBs, 181

Pedersen, L. H., 256–57

Pender, Dave, 45, 53, 228, 318n

Pentagon Papers, 52

Pepsi, 274

persuasion, 164

Pertschuk, Michael, 262, 264–65, 272–73, 316n

pesticides, 164

Pharmaceutical Manufacturers Association, 237

Phil Delta Theta fraternity, 16

philanthropy, 311n

Philippines, 212–22

philosophers, 21

Pier 54, 67

Pike Place Market, 198

Pike Street, 198

Pikes Peak, 49

Pinker, Steven, 288

Pioneer Square, 33, 170

Pitkin, Stan

  Bayley's praise for, 292

  in Cook trial, 96, 100, 110, 116, 119, 123, 131

  death of, 192

  departure from US attorney's office, 191

  description of, 81–82, 89–90

  in environmental control efforts, 165, 168, 172

  family of, 192

  Indian fishing rights case, 296

  at National Oceanic and Atmospheric Administration, 191

  in Seattle Seven trial, 132–33, 137, 140, 148, 159

  in water pollution control efforts, 165, 168

Plato, 120

Plattsburgh Air Force Base, 64

Playboy, 184, 312n

Poland, 8

Police Guild, 105

police officers
  blue wall of silence, 104–5
  bribery and corruption involving, 92–
      94, 96, 100, 104–17, 291–92
  1960s hatred toward, 130
  payoffs to, 93–94
  retired, 105–9
political parties, 287
pollution
  congressional reports on, 176
  Durning's speech on, 177–78
  industrial. See industrial pollution
  PCBs, 181
  pulp mill, 166, 176–79
  tolerance policy of, 177, 180
  water. See water pollution
Pope Leo X, 11
pornography
  bestiality, 187
  case law regarding, 185
  definition of, 185
  field research on, 186
  future of, 313n
  historical expressions of, 184
  KING-TV exposé on, 183, 187–88
  as misogyny, 185
  obscene, 183–88
  "prurient interest test" for, 185–86
  public opinion regarding, 185
  in United States, 184–85
  virtual reality, 313n
Port of Seattle, 85, 183, 203
Porter Hall, 19
Portland Retail Druggists Association,
      249–50
possessive individualism, 209

prejudice
  in Batesville, 14–15
  at Miami University, 22
  in Mississippi law enforcement, 26–27
prescription drugs
  direct-to-consumer advertising of, 252
  lack of prices in advertising of,
      246–52, 266
  Puget Sound pollution from, 180
President's Advisory Council on Execu-
      tive Organization, 198
price-fixing, 245, 256
Princeton University, 194
progressive termination policy, 209
Protestant Reformation, 10, 14
Protestants, 14–15
protests
  anti-war, 122
  First Amendment protection of, 131
  peaceful, 131
  Vietnam War, 119–20, 122
"prurient interest test," 185–86
psychic surgery/surgeons, 212–22
public corruption, 92–94, 96, 100,
      104–17
Puget Sound
  description of, 67, 75, 79, 131, 160
  estuaries of, 175
  fuel spillage into, 166
  homelessness in, 311n
  industrial pollution in, 166
  landfills in, 170
  mercury discharge into, 166
  orcas in, 180–81
  pharmaceutical prescription drug
      pollution in, 180

Puget Sound (*cont.*)

  pulp mill pollution in, 166, 176–77

  Shilshole Bay, 168

  water pollution in, 164–66, 180

pulp mill pollution, 166, 176–79

Purdue University, 45

Puritans, 208

Putin, Vladimir, 287

Q

Queen Anne, 33

R

race riots, 121–22

radicalism, 146

Rainier Brewing Company, 33

Rainier Valley, 91

Ramon, Frank, 95, 112–13

Rand, Ayn, 288, 299

Rawles, James Wesley, 308n

Reagan, Ronald, 277, 298, 308n

real estate commissions, 316n

Redford, Robert, 160

Reed College, 129

Refuse Act

  Durning's speech on, 177–78

  landfills on tidelands and, 170

  Mentor's prosecution under, 175

  water pollution enforcement uses of, 165–68

Rehnquist, William, 241

REI, 309n

Reich, Robert, 233

religion, 10–11, 20–22

Reppy, Bill, 43

Republicans, 8

residential real estate, 270–71

resignation, 278–80

Reuss, Henry, 176

Revelle, Randy, 253

Revlon, 205

revolutionary movements, 131

Ridgemont Theater, 186

rioting, 127, 141, 155–58

Ripley County, 15

risk-taking, 198

RMI Expeditions, 228–29

Roats Engineering, 174

Robinson-Patman Act, 198

Rockefeller, Nelson, 43

Rocky Mountain National Park, 29

Rodgers, Nate, 25

Roe v. Wade, 241, 285

Roman Catholic Church, 10–11

Rome, 27

Roosevelt, Franklin Delano, 8, 193

Roosevelt, Theodore, 243

Rosenberg, Susan, 297

Rosenthal, Benjamin, 262, 264, 299

Rossellini, Al, 84, 103, 256, 293

Rotterdam, 27

Rubin, Jerry, 125–26

Ruckelshaus, William, 163

S

Saint John's Lutheran Church, 7

Saint Lawrence Seaway, 27

Saint Vincent Hospital, 13

Salish Sea

  description of, 175

  orcas in, 181

salmon, 180–81

Salmon, Idaho, 30

Salmon Bay, 168

Salmon River, 30–31

same-sex marriage, 285

San Juan Islands, 80

Sandpiper, 171

Santayana, George, 71

Sartre, 21

Scalia, Antonin, 243

Schaefer, Robert, 256

Schumpeter, Joseph, 196

Seale, Bobby, 125–26

Seattle

    assistant attorney general
        job in, 89–90
    Boeing Company, 34, 67, 90
    businesses in, 309n
    camping in, 33
    capitalism in, 309n
    climate in, 32–33
    environmentalism in, 164
    General Strike of 1919, 121
    homeless in, 33, 311n
    illicit activities in, 93
    income inequality in, 311n
    law firms in, 68–69
    life in, 67, 90–91
    mountains of, 32
    neighborhoods of, 33
    pollution control in, 164
    restaurants in, 67
    riots in, 127–28
    Space Needle, 67
    travels through, 32
    World's Fair in, 28–32, 34, 67

Seattle Business, 280, 290

Seattle Children's Hospital, 215

Seattle City Council, 93, 253, 255, 295

Seattle First National Bank, 78, 282

Seattle Girl Scouts, 255

Seattle International Film Festival, 294

Seattle Justice, 292

Seattle Liberation Front (SLF), 122,
    126–30, 144, 294

Seattle Police Department
    bribery and corruption involving,
        92–94, 96–97, 100, 104–17,
        291–92
    present-day problems with, 310n
    tolerance policy of, 93–95, 97, 116

Seattle Post-Intelligencer, 104, 110, 164,
    221, 253–54, 256–57, 263, 273, 276,
    279, 293

Seattle Seven trial
    beginning of, 138
    Chicago Seven and, comparisons
        between, 151
    contempt citations during, 139, 143,
        149–51, 157–58
    courtroom disruptions during, 141,
        145
    cross-examination at, 147, 149, 159
    defendants in, 128–31, 137–42, 149,
        151–58, 294–95
    defense in, 133–35, 295–96
    description of, 124
    diary, 149
    documents in, 147
    follow-up after, 294–98
    Jencks Act and, 147
    judge of, 135–36, 138, 148–50, 296
    jury of, 139–40

Seattle Seven trial (*cont.*)
justice in, 160
marshals at, 140, 142, 155–56
media coverage of, 137–38, 142
mistrial of, 150–51, 158
opening statements of, 140–41
predictions about outcome of, 161
prosecution in, 131–33, 137, 139–43, 148
Red Parker at, 143–47, 158–60
riot at, 155–58
spectators at, 138, 141, 145, 149–50, 154
at Tacoma federal courtroom, 137
voir dire of jurors at, 139
weather conditions during, 138, 149
witnesses at, 142–46
Seattle Sundance Collective, 128–29, 160
Seattle Times, 85–86, 94–95, 104, 115, 117, 168–69, 213, 254, 258, 265, 268, 279–80, 293
Seeger, Pete, 51
Self-Induced Elimination, 55
Self-Renewal, 277
sexual abuse, 213, 285
Shakespeare, William, 186
share-the-wealth philosophy, 120
Sheppard, Harrison, 228
Sher, Byron, 242
Shilshole Bay, 168
Shorett, Lloyd, 83–86
Sierra Club, 177
Sigma Chi fraternity, 16
Silent Spring, 164
Sims, Ron, 271, 318n
60 Minutes, 183

skydiving, 48
Sloan Fellows Program, 238, 242, 259, 278
Smith, Adam, 196–97
Smith, Andrew V., 259
Smoking Control Advocacy Resource Center, 316n
Sneed, Joseph, 308n
Snoqualmie Pass, 32
social justice, 22–23
Socratic method, 40–41, 49
soft drink industry, 274
Solomon, Gus, 262
Space Needle, 67
SpaceX, 288
Spellman, John, 291, 293
Spiegel, Inc., 204–5
spirituality, 22
Spokane, 32, 61
Stall, Dick, 43, 45, 308n
Standard Oil, 197
Stanford Children's Convalescent Hospital, 46
Stanford Graduate School of Business, 238, 277
Stanford Law School
administration at, 44
atmosphere at, 44
competition at, 39
environment at, 39–40
Erxleben's teaching at, 242
examinations at, 42–43
grading at, 42–43
graduation from, 50
humiliation at, 41
life at, 38–40

Stanford Law School (*cont.*)
professors at, 40–42
reflections on, 49
Socratic method at, 40–41, 49
Stanford University
cheerleaders of, 39
diversity at, 38
first days at, 37–38
football games at, 38–39
founding of, 37
life at, 38–40
Miami University versus, 38–39
Starbucks, 309n
Steinbeck, John, 66
Steinborn, Jeff, 133, 151
Stern, Robert, 143, 294
Stern, Susan, 128, 130, 133–34, 138, 140,
142–43, 148, 151, 154–55, 294
Stouffer's Restaurants, 9
Strait of Juan de Fuca, 166
Stripple, Dean, 23
Students for a Democratic Society (SDS),
122, 124–25, 128, 143–44, 294
"Subterranean Homesick Blues," 128
suicide, 286
Sun Tzu, 71, 178
Sunrise Beach, 79
Supreme Court justices, 241
Swedish Covenant Hospital, 7
synagogues, 11
Syria, 70

T
Tai Tung, 67
Taylor, Elizabeth, 271
television advertising, 273–76

temporary restraining orders, 217
Tennessee, 81
Tesla, 288
Thanksgiving, 46–47, 49
"The Day After" (TDA), 126–28,
140–41, 144
Thiamine, 222
Thompson, Mayo, 225, 247
341st Combat Support Group, 58–59
Tigar, Michael, 134–35, 139, 141, 147,
151, 156, 159, 295
Tikkun, 294
Time, 44
Tocqueville, Alexis De, 50, 286
tolerance policy
of corruption, 93–95, 97, 116
of pollution, 177, 180
Tolson, Clyde, 234
Torve, Ted, 77, 79
trade regulation rules, 269
Trans-Alaska Pipeline Authorization
Act, 315n
Trans World Airlines (TWA), 213
traveling, 32, 35
tribal identity, 21
Trump, Donald, 241, 252, 286–87
truth, 21
truth-tellers, 261
Turner, Donald, 245
Tversky, Amos, 289

U
UCLA School of Law, 134
Udall, Morris "Mo," 92
Uhlman, Wes, 113–16, 253–55, 293
"Unchained Melody," 20

Undoing Project, The, 289

unions, 34, 121

Unitarian Universalist, 57

United Nations Charter, 62

United States

current fears in, 287

expansion history in, 208

future of, 287–90

optimism in, 289

pornography in, 184–85

United States Science Pavilion, 34

United Transportation Company, 166

University of California, Berkeley, 129, 279

University of Gonzaga Law School, 134

University of Kansas, 127

University of Michigan, 8

University of Michigan Medical School, 50

University of Montana, 135

University of Montana School of Law, 66

University of Pennsylvania

description of, 45

Law School at, 194

University of Providence, 61

University of Southern California, 39, 61–62

University of Toledo, 9

University of Washington

description of, 39, 43

Graduate School of Business, 278, 281

Husky Union Building at, 144

Law School, 294, 314n

Lerner at, 129

Unsafe at Any Speed, 190

Unsoeld, Willi, 228

Upham Hall, 21

US Air Force

basic training in, 56–57

discharge from, 69

enlistment in, 52–53

marching, 56

marksmanship training in, 57

Officer Training School, 54, 61

Self-Induced Elimination, 55

US Military

critiques of, 70–71

military ventures by, 70–71

used cars, 270, 298

V

valedictions, 279–81

Vanderbilt Law School, 81

veritas, 21

Versailles, 15

Viet Cong, 52

Vietnam Veterans Against the War, 297

Vietnam War

casualties of, 52

demonstrations and protests against, 119–20, 122

description of, 38, 40, 47–48, 51–52

draft for, 38, 51–52

environmental effects of, 52

leftist movements after, 119

legality of, 62

opposition to, 52, 62, 119, 129

origins of, 53

siblings in, 64–65

virtual reality pornography, 313n

Vitamania, 222

Vitamin B, 222

Vito's, 103

Volunteer Park, 33

Voting Rights Act, 285

W

Walker, Frank, 29–31

Wall Street Journal, 117, 252

Walla Walla, 130, 189

Walsh, Emmett T., 102, 292

Walters, Ken, 278

war, 64

Wasem, Cliff, 222–23, 225

Wasem's drugstore

  corrective advertising orders against, 224–26

  description of, 222–23

  Super B Vitamins advertised by, 222–26

Washington Committee on Consumer Interests, 265

Washington Post, 52, 242, 259, 275, 294

Washington State

  anti-Vietnam War protests in, 120

  assistant attorney general position in, 69, 75–76, 190

  Constitution of, 82–83

  environmentalism in, 163–64

  gambling in, 93, 95

  Harbor Line Commission, 83–84

  Industrial Workers of the World, 121

  labor history in, 121

  leftism in, 121

  life in, 67

  senators of, 200–201

  working class in, 120

Washington State Bar Association (WSBA), 245–46

Washington State Liquor Control Board (WSLCB), 255–57, 267

Washington Teamster, 267

Water pollution

  in Duwamish River/Waterway, 167, 169–70

  in Puget Sound, 164–66, 180

  Refuse Act and, 165

Watergate, 163

Wayne State University, 8

"We Gotta Get Out of This Place," 69

Wealth of Nations, The, 196

Weather Underground Organization, 122, 124, 128, 296

Weathermen

  bombings by, 296

  description of, 122, 124, 129–30

  drug use by, 145

  FBI infiltration of, 144–45

  follow-up on, 296–97, 311n

  Fortress of, 144

  hand signals used by, 145

  meetings of, 144

  Red Parker's infiltration of, 144–46

Weinberger, Caspar "Cap," 189, 194, 198

Wells Hall, 124

Wenatchee, 86

Western Washington University, 80

Weyerhaeuser Company, 166

Whatcom County, 81

"Where Have All the Flowers Gone?," 51

whistle-blowers, 261, 312n

Whitman College, 189

Whittaker, Jim, 228, 232

Whittaker, Lou, 228, 232

Whitten, Les, 127

Whiz Kids, 70

Whyte, William, 17

Wickwire, Jim, 232

Wilkinson, Charles, 210

Williams & Connolly, 134

Wilson, John, 104

Wilson, Marshall, 104

Wilson, Michael, 309n

With the Weathermen, 130

Wold, Darryl, 45, 308n

women's rights, 285

World Bank, 240

World Trade Center, 240

World War II Liberty ship, 27

World's Fair

   in Chicago, 35

   in Seattle, 28–32, 34, 67

Wright, Donald, 219

Wyoming, 30, 299

Y

Yakama Indian Reservation, 216

Yakutat, 106

Yale Law School, 44, 177, 272

yin and yang, 198

Yippies, 125

YMCA, 23

Youth International Party (YIP), 125

ABOUT THE AUTHOR

 Bill Erxleben is a former Washington State assistant attorney general, executive assistant United States attorney for the Western District of Washington, and Seattle regional director of the Federal Trade Commission (FTC). For his service at the Federal Trade commission he was given their Award for Distinguished Service, the agency's highest honor.

An award-winning teacher, Erxleben taught at the University of Washington's Graduate School of Business. In private law practice he was a partner in two Seattle law firms, Foster Pepper and Lane Powell. He served as president and CEO of Data I/O Corporation, a Nasdaq-listed technology company based in Redmond, Washington, and as chairman of the board of Advanced Digital Systems, a privately held Bellevue, Washington, technology start-up.

As a citizen activist, he served as cochair of a 1982 Washington State recycling initiative, Initiative 61 (the "bottle bill") and as cochair of PortWatch, a citizens oversight group covering the Port of Seattle. Twice elected to the Newcastle, Washington, city council, he was also the Democratic Party nominee for Washington State attorney general and the Washington State legislature. Currently, Erxleben serves as cofounder and cochair of Newcastle Watchdog, a citizens group promoting good government.

Erxleben is a graduate of Miami University (Ohio) and Stanford Law School, where he was a guest lecturer. Nominated by the FTC, he attended the Stanford Graduate School of Business as a Sloan Executive Fellow.

Erxleben has appeared before state legislatures and the US Congress, as well as federal and state courts, as an expert on consumer protection, environmental matters, and administrative reform. He has published law review articles and been a contributing opinion writer on public policy issues with Puget Sound–area newspapers.

Bill and his wife Gayle, an artist, have a son and a daughter, and live in Newcastle, Washington.

Made in the USA
Monee, IL
31 July 2021